AMONG CHIMPANZEES

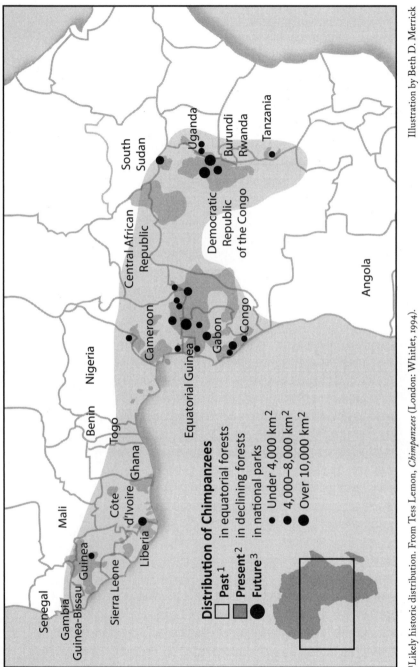

Distribution of Chimpanzees

Past[1]
in equatorial forests

Present[2]
in declining forests

Future[3]
in national parks

- Under 4,000 km²
- 4,000–8,000 km²
- Over 10,000 km²

[1]Likely historic distribution. From Tess Lemon, *Chimpanzees* (London: Whitlet, 1994).
[2]Current conservation areas. From *A.P.E.S. Portal* (http://apesportal.eva.mpg.de).
[3]Speculative future distribution if survival only in some national parks.

Illustration by Beth D. Merrick

Among
Chimpanzees

Field Notes from the Race to
Save Our Endangered Relatives

NANCY J. MERRICK

BEACON PRESS, BOSTON

Beacon Press
Boston, Massachusetts
www.beacon.org

Beacon Press books
are published under the auspices of
the Unitarian Universalist Association of Congregations.

17 16 15 14   8 7 6 5 4 3 2 1

This book is printed on acid-free paper that meets the uncoated paper
ANSI/NISO specifications for permanence as revised in 1992.

Text design and composition by Wilsted & Taylor Publishing Services

Map of Equatorial Africa showing chimpanzee habitat by Beth D. Merrick.

LIBRARY OF CONGRESS CATALOGING-IN-PUBLICATION DATA
Merrick, Nancy J.
  Among chimpanzees : field notes from the race to save our endangered relatives /
Nancy J. Merrick.
     pages cm
  Includes bibliographical references and index.
  ISBN 978-0-8070-8490-8 (hardcover : alk. paper) — ISBN 978-0-8070-8491-5 (ebook)
  1. Chimpanzees—Conservation—Africa, East 2. Wildlife conservationists—Africa, East.
3. Primatologists—Africa, East. I. Title.

QL737.P96M47 2014
599.885—dc23   2013045229

This book is written on behalf
of the amazing chimpanzees—
and in honor of those who have
loved them as much as I have.

It is especially dedicated to my
friend Bandit, an uncommonly
intelligent chimp whose life
made mine so much richer.

To Jane, who fights every day
on behalf of chimps.

And to David, who fights
for peace and humanity.

❧ ❧ ❧

Treat the earth well;
it was not given to you by your parents;
it was loaned to you by your children.

KIKUYU PROVERB, KENYA

CONTENTS

PART III. GREAT APE ADVOCATES/
WHAT WE LEARNED, 2008–2011

PART IV. MAKING IT HAPPEN

In every person's life, there are pivotal moments, events that alter our perspectives and leave us changed forever. One of those moments in my life came in 1986, when I attended a conference on chimpanzees that brought together chimp researchers from all over the world. One after another, as each of us shared the stories of the chimpanzees we were studying, we were shocked to recognize a terrible commonality: in every study site, there was habitat destruction—whether due to human population growth, logging, mining, or cattle grazing. Chimpanzees were being caught in snares, losing their arms or legs or even their lives. Some were hunted for the live-animal trade, the mothers shot in order to steal their infants for medical research or for entertainment or to become pets. We heard about the bushmeat trade—the *commercial* hunting of wild animals, including chimpanzees—very different from the subsistence hunting that had enabled forest people to live in harmony with their world for hundreds and hundreds of years.

During one afternoon session, we also heard about the sometimes horrible conditions some captive chimpanzees face. We saw secretly filmed footage of chimpanzees imprisoned in the sterile, steel-barred five-by-five-foot cells of a medical-research lab. The images chilled my soul and filled me with sadness—and anger. I arrived at the conference as a scientist, having realized my childhood dream of living with animals in Africa and writing books about them—and even acquiring a PhD along the way, thanks to Louis Leakey. But I left as an activist, knowing that I would have to leave the forest and the chimpanzees I loved to do my bit, to do everything I could to try to save them. I have not spent more than three weeks consecutively in any one place since; instead, I travel constantly on their behalf.

The chimpanzees and the other great apes face an uncertain future.

Chimpanzees are already extinct in four of their original twenty-five range countries and nearly so in ten more, and it is estimated that their populations could decline by another 80 percent in the next thirty to forty years.

Local people living in poverty are cutting down more trees to try to eke out a livelihood for their families, even as over-farming depletes nourishment from the soil. Foreign companies acquire land for logging or mining concessions or for intensive farming, securing it from government officials who are often corrupt. And as humans encroach ever deeper into the forest, so the danger of passing human diseases to the apes increases, for they are so like us biologically that they can catch our infectious diseases. And we can catch theirs.

I have seen the desperate poverty of so many of the people living around wilderness areas. We cannot hope to save the chimpanzees—or any other wildlife—if we do not help the people improve their lives. We must fight poverty on the one hand, greed and corruption on the other. And above all, we must try to educate young people to be better stewards of this planet than we have been. We also need more and more people to learn about the problems, to commit themselves to doing their best to help, and to become powerful voices for the great apes. Otherwise, our grandchildren may know a world where the last of the great apes live in zoos, or small forest patches, with little hope of long-term survival.

❊ ❊ ❊

One of the aspects of my life at the Gombe Stream Research Center I loved was working with the students who came to learn about the chimpanzees and to help collect data for their PhDs or for our long-term study. Many of them have gone on to become respected scientists, doctors, teachers. One of them was Nancy.

I remember Nancy from the days when I taught human biology at Stanford University, and I remember how pleased I was when she was picked out of many applicants to join our team. Nancy went on to become a doctor—and an excellent one, I am told. I would have expected no less. But she did not turn her back on the chimpanzees. Indeed, more than very many of my ex-students, she has risen to the challenge. I have been amazed and delighted by the way she has flung herself into learning ever more about the problems apes and people face in Africa, and by her determination to do all she can to help—even to the extent of involving her family.

Nancy has also been a great supporter of Roots & Shoots, the program for young people I began in Tanzania in 1991. Roots & Shoots started with twelve high school students on my veranda in Dar es Salaam, but it now has members of all ages, from preschool through the university level, in more than 120 countries—and growing. There are groups right across Tanzania, and it is expanding in other African countries and throughout the world. Its recent expansion across mainland China means that these youth are now a vital part of our growing global family of young people who are learning, through service projects, to make the world a better place for people, other animals, and the environment we all share.

Roots & Shoots is creating leaders for tomorrow—young people who communicate with each other, who understand that despite differences in culture and skin color, the same human heart beats within. In this way, we are trying to build a better world for tomorrow, based on understanding, love, compassion, and respect for all living things. Nancy started one of the first groups in California and has been involved ever since.

In this delightful and insightful book, Nancy shares the stories of people who have made enormous differences in the lives of chimpanzees, often sacrificing comfort and risking health and even their own lives—people who understand that it is up to us to speak out for those who cannot speak for themselves.

I was so young when Nancy's love for the chimpanzees began. And she was even younger—just nineteen years old. Our friendship, and our love for life and living, has remained undimmed. She moved away from the forest in pursuit of her career, but she describes a pivotal moment of her own that brought her full circle. Her personal story, and the stories of others she has met and admired, reminds us that every one of us can become involved. If we are passionate, determined, and not afraid of hard work, we can truly make a difference. The chimpanzees, the gorillas, and the bonobos need us all if they are to survive, and the forests do, too—and we need the forests, most desperately. Just remember that when we get together, and take action together, we can be a strong voice for the natural world.

Nancy tells a tale that is about commitment and transformation. I hope that you will enjoy it as much as I did, and that you, too, will join us and get involved.

Jane Goodall

The disturbing e-mail arrived on June 16, 2009, its subject header read-ing, "Decimation of Chimp Population in Tanzania." I agonized for two days before opening it, hoping its contents would not be as devastating as I feared. Finally, it was time. I clicked on it and found an update from the *Scientific American* website:

Tanzania's chimpanzee population has plummeted to just 700 today, according to a report from the Tanzania National Parks Authority. The Parks Authority blamed disease and predation—by humans and other mammals—for the dramatic losses. The country's chimpan-zees are located in just two habitats, making them highly susceptible to population-destroying illnesses.

And there it was—exactly what I had dreaded. It appeared that even in Tanzania, home to Dr. Jane Goodall's famous research center, chimpan-zees are threatened with extinction. If true, it meant that one catastrophic epidemic or even just continued habitat loss could spell disaster for these last Tanzanian survivors.

An e-mail from Dr. James Moore, of the University of California, San Diego, revealed that the faulty estimate of 700 was not that far off from current estimates of 1,000 to 2,600 chimpanzees.[1] One hundred of the chimps make up three small adjacent communities at Goodall's research site in western Tanzania. This is a population so small that it is teetering on the edge of biological nonviability. The others remain in areas to the south where human encroachment is fast approaching. The message hit hard because it cinched the truth—the situation was even bleaker than what we had guessed while visiting Tanzania some months before. This was final confirmation that it was past time to investigate the full extent to which chimpanzees are at risk across Equatorial Africa.

The truth was tough. One hundred years ago, chimps numbered in the millions, and although an estimated 150,000 to 300,000 remain, their numbers are plummeting even in remote forests. Exponential human population growth means that critical swaths of forest are becoming fragmented or disappearing, and chimps living in unprotected forests—a majority—are in immediate danger every day. In fact, many chimp populations can no longer survive in what little forest area they are left with. Field researcher Matthew McLennan writes,

> I just got back from Uganda last week. While it's good to be back home . . . I know I'm going to worry about the chimps at my site—there seems to be no end to the forest clearance, and there really is hardly anything left!

And, so, a 2009 e-mail lent new urgency to a task I already had under way—telling tales of the remarkable chimps and why they matter. It seemed a sacred debt I owe as one who has been blessed to know chimps. I have experienced the joy of walking with chimps, tickling and laughing with them, even having tears wiped from my eyes by my friend Bandit, the most intelligent and remarkable chimp I have known. I have witnessed their almost human dramas: a female selflessly adopting an orphaned infant, a group rolling a log to keep a lion at bay, an adolescent son mourning the death of his mother. I have seen them lie on their backs to wonder at the night sky, legs crossed, arms folded behind their heads.

My life with chimps dates to 1972, when I arrived at Dr. Jane Goodall's camp in Tanzania as a Stanford University student, working as a field assistant. As I witnessed the tremendous intelligence and complexity of the chimps, my human-centered worldview was thrown into disarray. They were like children: excitable, curious, and often unable to control their very real emotions. Unbeknownst to me at the time, my Gombe arrival was the start of a path to working with some of the world's most fascinating scientists and conservationists, people whose passions would make a difference for chimps and people of Africa. It was also the beginning of a lifelong fascination with chimps, without a doubt the most intriguing creatures on Earth. It is impossible not to be surprised by how human their laughter is as they tickle one another, impossible not to be touched by a usually fierce dominant male joyfully chasing a juvenile around a tree, then reversing and letting the youngster chase him round and round.

This book, so influenced by that e-mail, is both a chronicle of my personal search to learn how chimps are faring across Africa and in captivity and my eyewitness account of a very critical period in their existence. At times, it has been overwhelming to see how imminently threatened chimpanzees are in today's world. But to allow a world without chimps is unconscionable—so you and I must get involved or risk losing them forever. This book recounts my journey among the inspiring people fighting to save them and is a call for us to join them in order to save humankind's closest relative, the remarkable chimpanzees. Let us be a voice for the chimpanzees, beings who so deserve to be heard.

PART I

RETURN TO AFRICA, 2008

CHAPTER I

DÉJÀ VU IN PARADISE

"How long until we get there?" he asked, half puzzled, half concerned.

Gary was watching the bow of the water taxi taking us to Ngamba Island. The lake was choppy, and the waves were battering our weathered boat. I could see now that he was watching the seam between two planks in the ship's bow. Each time the waves slapped the boat, the planks separated just enough to allow a trickle of water onto the floorboards. No doubt he was wondering whether we'd make it without the boat being swamped.

"I bet we're getting close," I answered, telling a half-truth, then went back to studying the Ngamba Island visitor-information book. The boat trip usually took just ninety minutes, but our nine-mile voyage was going to be considerably longer—the chop of the lake was seeing to that.

Here I sat in an African dinghy, off to share the magic of chimps and Africa with the three people who matter most to me: my husband, Gary; my nineteen-year-old daughter, Kate; and my sixteen-year-old son, Bryan. I was glad they had agreed to come. The kids were pretty grown up, and it would be understandable if they didn't share my love of Africa and animals. But here they were, taking a leap of faith by coming along on this three-week journey.

"You won't believe the family vacation we're planning," I remembered telling the kids months ago. "We're finally taking that trip your dad and I have talked about ever since we got married. We're going to Africa this summer to see the chimps."

Bryan smiled vaguely, but Kate lit up. "That's amazing!" she said. "Are we going to Gombe?"

Gombe National Park, in Tanzania, was where I had first developed a fascination with chimpanzees while working as field assistant to Dr. Jane Goodall. It had been a magical time in my young life and a first big departure from my sheltered upbringing.

"You bet we are. And what's more, we're also going to visit a chimp sanctuary on a tropical island in the middle of Lake Victoria."

"You're kidding!" shouted Kate.

"Awesome," said Bryan in his usual teenager monotone.

Gary spoke up. "Yeah, so what do you think? Mom is giving us the choice of a week of volunteering there or going just as tourists for a couple of days and taking it easy."

"Awesome! Let's go for the week," said Bryan, finally sounding animated and not noticing the somewhat disappointed look on his father's face.

With that, the matter had been settled—much to my relief. It would have been torture for me to sit in camp being pampered as a tourist when we could instead be immersed in chimps and working alongside their African caregivers. After all, how long had I dreamed of my family seeing the astounding lives of chimps with their own eyes?

As I sat daydreaming, I saw young Jane's face and then my nineteen-year-old former self, there in her concrete-block home on the beach at Gombe. Leaning toward her, I had half-whispered, half-pleaded, "Dr. Goodall, I came here wanting to study chimps, not baboons. I've spent the summer studying them in zoos, and I know this is what I want to do! Please let me switch."

It was 1972, and I was an uncommonly innocent college junior from Pasadena, newly arrived at Gombe. East Africa, with its wildlife, its poverty—even genocide, just a few miles away in Burundi—was about to alter my world in profound ways. After those seven months in Tanzania, I would have three more years working with chimps back at Stanford University that would ensure a lifelong interest and commitment.

Ultimately, I became a doctor rather than a primatologist, a rather circuitous route for someone so intrigued by chimps. But my interests were in conservation and advocacy, rather than in untangling the ins and outs of chimp behavior. I wagered that it would be easier to return to East Africa someday to address conservation issues if I were a doctor with skills to also help humans.

After unending years of medical training and fellowship, I married and became physician, wife, and mother. Although they were great roles, they nevertheless complicated my chimp ambitions. So, in homage to chimpanzees and Jane, plan B was to advocate through conservation and animal-welfare organizations and to promote her environmental youth program, Roots & Shoots. But now, with my children nearly grown and my husband near retirement, it seemed time to make good on that long-ago intention. It was time to head back to Africa to begin researching a plan—and to acquaint my family with chimps in hopes that they would fall as much in love with them as I had.

A bucket's worth of icy-cold water thrown by the lake into the water taxi quickly brought me back to reality, and I went back to studying the information book, which described the Ngamba Island Chimpanzee Sanctuary, operated by the Chimpanzee Sanctuary and Wildlife Conservation Trust, also known as Chimpanzee Trust Uganda, to which we were en route. The Ugandan sanctuary, it said, was home to chimps who had been rescued from the illegal pet trade and the black market. The sanctuary had opened in 1998 with just ten chimps, but the population had quickly grown to forty-two. The book described every one of them, telling readers about their personalities and quirks, and detailed the sanctuary protocols.[1]

VISITOR SAFETY INFORMATION
CHIMPANZEE ESCAPE PROTOCOL

- Two Emergency Assembly points (EAPS) have been erected on the visitor side of the Island.
- In event of any chimpanzees escaping into the campsite, a whistle will be blown. Upon hearing the whistle, everyone on the island should move to the EAPS. If the chimpanzee approaches towards you, enter the water but don't go in deep water as chimpanzees cannot swim.

I tried to picture myself making sure to stay in shallow water while a chimp soundly pummeled me into small bits. "What are chimps doing escaping?" I wondered. Then, deciding it was better not to think about it, I joined my husband in studying the leaky boards of the boat.

Patrick, the cook, who had managed to sleep sitting up throughout the entire jarring boat trip, was starting to stir now. We had passed many large islands, each one raising our hopes that it would be Ngamba. But the island we were approaching now looked especially promising. There was a dock with a moored water taxi, blackbirds chirping along the length of the long rope that held it fast, a few tents and monitor lizards along the water's edge, and some platform structures farther off. Storks waded along the shore, and weaverbird nests hung from bushes like ornaments from a Christmas tree. In the distance was the sound of chimps excitedly hooting. At long last, we were arriving.

❧ ❧ ❧

"Let us to hurry, please." An animated African man in a dark-green Ngamba Island jumpsuit was helping Kate off the boat, practically lifting her off her feet in his haste to disembark her. "You have not to travel this long way so as to sit in a boat," he said with a wide smile. His name was Amos, and he was not only a chimp caretaker but also the sanctuary's bookkeeper and gift shop coordinator.

In an instant, he was herding us up the hill to watch the delayed 2:30 feeding. "We have waited to give food to the chimps so as you could be here. All the chimps have come from the forest, and you can hear how much they want their fast so as to end," he explained, as if we were about to witness the eighth wonder of the world. Bryan, a cross-country runner, bounded alongside Amos, unconcerned by the toll the hill and the humidity were taking on the rest of us.

We climbed the stairs up to the viewing area, fifteen feet above the chimps who had gathered in the clearing below. The African staff and a small number of tourist-volunteers were arrayed at three points of the thirty-foot-long platform, each holding a bucket of carrots, jackfruit, limes, papaya, pineapple, yams, and other fruits and vegetables. Seeing us, they started throwing the food to the chimps. Immediately, all forty-two chimps turned up their pant-hooting to a deafening pitch, some even screaming as they spotted the flying food. (A pant-hoot is a loud call chimps make when excited, such as when arriving at a fruit tree.) The adolescents and less confident chimps hugged one another with fear grins, others with excitement.

"That one there, he's the alpha!" Amos shouted to us. "His name is Mika. He gets the best fruit to keep him happy." A keeper lobbed a pie-sized wedge of jackfruit to the very large and handsome Mika. His hair stood on end all over his body, and he swaggered upright for a few feet as he approached it. The other chimps stayed away, fearing attack and knowing that their turn would come soon.

With Mika fully occupied with his jackfruit, the keepers began throwing food to other high-ranking males and a few particularly aggressive females. The low-ranking adolescents moved to the periphery, hoping stray fruit might fall near them. A few, like Bwambale, began doing fantastic leaps into the air, hoping to get the keepers to throw them some food. Others remained hidden in the high grass around the periphery, waiting for leftovers once the others had finished. Low-ranking Sunday collected an enormous armful of carrots, a food that was of little interest to the others. He finally picked up so many that he had to walk on his hind legs, cradling the carrots with both arms. Sunday was the tallest chimp I have ever seen—and, no doubt, his carrot diet accounted for the fact that he was also the skinniest.

Ikuru, the lowest-ranking female, was so nervous that she was unable to be strategic. As Mika ate, she nervously moved up to him, grunting with fear and seeking reassurance by extending her arm. Mika swatted her away and, when she failed to depart, gave her a resounding slap on the back that sent her off screaming.

Pasa, an adolescent, moved quietly to the area below us. She had spotted an avocado next to the electric fence and was determined to get it without being detected or shocked. Stealthily, she grabbed a long stick and pretended to play with it, but every once in a while, she peered over her shoulder at the more dominant chimps. Whenever they were looking elsewhere, she used the stick to prod fruit away from the fence to where she could safely pick it up and eat it.

I took a moment to watch my husband and children and was rewarded by the look of incredulity on their faces. It was obvious that they were registering just how smart and complicated chimpanzees are and that their human-centric universe was being turned upside down and punched inside out. It seemed that Ngamba Island might just be all that I had hoped for—a means of instantly immersing them in the wonder of chimps.

As feeding ended and the last chimp moved off to the forest, Amos showed us where we would be staying. It was just a hundred yards from the staff quarters and the observation platform to the tented camp provided for visitors. We walked past the pit toilets along a sandy pathway demarcated by small, carefully placed stones. A dove whose nest lay along the path noised her annoyance at our invading her space. Straight ahead were our canvas tents, well appointed and roomier than we needed, but comfy. On the deck of each, which reached along the water's edge, were two armchairs from which to survey paradise. Lush reeds rose from the water, flush with wading birds and pairs of swimming ducks, even an otter. The fresh air held the wonderfully blended aroma of the brush and fresh water.

Amos told us that this is an island where chimps are king, 98 acres of it thickly forested and the domain of the chimps, the other 2 more sparsely vegetated acres parsed between staff, visitors, and a holding facility for the chimps to sleep in at night. Although we would get to enjoy the comforts of this beautiful tented camp throughout our stay, our job as volunteers would be to clean cages, prepare food, help with community outreach, type up observations of the chimps, staff the gift shop, and generally pitch in.

"The morning starts with an hour's walk with the young chimps for interested visitors, then release of the other chimps for the morning feeding," he said. "They come back from the forest for feedings at 11 and 2:30, so you need to be back at 2 to prepare the buckets. And we'll make porridge at 6, when the chimpanzees come back to the holding facility for the night."

"Now you need to meet Dr. Fred," Amos announced in his broad, warm manner. "We will go and see him." Dr. Fred, the island veterinarian, had missed his time off in recent weeks due to an immense backlog of sanctuary duties. He was small and slight, professional, and always serious. Most of his sentences ended in a question.

"You are enjoying Ngamba Island, are you not?" he said when we met him moments later. Dr. Fred's words invariably made us feel important. "We are so pleased to have you here and look forward to learning from you all that you have to share. You will educate us about observations, for some of us are not so good as yet."

"And tomorrow," he said, looking as though he was bestowing a great gift, "you will go on the Forest Walk. We will meet at 6:45 a.m. Wear no jewelry, and you will come to the kitchen first thing. You will enjoy it?"

✦ ✦ ✦

Day Two, 6:50 a.m.: There would be no going back once the gate was locked behind us. We walked through a safety door in the electric fence, entering the chimp forest. As they released the chimps from the holding area into the forest where we now stood, we would be on even terms, chimps and humans locked in together, nothing separating us or protecting us. This was the beginning of the Forest Walk, a one-hour venture into the chimps' forest accompanied by seven chimps, Dr. Fred, and Amos.

"Ready?" one of the caretakers yelled from the other side of the electric fence.

"Ready!" confirmed Amos.

I had a "Maybe" stuck in my throat somewhere, torn between trusting these men versus my own knowledge of how unpredictable captive chimps can be.

The grill lifted from the chute, where a small group of chimps awaited their release. My family, Amos, and Dr. Fred stood in a line, facing whatever was about to emerge. My mind wavered between recollections of cute five-year-old chimps on the Forest Walk brochure and the previous year's evening-news report of a chimp owner mauled by his pet. Despite all my experience with chimps—or perhaps because of it—my heart raced with both fear and excitement.

Out of the chute peeked the wrinkly, charming face of a nearly full-grown chimp. It was Nakuu, a petite adolescent who seemed excited to see us. Behind her loped two larger adolescent females, a fully grown female that limped a bit as she walked, a mischievous young male, and two more playful adolescent females. They were wide awake despite the dawn hour and pleased to be in the enclosure without the more volatile and dominant adult chimps.

Nakuu strutted purposefully toward us, first studying Kate, then me, next Bryan, and finally Gary. Having made her selection, she walked up to Kate, placed her hand on Kate's wrist, and started to climb up her. "What's she doing?" Kate asked, looking one part nervous and two parts delighted. Nakuu proceeded to place herself squarely on Kate's back, ready for a piggyback ride into the forest.

Like preteen girls at a dance, the other three of us stood a little nervously as we waited to see what the other chimps would do. Bili, a husky "big girl" of a chimp, started to move toward Bryan but finally opted for sturdier-appearing Gary. She raised an arm, gesturing for Gary to help lift her onto his back—all seventy-three pounds of her. Gary obliged, but the corners of his mouth were twisted up as though he was embarking on a bad blind date. Bili, by contrast, had the pleased look of having just been selected Rose Queen as she settled herself onto his back.

It was eight-year-old, even-tempered Pasa who approached me. As she crawled onto my back, I felt her coarse hair and the rough pad of her foot and whiffed her musky smell. I gratefully propped her feet up on my hips, and we set off on our hike across the island, Dr. Fred leading and Amos bringing up the rear. As we walked, the tall canopy of trees lent a fairy tale feel to this dense forest in which we found ourselves bearing chimps. We walked single file, except when some of the other chimps bolted off the path for a game of chase. It felt as though we had wandered into a wonderful, impossible dream.

After ten minutes, Pasa proved too heavy, so with Amos's help, I talked her into crawling back down and walking. Reticently, she complied. She gamboled past Kate, taking a quick swipe at Nakuu, who remained perched on Kate's back. Nakuu screamed for a moment, temporarily damaged by Pasa's aggression, but quickly recovered. Kate, however, did not improve as quickly, and she looked nervously at Amos.

"Ah," he commented. "Pasa is unhappy that Nakuu is getting a ride but she is not. She is letting her know who is boss." We looked at Nakuu, who defiantly remained on Kate's back—just this once, a low-ranking chimp triumphantly getting the better of her betters.

We walked another ten minutes through the forest, and as we did, I thought of the misgivings I had had about taking my family on this trek. I know only too well that captive chimps can be impulsive and dangerous. In fact, we couldn't have imagined doing this walk had it included the fully adult chimps. The adults are about five times stronger than humans, despite their shorter stature, and because most of them have been mistreated by humans at some point, they are often erratic.

I had studied wild chimps at Gombe without any fear and in much different circumstances. There, I followed closely behind them as they went about their lives, largely ignoring me as I did my best to try to keep up each time that they moved. But the situation here at Ngamba Island was remarkably different than anything I had ever experienced. We were walking together, chimps and humans, enjoying one another's company.

"Let us sit down, yes?" Dr. Fred suggested. Gary and Kate had walked half the island carrying their sixty- and seventy-five-pound chimps and were eager to rest. The chimps climbed down, looking as though they knew exactly what was next. The adult female, Ikuru, moved toward me, limping on her injured right hand. Then she abruptly placed herself in my lap, giving me a long, doleful gaze.

"What?" I asked her, knowing she wouldn't be responding.

Amos smiled, happy to translate. "She wants to be groomed."

I could scarcely believe it. How many times at Gombe had I wondered what it would be like to be part of a grooming session? What was it about this activity that drove them to spend so much time at it? Perhaps, in this surreal moment, I was about to have answers.

Wishing to impress my new best friend with my knowledge of chimps, I started in combing through her fur with my fingers and pretending to pick out little bits of dandruff and dirt while smacking my lips. Ikuru looked up at the sky, nonchalantly handing me her left arm to groom—and, periodically, other limbs. I guessed from her endearing looks of deep appreciation that, given her low-ranking status, other chimps probably didn't spend much time grooming her.

When it came time to return to camp, Ikuru looked hopefully at me, longing for a piggyback ride, but she was too big. We would have to work out some other plan. She handed me her right forearm to support so that she wouldn't have to put weight on it to walk, and with a little practice we mastered it, limping along together at a fairly good pace. Dr. Fred laughed, saying, "It is good to be here, is it not?"

Even the far side of the island was a wonder. We found trees full of hundreds of sleeping fruit bats. As we gazed up, there was certainly nothing scary about them. They were vulnerable and cute as they hung upside down, their wings folded up and inconspicuous. Another of nature's mysteries could be checked off my list, knowing now where bats go during the day.

After soaking up a few minutes of sunlight on the rocky beach, we headed home. The more direct route back made for a shorter hike. The chimps moved more cautiously now, sometimes sidestepping the path unexpectedly. We could see they were avoiding lines of *siafu*, stinging fire ants, and we took it as a signal to do the same ourselves.

As we got closer to camp, the chimps erupted in play. They chased one another, frolicked, and laughed (a breathy exhalation laughter that sounds like "Huh-huh-huh"). Even Ikuru became silly and joyful. Walking ahead, she turned a somersault and landed splayed out on her back, a signal for me to groom her. This time she groomed me back, gently moving her fingers across my arm as though there were bugs to remove.

"Now we must play with them," Amos announced, smiling, as we arrived back in a clearing near the gate. He looked like the biggest kid of all as he set about tickling any chimp within reach. They ran up to him, like kids to Santa, looks of "Oh, please, play with me!" written on their faces. Amos bent over with a chimp play face—an enormous, funny smile—and mimicked their laughter. We immediately jumped in, tickling and poking. Amos grabbed Pasa's arms, Bryan grabbed her feet, and they swung her back and forth until finally giving her a heave-ho into the tall grass nearby. Soon, we were swinging happy chimps as fast as we could throw them. Bwambale lay laughing in the grass where we had lobbed him. He reached over and poked Kate with his foot to get her attention, then playfully threw himself on his back between us. With his hands and feet straight up, it was crystal-clear he was ready to be flung again. We laughed and tossed until we couldn't toss anymore.

Knowing our romp with the chimps was fast coming to a close, I tried to etch a permanent mental snapshot into my brain and to recall the last time I had felt so utterly exhilarated. Long ago, I had known and worked with chimps for several years, but this was an altogether new experience. Just this once, I was breaking all the rules and getting to be one of them, if only for an hour. It was truly a perfect hour.

And so, fueled by this Forest Walk, I was back, ready to immerse myself in chimps and East Africa once again, ready to delve into why this beautiful sanctuary was acquiring new wards at a pace far more rapidly than ever imagined and to face up to any potentially alarming news.

"Never put a period where God intended a comma," I thought to myself. It seemed it must be time to correct the punctuation in my life by resuming a journey that I had strayed from.

CHAPTER 2

SANCTUARY

There are now chimpanzee sanctuaries throughout Equatorial Africa—a surprise, given that just one existed in the 1970s. I had imagined that each contained a handful of chimps. Past estimates of the chimp population were on the order of one million, so I had worried little about them. After all, Africa is full of untouched forest, I had thought.

I tried to stay abreast of chimp-conservation issues over the years by joining organizations like the Jane Goodall Institute and keeping in touch with friends who study chimps. When I heard of the need for a wildlife corridor at Gombe in 2003 to maintain the forests connecting adjacent chimp communities, I assumed it was an isolated problem. I never suspected how illustrative it was of difficulties chimp populations face throughout Equatorial Africa.

All these years, I considered myself a chimp expert, yet I had virtually no idea. Here at Ngamba Island, I was about to finally start learning the truth.

✢ ✢ ✢ ✤ ✤ ✤

Chimp caretaker Rodney took us to the kitchen to teach us the ropes of preparing chimp food. He was tall and attractive—and, having finished university, he was also quite articulate. Decked out in his designer sunglasses and jumpsuit, he looked more like a misplaced rock star than a chimp keeper.

"There are four feedings each day, and the list tells you what foods need to be prepared," he told us. "You'll be pros in no time."

Rodney appeared happy to hand off fruit cutting to us, a task he no doubt found poorly matched to his abilities. He seemed better suited to his work as community-outreach coordinator, for he had an uncanny ability to engage children in appreciation of all things conservation. For now, however, Rodney focused on teaching us how to cut and sort the food.

I glanced over at Bryan, tall and skinny in his green Ngamba Island jumpsuit, curly brown hair reaching down to the collar. I had finally grown to love that long hair, which was such a part of his teenage identity. He was his own man these days, always adamant about doing things for the right reasons—and sometimes for the right girl.

Kate, looking a bit more disheveled in her jumpsuit, seemed glad for the company of her younger brother. He had always been her foot soldier for whatever new undertaking was going down. Her cautious nature was often trumped by her natural curiosity, so it was good to have her brother as backup. Bryan lifted the heavy bags to the sink and answered Kate's questions about just how the yams needed to be cut.

And there was Gary, surveying the whole scene, ready to provide whatever help the other three of us could possibly need. Although I was the one frequently asking Rodney whether we were covering our duties, it was quieter Gary, behind the scenes, who had things under control. Just now, he was focusing on how to keep Kate from slicing her finger as she cut up yams.

"So, who's going to prepare the jackfruit?" asked Rodney. We looked blankly from one to another and back to Rodney. He was holding a very large, prickly white fruit that could have been the egg of an alien creature. By default, the honor went to the youngest and lowest ranking. Bryan amiably accepted.

Rodney chopped the sticky jackfruit into rounds and then triangles, making Bryan his apprentice. After two minutes, it was Bryan's turn. Rodney peeled away the knife, now firmly cemented to his hand by the tarlike sap of the jackfruit, and gave it to Bryan, who finished the job. The rest of us sorted it into buckets while Bryan and Rodney went outside, trying not to get their hands stuck to the doorknob on their way out. It would take fifteen minutes of washing with cooking oil to finally remove the sticky debris from their hands.

❧ ❧ ❧

The previous day, we had met Lilly Ajarova, executive director of Chimpanzee Trust Uganda, in her offices on the mainland. Lilly, a highly educated Ugandan woman who was professional and well spoken, was overwhelmed that morning with Ngamba Island's financial pressures. Still, she took an hour out from the morning's emergencies to welcome and brief us. She wanted to imbue in us the obvious passion she had to save Uganda's chimps—both those in their native forests and those that can no longer live there.[1]

We learned that only five thousand Ugandan chimps remain in the wild, down from fifty thousand in the 1970s.[2] The explosion of Uganda's population has led to clearing of native forests for subsistence farming, growing of cash crops like tobacco, and harvesting of trees for fuel for cooking or construction timber. As human-population growth has exploded, the chimp population has reciprocally waned, and this explosion has brought with it a sharp increase in the number of chimps needing sanctuary at Ngamba Island.

Uganda's chimps, we learned, are still being killed in large numbers, some caught in snares set to trap small animals, others hunted as part of the bushmeat trade. Some are killed as pests, a result of farms and cities increasingly encroaching on their wild habitat. A shocking one in four wild chimps loses an arm or a leg to snares and steel traps. And often, when an adult chimp mother is killed, her infant or juvenile is seized and sold at the local market or smuggled out of the country to places like the Middle East to become a pet.

For every confiscated baby chimp turned over to a sanctuary, an estimated ten other chimps have died—some adults in the process of trying to protect the infant, some infants as a result of maltreatment or depression.[3] Chimpanzees are subject to many of the same psychological disorders that affect humans, including depression and posttraumatic stress disorder.[4] In every case, the young survivors have been traumatized by witnessing the killing of a parent, much as a human child would be, and further damaged by being raised without parental love and care. Lilly had rescued far too many of these shell-shocked infants, who trembled and cowered at any approach by a human being.

"Do you have any other questions?" Lilly asked at the end of the briefing.

"I do," said Kate. "Isn't Swahili a national language here? Every time I try to speak it, most people laugh or just don't answer." Kate had studied a semester of college Swahili in preparation for the trip.

Lilly looked at the floor, and there was a difficult pause. Finally, she spoke. "I think that's because many of us have very bad memories of when Idi Amin was in charge," she confided.

I felt uncomfortable, remembering stories I had heard of the crazed Ugandan leader.

"His soldiers said that we must all speak Swahili. They did some very bad things to us, and now, none of us want to be reminded of that."

Kate knew right away that she had stumbled into awkward territory, and we all said very little except how sorry we were. I could only imagine what Lilly had endured. I had been in Tanzania in 1972 and knew of the reign of terror Idi Amin had created. Thousands of Ugandans suffered abduction, torture, and murder, and the entire Asian community was forced to leave the country on three months' notice. Huge numbers of wild animals had been slaughtered, and some populations were only now starting to recover. It was little wonder that, even this many years later, Idi Amin was still widely referred to as the Butcher of Uganda.

✦ ✦ ✦

Rodney and Bryan came back into the kitchen, fresh from their fifteen minutes of hand scrubbing.

"You don't want to cut the jackfruit, trust me," said Bryan, holding up his hands, still smeared with cooking oil and small islands of goo.

"This is my job every day," Rodney reminded him. "Just wait until the cage cleaning."

✦ ✦ ✦

By 5:30, the chimps had started to reassemble near the viewing platform, anticipating their 6:30 return to the holding facility for the evening's feeding and to spend the night. Enjoying the cool evening, they played, climbed trees, and groomed one another. The adolescents scaled the eighty-foot trees with ease to graze on their fruit.

"The female threatening one of the males is Megan," Kate explained to a tourist, pointing to some chimps near the platform. "She's a very aggressive and high-ranking chimp, even among the males." Kate had mastered the names and identities of many of the chimps in just a few days, having quickly figured out that chimps can be readily identified not only by facial characteristics but also by personality.

Only a few chimps were eager to enter the holding area when the chute opened at 6:30. The holding area consisted of four adjoining open-air cages with connecting doors that could be closed to control the movement of the chimps. The keepers kept the chimps here to sleep, concerned that their habit of making new nests in the trees each night would cause significant damage to the small forest. Having them here also allowed the caretakers to check for wounds and other health problems and to account for the chimps' whereabouts.

By 6:35, the holding area was filled with screams, threats, chasing, and fighting as the chimps entered and sorted themselves out for the night. Mika entered the area in hot pursuit of Connie, who was in estrus. Connie, who had put up with Mika's overtures for most of the day, looked tired and annoyed.

The chimps pressed themselves against the cage bars as the keepers handed out a few pieces of fruit. Rodney put whole papayas far too big to fit through the bars into the outstretched hands of Tumbo and Megan. Those chimps were the keepers' favorites, especially Tumbo, a gray-haired adult male and good-natured former circus chimp. Our curiosity about why they had been handed fruit too large to draw into the cage was short lived, as Tumbo pressed his mouth through the bars and started to eat away at its thick middle until he had whittled it down enough to pull it through the bars and gulp it down.

"I require assistance now with porridge," Amos said. Following his instruction, we happily grabbed buckets, dumping large cans of Ovaltine-like powder into them and filling them with water until we had concocted a gooey potion that Amos deemed "perfect."

"Try some of it," Amos prodded me. I checked his face for a smile, but he was serious. "I used to drink this as a child. Many children have this every night." I watched a bubble break as it reached the surface, throwing brown powder on top of the mudlike porridge.

I looked at the cages, where forty-two pairs of outstretched hairy hands held shiny silver bowls outside the cage bars. It was like a scene from *Oliver Twist* as the keepers filled each bowl. The chimps pressed their lips to the bars and sipped their porridge. Little Kikyo finished his porridge and then moved below his pal Rambo, stretching his lower lip through the bars and catching each bit of porridge that accidentally overflowed from the corners of Rambo's mouth. When snack time came to a close, the chimps politely handed their bowls to the keepers like well-behaved children.

"Which is your favorite chimp?" we asked the head keeper, Gerald.

"It is Katie, for she has been very kind to us. The chimps all used to drop their bowls on the ground when they finished. But Katie always would hand the bowl to us. She would seem most unhappy with the others, and she taught them to do it, too." Perhaps, in reality, the keepers had simply rewarded her with second helpings and the others had caught on. No matter. Katie was definitely cool.

It was getting dark now, and some of the chimps were settling into the hammocks that hung from the ceiling bars. A multitude of negotiations and disputes ensued as the chimps maneuvered themselves into their best possible scenario for the night. Sunday stood pressed against the cage bars, still holding his porridge bowl in hopes that Stany, another keeper, would refill it. Rambo held his open palm to the mouth of Kikyo, whimpering and begging for bits of papaya. And Kidogo had just perfected her comfy nest of hay on the floor when an unruly male on the platform above peed on it.

Mika was among the last to head to bed. He climbed up to Okech's hammock, pushing Okech out of it. The other chimps barked as they watched, likely relieved that it wasn't their hammock that was being taken. Okech didn't protest and instead simply moved into one of the twine hammocks. Meanwhile, Mika turned over in his hammock to gaze adoringly at Connie, one hand tucked under his head for a pillow. The hapless Connie rolled over, turning her back to him and probably thinking of the long night ahead.

❊ ❊ ❊

"So, how do you find your stay so far?" asked the affable Gerhardt over dinner one evening.

Gerhardt had a delightful Austrian accent and an extraordinary English vocabulary. Often, I delayed responding to his questions because I was so absorbed in the pleasure of just listening to him.

"Awesome," said Bryan in his own succinct way.

We had been enjoying breakfasts, lunches, and dinners with fellow volunteers Gerhardt and his wife, Sonja. The two had traveled all over the world and knew more about the United States than we did. Each day, there was also a new mystery couple, depending on who had booked an overnight stay. They came from all over the world—Spain, South Africa, Singapore, Australia, and Malaysia—and each night was an adventure, a new set of stories and wonderful political discussions of the world's ills. A pair of German researchers from the Max Planck Institutes and a charming Dutch business student added to our international cadre, as did the inspirational Ugandan staff, particularly Stany and Gerald.

The pair had been part of the Jane Goodall Institute's efforts to establish the sanctuary ten years before, constructing buildings, bringing the chimps to the island, and even relocating an entire fishing village to a nearby island. Respected and congenial, they had created a harmonious human community in which everyone did their part. They cared deeply about the chimps and worked tirelessly to educate visiting students and tourists in hopes of recruiting new foot soldiers in the battle for chimp conservation. Like the other sanctuary workers, they spent weeks at a time away from their families just to keep Ngamba running. But there were bigger sacrifices still, we learned that evening as we sat around the campfire.

"Perhaps I will see you on my book tour," Stany said casually. "You know, I hope to be in the States next year." The book he was referring to, written by a former volunteer, told Stany's harrowing story of rescuing eleven chimps years ago during a time of genocide in nearby Burundi. In the initial days of violence, Stany and coworker Debby Cox had remained with the chimps to protect them from any brutality. But one evening, as Debby drove Stany home, they were pulled over by Tutsi soldiers. Stany, a Hutu, was forced to the ground, where he was kicked in the head and beaten. The soldiers were preparing to shoot and kill him when their leader arrived, just barely in time. "He's not worth wasting a bullet on," Stany recalled the man shouting at the soldiers. "Tell the white woman to come get her trash."

It was clear that they needed to get themselves and the chimps out of Burundi. It took months, but finally, Debby and Stewart Hudson, director of the Jane Goodall Institute's US headquarters, arranged the transport of the twenty chimps so that they could be flown to safety at Sweetwater Sanctuary, in Kenya. Evacuating the chimps, however, meant that Stany would have to leave his wife and children alone for weeks until he could return.

Things worsened further when Stany's passport was seized as he left the country, preventing him from returning to Burundi. As days passed without his return, Stany's family realized something was wrong and that it was time to flee to the countryside for safety. For the next four miserable years, they subsisted on little or no money, trying to survive the genocide. Meanwhile, Stany remained apart from them, knowing nothing of their whereabouts—or even whether they had survived. Finally, the family was located when Debby heroically went to search for them, and they were eventually reunited with Stany in Uganda.

None of us could match a story like that, and none of us tried. The equatorial stars were out in force, and life in this international group of camp-fire soul mates felt rich. We simply relaxed there on the beach, exchanging stories and enjoying the sounds of nesting hamerkops (wading birds) and chirping frogs. Amos told jokes while Dr. Fred tried unsuccessfully to get us to sing. The South Africans told of elephant safaris, and the Austrians taught us about Texas. It felt like a small, very connected planet.

CHAPTER 3

NEW ARRIVALS

It had occurred to me that cleaning chimp dung and following wild chimpanzees is probably not the average family's idea of a vacation—even in the case of my somewhat quirky family. Perhaps I had brought them here less for their "edification" than for my desire to relive a delightful past, adorned with both chimp and human characters.

It was refreshing to find out how normal these sanctuary chimps are. All had undoubtedly been traumatized early in their lives by witnessing the killing of their mothers and being taken captive by humans. They could have been remote and disturbed. But instead, they had become a true community, one in which they played, groomed, and restored one another. What a testament they were to the healing that is possible when these intelligent beings are lovingly nursed back to mental health.

✻ ✻ ✻ ✻ ✻ ✻

One morning, Dr. Fred announced that two baby chimps, Mac and Afrika, were on their way to the island to begin new lives here. They were deemed safe to begin life at Ngamba now that they had completed a three-month quarantine that guaranteed they were free of tuberculosis and other disease. Mac, we were told, was eighteen months old, and Afrika was a little over two years of age. Their arrival was certain to be both exciting and troubling, the latter because these babies were far too young to be orphans. Wild chimpanzees remain constantly with their mothers up to about age seven, as they near early adolescence, and their years of early development and dependence mimic that of humans. If these infants were still in the wild, where they rightfully belonged, they would be carried by their mothers, constantly under their protection, and still suckling from their breasts. Instead, it was their human keeper, Philip, who was caring for them, trying to gently nurture them back to physical and mental health.

The chimps arrived in a large plastic carrier, and it took most of Philip's strength to move it into the holding facility. Soft, nervous sounds were just barely audible from inside. Gerald and Rodney followed, checking that the door to the connecting cage was closed and that its two chimp occupants could not enter. The other Ngamba Island chimps were out in the forest, ensuring that there would be relative calm when the babies were allowed out of their container and into the room they would occupy for the next several months. The infants' faces could just barely be seen through a grill in the carrier as they hugged one another and studied the room.

Philip bent over quietly with the brave facade of a parent giving his children up to an orphanage. As he opened the cage door, nothing emerged except a few soft scared whimpers from the pair inside. But finally, a tiny, hairy face peered back at Philip. "Come, Mac," Philip whispered. "Come on." Mac looked hesitatingly at Philip but finally began gradually releasing his viselike grip on Afrika. Then, at last, as though an unsuspected burst of adrenaline had exploded inside his tiny body, Mac thundered out of the container, stamping his feet and arms like an alpha male. The proud smile on Philip's face told us that all was going inexplicably well—that is, until Mac caught sight of others in the room. Instantly, he ran back to the container and slammed his bottom down on the floor, not feeling so brave after all.

Finally, Afrika's head cautiously emerged atop of his, and Mac crept over to Philip and climbed into his arms. Afrika followed along behind him and began walking the cage perimeter, cautiously eyeing the humans who watched outside. Eventually, Mac climbed down, and the two walked around the cage, embracing one another.

After a few minutes, Philip quietly slipped out of the room. By now, Afrika was engrossed in a hanging rope that she had discovered she could dangle and swing from. Mac had discovered the adoring humans just outside the bars and was laughing as one of them began to tickle him. As soon as Afrika noticed, she ran over and began swatting at the people, as though she was protecting her baby. Once the tickling stopped, she kept Mac in her embrace, guiding him around the cage and waving her arm at anyone that dared coax him to approach.

Within two hours, the youngsters were surprisingly at ease. Afrika continued to swipe at observers too attentive to Mac, but now her actions were in fun, done because she hoped to steal some of the attention. As Afrika came to my spot, she laid her back up against the bars and I reached under her armpit and about her neck, tickling her. A big chimp play face appeared, and I could hear her laughing. She tumbled over, grabbing at me teasingly and inviting more tickling, then burst off to the next observer.

By the next morning, Afrika was brave enough to sit up against the bars of the adjoining cage where adult male Asega sat. The two had studied one another for an hour, and Afrika had been running up to within a few feet of Asega, then charging away in flirting retreat. But this time, she planted herself squarely up against the bars. Asega gently reached through and began grooming her, no doubt her first contact with an adult chimp since the disturbing day of her capture and a pivotal first moment in her journey back to a more normal chimpanzee life.

The babies' introduction to the group was expected to take many months. If all went according to plan, they would be introduced within a few weeks to some of the most nurturing female chimps, who likely would "adopt," carry, and protect them. Next, they would meet some of the gentle-natured males in hopes the males would shield them from other, more aggressive chimps. Ultimately, they would join the entire group and become full members of the community.

As Mac reached his hand toward me, I thought about their tragic stories. Before being rescued, Afrika had been kept in a cage so small that she was unable to move in it, and her only social contact was when her captor threw food in. She was kept like this for more than two months, and when she was rescued, she was not only emaciated and depressed but also barely able to walk. The laughter and adjustment we were witnessing now was evidence of the nurturing care the sanctuary provided. Young chimps deprived of social stimuli in labs generally suffer permanent damage, rocking and pulling out their own hair—basically, losing their minds. But these youngsters were en route to a healthy, reasonably normal life. We tickled Mac some more, celebrating that at least some part of his young life had gone right.

⁕ ⁕ ⁕

Chimps, like people, come in many flavors, and one of our favorites was Tumbo. One of four former circus chimps in the group, he was particularly clever at conveying his desires to humans. At feeding time, he would confidently clap his hands and gesture to the keepers to throw him some food. Calm and smart, he used intelligence rather than aggression to achieve high rank. But his real charm was that he was a peacemaker. When other chimps were upset, he would calm them. If there was a fight, Tumbo would begin a charging display to stop the fighting by drawing attention to himself.

We enjoyed learning more about our friend, the lanky and carrot-loving

Sunday, who was also an accomplished escape artist. In years past, he had become so good at getting out that the keepers had kept him in the holding area for weeks at a time. One day, after he escaped, he spotted some fishermen in a motorboat pulled up next to the shore. Fascinated by the boat, he moved intently toward them, at one point standing up on his hind legs to get a better look inside. Seeing the upright chimp, the fishermen panicked and started making as much commotion as humanly possible. Still, the chimp kept coming. The captain grabbed for the engine throttle and tried to move the boat away from shore, but by this time, Sunday was just a few feet away. He jumped into the boat as the screaming fishermen threw themselves overboard into the water. Meanwhile, the boat—and the chimp—motored off into Lake Victoria at full speed.

Alerted by the fishermen, the keepers jumped into a boat and went in search of Sunday. They quickly caught up to him, finding him standing at the helm, piloting the boat. Eventually, he was darted and subdued so that he could be safely returned to the island, but the legend of his escapade lives on, no doubt bringing new meaning to the term "Sunday driver."

The week with the chimps also brought daily surprises. We watched as Mika stole a keeper's keys, breaking one of them in the lock as he tried to work it. A second Forest Walk proved as eventful as the first when Kate accidentally sat near a nest of ants and they began crawling into her pants legs. The day was saved when Ikuru came to her rescue, picking the ants off one at a time and devouring them. As Gary stood watching, Bili sat at his feet, fascinated by his shoelaces, which he had double-knotted. Overcome by curiosity, she tugged at one of the laces, creating a knotty mess. Undeterred, she managed to not only unknot the lace but also to completely undo it. She then promptly began working on the other lace with a look of such intensity that she might well have been performing surgery.

Our favorite chimps, though, were the two newcomers, Mac and Afrika, innocent, delightful children that we never tired of watching. Although they should have been spending these early years in the constant company of their mothers, they were instead now well embarked on their introduction to the Ngamba Island Home for Orphans.

❖ ❖ ❖

The day before our departure, a group of Ugandan secondary school students visited Ngamba. Gerald, in his usual respectful manner, addressed them as "Ladies and gentlemen," preaching to them about each student's responsibility to protect wild chimps living near their villages. I joined in, sharing stories of their intelligence and abilities. The students were fascinated, as was their teacher, a gifted young woman whom the students revered. She had read Jane Goodall's books as a young girl, and seeing the chimps obviously meant a lot to her.

At the end of the class visit, we left the observation platform, excited by the visit. As I rounded the last banister, there stood one of the girls with whom I'd been talking, obviously waiting for me.

"Thank you so much," she said. "I am so glad to know of the chimps."

"Oh, you're welcome. It was truly my pleasure," I said. "Aren't they amazing?"

She glanced down at her feet and then said, "I have to tell you. I have never talked with a white person before. I have heard many terrible things. But it was very good. I think you are not so bad."

I took it as the compliment it was intended to be, and we walked together to the beach. Later, I gave my signed copy of Dr. Goodall's book *Reason for Hope* to the teacher, knowing how much she admired Dr. Goodall and certain she would inspire future generations of students. It felt right, as though this book, which had traveled halfway around the world, had finally arrived at its destination.

❧ ❧ ❧

The next day, Gerald, Rodney, and Stany walked us to the boat for our departure. We felt just like the high school students of the day before as Gerald issued us our instructions: We were to return home and spread the word of what we had learned. We were to report to the world beyond Uganda of the threatened chimps, of the need for resources to keep Ngamba Island afloat, and of the Ugandan people and the many challenges they face daily.

"One last photo," Gary declared. We all pant-hooted as Patrick snapped our picture. "Good-bye, Secretary," Gerald grinned, using the pet name he'd created for me one day while I was transcribing the keepers' notes.

"*Welaba, Mzee,*" I said, using the Lugandan word for "wise man" and the little bit of that language that he had taught me in order to say good-bye.

We left Ngamba on a speedboat, thinking of the thousands of chimps whose lives hang in the balance. As more roads are cut into their forests, it seems, more chimp orphans will continue to arrive at Ngamba. Only efforts to educate and improve the well-being of the local people, coupled with effective conservation programs, will be able to protect the chimps and other African wildlife. Yet here was Ngamba, its gifted educators and dedicated conservationists just barely getting by on a shoestring budget. We tried to imagine what we could possibly do to help.

Kate, seeing how preoccupied I was by all of this, opened her copy of *Reason for Hope.*[1] "There's a great paragraph I've got to read you," she said, and as she did so, I hoped for inspiration and a solution.

"Yes, I do have hope," Dr. Goodall had written.

> I do believe we can look forward to . . . a world in which there will still be trees and chimpanzees swinging through them, and blue sky and birds singing, and the drumbeats of indigenous peoples reminding us powerfully of our link to Mother Earth and the Great Spirit— the God we worship. But . . . we don't have much time. The planet's resources are running out. And so if we truly care about the future of our planet we must stop leaving it to "them" out there to solve all the problems. It is up to us to save the world for tomorrow: it's up to you and me.

"Amen," she whispered, closing her book.

"Amen," I echoed, now more pensive than ever.

CHAPTER 4

FULL CIRCLE

We began the second leg of our trip, flying eight hundred miles to the western edge of Tanzania, en route to Gombe National Park, where I had worked years ago. We would spend the night in Kigoma before taking a boat on to Gombe for a two-night stay.

My children had briefly visited there two years previously with Jane's Roots & Shoots, an environmental youth program. During their brief visit to Gombe, they had seen just a couple of chimps, and only from a distance. Much of their Tanzanian visit had instead been spent at the base of Mount Kilimanjaro, where, along with some Tanzanian Roots & Shoots members, they had nurtured seedlings at a tree nursery. Moved by their experience, the American youths went on to raise $18,000 back in the United States to help their Tanzanian friends create new tree nurseries.

By now, my entire family was indebted to Jane in so many ways.

❖ ❖ ❖ ❖ ❖ ❖

The African businessmen seated in front of us, attired in handsome suits, were absorbed in their newspapers. A woman across from us was bringing her cleft palate baby home from the Dar es Salaam tertiary-care hospital. The plane was full of African travelers on life's errands, and only a very small minority of seats belonged to tourists like us.

The plane landed at the small Kigoma airport, and after disembarking down a short flight of stairs, we entered the two-room terminal, where our bags would be delivered. As we walked, we scouted for Jane, having heard she would be leaving for Dar es Salaam on the plane that we had just arrived on. We had hoped to at least get to say hello, but we were sadly disappointed when we were unable to spot her.

About then, an old Land Rover in need of paint drove up to the terminal to collect us. The ape-like creature painted on the side of it looked more like Bigfoot than a chimp. Lettering on each side read "Chimp Adventures."

"Gombe Stream," called a young African man as he emerged from the van. "Those going to Gombe Stream, this is your ride."

"Here we are," answered a gray-haired man and his teenage son, much to our surprise. "Who are they, and how can they fit all of us in this van?" we wondered.

"Us, too," called out an elderly woman and her daughter.

They packed us into the van as though fitting circus clowns into an MG Midget. "Lairmore-Merrick family—we'll be dropping you off at the Hilltop Hotel for the night," the man announced. "The others of you we'll be putting on a boat and taking you out to Gombe straightaway."

I sulked, thinking of "undeserving" strangers getting a head start on us at Gombe while we waited overnight in Kigoma. As we learned the next day, however, the "undeserving" strangers were remarkable people. Mike was a Royal Canadian Air Force doctor whose most recent assignment had been directing a staging-hospital operation in Afghanistan; he and son Ky had traveled the world—as had Andrea, an Australian NGO specialist, and her Canadian mother.

The short drive from the airport to town seemed vaguely familiar, but unlike years before, there were now endless shops, and people swarmed the streets. Bright cloths hung in front of the mercantile shops. Shop signs were written in English and Swahili, with images of Hollywood movie stars and the Coca-Cola logo painted on some, pictures of fancy African ladies on others. The men had on cotton trousers and shirts, while the women wore more traditional fare, including half of an African cloth wrapped on their heads or used to tie their babies to their backs as if they were papooses. As we drove toward the lake, I recognized the wet-earth smell.

The Hilltop Hotel was located on a ridge directly along the lakeshore, and the van bumped along a lengthy red-earth driveway until we finally arrived at the hotel sentry gate. There stood the guard—a splendid elderly man, rail thin and almost toothless, wearing a violet military uniform with epaulets. A beret was tipped nattily toward his right temple. He snapped to attention as we approached, saluting us as though we were royalty. His remaining teeth shone as he proudly grinned at us, fully aware of his own noteworthiness. He waved us in, and we headed down the last jarring segment of the driveway, watching men alongside the road who were crushing rocks with pickaxes to create a new gravel surface. We arrived to find a young African man sunning himself at the parking area, almost asleep.

He was the all-purpose lobby employee—greeter, desk clerk, bellboy, concierge, and bathroom attendant all in one. We followed him into the lobby, passing a number of weathered taxidermied antelopes.

"Welcome to the Hotel California," I expected him to say, for that was just how strange this place seemed. It was huge—set on three acres, with expansive lawns, a dining room, and more than fifty rooms—yet totally devoid of guests. There were overstuffed expensive chairs carefully placed throughout the lobby, contrasting with tattered posters and cracked walls with missing paint. "Business center open 24 hours daily" read a sign behind the clerk. We guessed the "center" likely consisted of an old manual typewriter and a broken adding machine.

Our new African friend checked us in, then insisted on carrying our bags to the rooms. We walked out into the sunlight, finding long green lawns and beautifully kept grounds with three gardeners at work. There on the grass were eight zebras, roaming freely. They seemed every bit as odd as the antelopes in the lobby, particularly since we knew they are not native to the area and belong, instead, on the Serengeti, hundreds of miles away. Realizing the heart attacks the small herd would cause hotel risk managers in the United States, we tiptoed past them, only a few feet away, and wondered what would happen if we accidentally startled them. I could picture Bryan rolling his eyes, prompted by this little hotel trying to be something it clearly was not. The young man delivered us to our rooms, the packs on his back stacked three high.

As we settled into our room, a group of vervet monkeys came tapping on the windows, gazing inside and helping us understand how zoo animals must feel. An occasional zebra strolled by. I gazed fondly out the window at Lake Tanganyika, thinking of wonderful times past and new adventures ahead. In the morning, we would go by boat to Gombe.

❊ ❊ ❊

"Wow—it's still the same," I thought to myself. "Thirty-six years later, and it's still the same."

I prepared to step off the boat onto the beach of Gombe National Park, one leg wanting to run through the water and up the beach and the other seemingly still weighing whether this was a good idea or not. Thoughts of wild chimpanzees, sunset swims, and hikes through the glorious Tanzanian forest emerged. But what if my memories had become inflated over time? What if the reality of this place wouldn't live up to the stories I had told my family all these years? Was it possible this could turn into a let-down, an embarrassment?

It was too late now. My nineteen-year-old, the same age I had been and wearing the same grin I had worn when I first wandered off the boat onto these shores, was already on land.

"Dr. Tony!" she yelled. It was Dr. Tony Collins, Gombe's heartthrob from my time here long ago, now bald and slight. But there he was, thirty-six years later, standing at the dock, now a key player at Gombe, a well-known conservationist and baboon researcher, and acting director of the facility. "*Karibuni*," he called, welcoming us. "Your timing is perfect. The chimps are just outside camp, and Jane is here."

With that, both legs agreed that disembarking would be an excellent idea. I smiled with relief, feeling somehow that life was coming full circle. I was about to see how Gombe had fared over all these years.

❖ ❖ ❖

Knowing that Gombe must have changed greatly over the years, it was surprising to me how familiar things appeared. The kitchen and the photography lab looked just as they had in 1972, and the only thing new was a row of offices where the dining hall had stood. I thought of Gombe past, when its inhabitants were fifteen to twenty undergraduate and graduate students, plus the Tanzanian camp and field staff. Those had been the grand old days of Gombe—coming just twelve years after Jane herself had first arrived—a time when every day yielded exciting new discoveries about the hitherto unknown world of wild chimpanzees.

Tony walked us into an office to chat. Gary and Bryan joined him on the bench, while Kate and I took seats across the room, and we plied him with questions about how he and his family were doing and how he had managed to stay at Gombe for so many years. Finally, we asked him about what he was doing currently.

"Just kind of hanging about, I suppose," he offered in his understated Scottish way. The truth was that he had continued the baboon studies that he had initiated in 1972, focusing on a group known as Beach Troop. Troop members had been wildly successful at breeding new generations, and as with a dividing cell, there were now numerous new troops.

"Ah, yes, I'm afraid I have years' worth of data to crunch in order to be ready for a paper I'll deliver at an upcoming primate conference. Kind of disturbing, actually."

It was obvious that Tony was still his generous self, the guy who literally emptied his pockets of every bill and coin when approached by a beggar. It wasn't a surprise that of the thirty-five or so PhDs who had studied at Gombe, it was Tony who had remained there all these years, ever faithful to Jane and Gombe.

"I'm afraid Jane took a bit of a spill and tweaked her shoulder," he told us. "Fell down the path."

I offered my services as a physician, but he merely said, "I'll mention it."

Knowing that we would see him later, we left Tony to his data and went in search of chimps with Imani, our guide, and Juma, the national park ranger.

❖ ❖ ❖

Gombe legend has it that the chimps can sense when Jane is present and come down to the valleys to be with her, and we soon came to believe it. We had walked for only five minutes when we met up with two chimps, an adult male named Zeus who was feeding on palm nuts in a tree, and the infamous male, Frodo, crossing the stream to join Zeus.

"Wouldn't you know we'd run into Frodo!" I said to the others. "Be careful, because he's the one that likes to toss people around when he gets excited."

Some part of me was happy to see him, nevertheless, because I had known his mother, Fifi, so many years ago. Frodo was huge, among the largest wild chimps I have seen, yet almost gentlemanly as he walked past us. Perhaps age had tempered his past aggressive behavior. He moved effortlessly into the tree with Zeus and began eating palm nuts. Two African field researchers sat below with their check sheets, recording data.

After watching Zeus and Frodo for a number of minutes, we moved on and quickly found more people and chimps. The group included Mike and his son Ky, who we had met the previous day, and their guides. They were watching two families of chimps: Frodo's sister, Fanni, with her three children—eight-year-old Fundi, four-year-old Familia, and six-month-old Fadhila—and Sandi with her children Samwise, who was seven, and two-year-old Siri. It was a typical warm afternoon for the chimps. The older children played boisterously in the bushes near where Sandi and Fanny sat grooming. Little Fadhila stayed right by her mother's side, one hand touching Fanny's back, ready to grab on should she suddenly get up and move. Fundi's laughter was infectious as he hung upside down from a branch and playfully slapped at Siri and Familia while they roughhoused.

We watched for some time before striking off with our guides for Kakombe Falls. The path was steep, with huge drop-offs to the right, reminding us we were in the mountains of the Great Rift Valley. But it felt good to be back on these paths. Bryan offered some encouraging words to Kate, knowing her fear of heights and difficult hikes, and she bravely mumbled something congenial back. Once we finally arrived, we allowed the waterfall mist to drench us, and the photo commemorating our visit shows a family of happy, half-drowned bilge rats, not quite ready for a Christmas card.

Talking with the guide on the way back, we learned that none of the Tanzanian field assistants and very few of the chimps who I had known were still there. I could count the chimp survivors on one hand: Gremlin, a delightful two-year-old back when had I met her; Wilkie, who was born during my stay; one-year-old Freud; and Sparrow, just twelve years old in 1972. I had expected to see more familiar faces, and I wondered how the Gombe populations were doing overall.

Tony met us once we arrived back at the beach and invited us to Jane's house for a visit. "She's just back from walking in the forest—alone," he said.

This was her precious one-week stay at Gombe, and Tony had been unable to convince her of the danger of roaming unaccompanied. We knew she must love Tony for his gentle ways and for his abhorrence about controlling anyone.

We walked toward Jane's house, which stood just as it always had. It was a mostly cement rectangular structure, lodged adjacent to a small stand of trees and placed squarely facing Lake Tanganyika. Vines grew along parts of it, and much of its cement-block surface was cracked.

We entered the living room, where Tony instructed us to have a seat while he went to check on her. Every one of us was excited to be here, but Imani, our shy African guide, seemed particularly awed to be a guest of Dr. Jane Goodall's. Every now and again, he looked at the floor and his eyes flashed in amazement.

After a two-minute wait, out came Jane. As always, her hair was in a ponytail and she was wearing a button-down shirt. As I watched her, I thought how years ago I could have predicted that this was where I would find her still, at age seventy-four, looking as natural and poised as ever.

Still, the more I thought about it, something seemed not quite right. She was keeping her right arm folded in front of her, as if it were in an imaginary sling. Was she nursing her shoulder but trying to be inconspicuous about it?

"Hello, Nancy, and all of you." She seemed genuinely glad to see us. After hugs all around, we took our places on the sofas.

"Jane, we won't stay long," I said, "but it is so good to get to see you."

"We heard you had a bad fall," Gary added.

And with this, she told us of her "battle with a rock of gigantic proportions," telling it with an eloquence hardly expected from a woman in pain, or at least not an American one. She had climbed up an impossibly steep Gombe trail in pursuit of a lone chimpanzee. The ground had been "skiddy," she said, and there had been only grass and brittle vines for handholds. Much to her relief, she spotted two huge rocks above her. She successfully pulled herself up onto the first, but when she reached for the second, it detached itself from its hollow, striking her shoulder and knocking the wind out of her, and sending her tumbling back down the trail. "Three tumbles, and I'm thinking that when I get way down to the bottom, every bone will be broken, and I'll probably be dead." The rock, found later, weighed in at a bone-crushing 131 pounds, and it seemed almost a miracle that she had survived.

"I lay there for I don't know how long. After that, it took me a long time to get myself up to the top of that beastly trail, to where the trail along Peak Ridge leads down to the beach. I was absolutely covered in blood from gouged-out arm flesh; I had a bruised face, and was thinking I had broken my jaw and my shoulder. Thankfully, I'm a tough old bird!" She looked around the room once again, as though gauging how the story was registering with each of us. Perhaps our dropped jaws were a giveaway.

"Tony climbed up the next day and found the rock. When he got back, he said, 'Jane, it's enormous, much bigger than you said.' I told him that if it had landed on my head and not my body, I would surely not be here!"[1]

"Oh, my gosh, you really are lucky to be alive," whispered Kate, looking astonished.

"Mmmm . . . and she was back out in the forest alone again today," Tony told us.

Jane gave him a quick glance that combined both minor annoyance with and appreciation of his testimony to her bravado.

"Perhaps you should get an X-ray tomorrow when we return to Kigoma," suggested Dr. Shadrack Kamenya, the park's director of conservation, who had joined us.

I offered to examine her, but ultimately she allowed me only to palpate her shoulder through her blouse as she sat on the sofa. At one point, I mentioned that if we were in the United States, I would insist on driving her to the nearest orthopedist to be examined. When she looked me squarely in the eyes and retorted, "Thankfully for me, we're not in the States," I knew that the conversation was over. I had met my match. We turned to more congenial conversation, talking of days gone by.

Jane spoke of her deceased second husband, Derek Bryceson, and his contributions to Tanzania as director of the national parks. We told her of our travels and praised the programs of the Jane Goodall Institute, its chimp sanctuaries, and its programs to help local people.

"Yes, and we must extend those programs to help the refugees," she said. She talked of the urgency of finding funds to help refugees being sent back to the Democratic Republic of the Congo from nearby Tanzanian camps. "It is absolutely unthinkable that they are sending refugees back to Congo with nothing more than three months of provisions. They don't even know what they're going back to or how they'll survive."

The conversation turned next to Jane's joy at the success of the recent first International Roots & Shoots Youth Summit. Bryan had been fortunate to be one of the student representatives from the United States.

"It was awesome!" Bryan said. "The people there had accomplished such amazing things. The only bad thing was going back home to people that just don't care."

Jane looked alarmed. "You have to keep that spirit of the conference. You can't just give up." She encouraged him to keep the community alive through the Internet, letters, and projects. "Why don't you reconnect with Shadrack at Lugufu Refugee Camp when you get back to Kigoma. Keep sharing your ideas."

Tony had remained fairly quiet throughout the conversation, seeming to keep an eye on Jane. I, too, was watching for signs that she might be in pain and that we ought to go, but she seemed surprisingly resilient. It was a joy to be back in her living room, like in the old days. There were no crowds of people wanting her autograph or a photo, no assistant stealing her off to her next appearance, like when she lectures in the United States.

"How about we have some whiskey?" suggested Tony. "It's a tradition." Tony retrieved the whiskey and poured each of us a glass, diluting it with club soda. This was a rite of passage for me—to sit in Jane's living room sharing a dram of whiskey. My children sat looking incredulous at finding themselves in Dr. Goodall's living room, even being offered whiskey—which, by the way, they declined. We chatted, signed the guestbook, and savored the moment.

"Too bad we don't have some of the whiskey from the *choo* bottle," said Tony. Gary, Jane, and I started laughing.

"Tell the others that story," Gary said.

Tony, a master of maintaining a straight face, recounted the story: "Well, Julie Johnson had the most wonderful bottle of Vat 69 blended Scotch whiskey that she saved for the longest time, waiting for a really spectacular occasion. And one night, we had a party, and somehow, no doubt in someone's drunken stupor, that bottle of whiskey ended up unopened in the bottom of the latrine.

"No one could stand the thought that this perfectly amazing bottle of whiskey was sitting there untouched, so Julie volunteered that whoever could retrieve it would get to keep it and get another bottle besides. Pretty soon, everyone was in on it. Over the next two weeks, some remarkable feats were attempted, none of them successful. Finally, Jim Moore and Caroline Tutin got it out using Grub's fishing tackle with a snare loop." I laughed, picturing the two of them fishing for whiskey with equipment borrowed from Jane's young son, Hugo—nicknamed Grub—while wearing clothespins on their noses so as to avoid succumbing to the smell of the *choo*, or pit toilet.

"The minute they got it out, we took the bottle to the infirmary, wiped it down with antiseptic, and promptly consumed it." It was a legendary Gombe moment.

"All right—it's time we go and let you get some rest," I said, guessing that Jane must surely be exhausted. Still, the indefatigable Jane took her time, deciding to sign picture postcards to send to our friends at the tented camp.

"Can you remove the cap from my pen?" she asked me, still nursing her arm. She then inscribed the cards with "Welcome to Gombe. Best regards!—Jane Goodall." As she handed them to me, she instructed me that I was to tell each of them to join the Jane Goodall Institute in their respective countries as soon as they got home.

As a grand finale, Tony proposed that photographs of our grand event be taken out on the steps. Jane quite agreed that this was very necessary.

My husband's dreams had been answered, as for years I had kept him from requesting our snapshot with Jane, trying to spare her yet another flash photo!

We marched out to the steps, where we arrayed ourselves in what seemed like twenty different groupings, each one captured in photographs by at least two cameras. Then we kissed good-bye, wishing Jane well on her return to Kigoma in the morning. We headed for the water taxi, feeling high as kites and a little tipsy from the whiskey. The boat delivered us to the tented camp twenty minutes away, where dinner was waiting.

As it turned out, the other four had a story of their own. They had chanced on Jane while she was out walking in the Gombe forest. They had tried to be polite and not bother her, but Jane seemed quizzical when they started to depart so quickly. "Don't you want a picture?" she asked. Well, yes, of course they did, and so they flanked her and had their pictures taken with the magnanimous Dr. Jane Goodall at Gombe.

Jane's shoulder proved to be dislocated—a stunning revelation when I heard about it days later, back in the United States. How could she possibly have endured it? I wondered, never having seen another human being tolerate an injury like that without an immediate visit to the emergency room. I had always known how she treasures her all-too-infrequent week-long visits to Gombe and her time hiking alone in the forests, unfettered by VIPs or camera crews. But it took on a whole new dimension now with the realization that she had chosen unimaginable physical pain over the mental anguish of giving up even a single day at her cherished Gombe. This place was truly her soul, the site of fond memories of solitude and discovery and a simpler time. Only now could I fathom the full extent of her sacrifice in traveling the globe three hundred days a year to save her chimpanzees—and of the pain of willingly giving up Gombe's natural world for the madness of constant travel, interviews, lectures, and inspiring the world.

❧ ❧ ❧

The next day brought more good luck. Once again, it took only a short walk from the beach to stumble on a sizable group of chimps. Sparrow, Fanny, and their families were socializing there, along with two newcomers, a young adult male named Titan and Sifa, a female in estrus. Likely, Sifa was staying with the other two females in order to defuse the constant attention of Titan.

Titan, the equivalent of a sixteen-year-old human male, seemed excited, if a bit confused. He would playfully wrestle with the youngsters for twenty minutes at a time, but as soon as he noticed Sifa moving away, his hair would stand on end and he would become agitated.

"Hoo-ha, hooooo-ha, hoo-ha," Titan's pant-hoot was becoming higher pitched and faster, and he was rocking back and forth where he sat.

"Over here, sir. You need to move over here, sir," the guide called to Mike.

Just then, Titan jumped up and ran toward Mike in hot pursuit of Sifa, with whom he was fully fed up. Fanny grabbed her baby and ran into nearby bushes, making a loud barking noise, followed by Familia and Fundi. Sparrow and family disappeared in the opposite direction, but we could hear their screams. As Titan charged through the bushes after Sifa, the others ran after him, maintaining a safe distance.

I looked for Mike and found him still frozen in place. Titan had long since charged past him, not paying any attention, but Mike remained there, immobilized, wearing a fear grin. The guide walked over to him. "Let me feel your heart," he teased, placing his hand on Mike's chest and pretending to count the uncountable pulsations. Mike stayed close to the guide after that.

We tried to keep up with the chimps, but by now they had scattered and were difficult to find. We eventually gave up and, instead, went off to pursue our heart's content, whether a swim in the lake or a hike to the waterfall. The four of us chose a walk to "the Peak," where Jane had gone in her early days of research to try to spot chimps in the valleys below.[2] The view seemed like a fitting last stop, knowing as we did that we would be leaving Gombe to return to the tented camp in another two hours.

It was another tough climb, replete with an unexpected reunion at the top with Mike, Andrea, Ky, and their guides. We celebrated with water-bottle toasts and photos. But when it was done, I was unexpectedly overcome with emotion. It had been good to know that Gombe was still thriving and to see the healthy descendants of the chimps I had known back in 1972. But at the same time, I felt concerned. When I stood at the lookout spot and gazed across the lake, I could no longer see the Democratic Republic of the Congo, thirty miles away. The sky was no longer the deep blue I remembered. Now, there was a gray haze that dulled the sky, and there was even the smell of smoke. Villages that had been home to a hundred people now were ten times that size—one village even had a population of five thousand. And Gombe National Park itself seemed like a cutout, a forested area surrounded by lands devoid of vegetation. Paradise had been all but paved.

As we walked back to the beach, our guide took us an unusually round-about way, departing from the more direct route the others had taken. I was feeling hungry and tired, even a bit irritated. Just then, the guide brought us to a clearing in the forest, where we stopped for a look.

"Do you recognize it?" he asked me.

"No—I'm afraid I don't. Why, should I?"

"This is—I think it was called Pan Palace," he told me, smiling, "to feed the chimps bananas."

It was hard to believe, but the meadow was where "Camp" had been. The building and the feeding station had been removed years ago by IMAX cinematographers so as to allow for better filming in all directions and more natural shots. Now, the entire area was overgrown by bushes and grass, as though nothing had ever stood there.

"And what about this place?" he asked me, guiding us to a dismal old hut thirty feet away. As I opened the rusty door, it all came back to me. This was where our offices had been, where we had worked every day, waiting for chimps to turn up that we could follow and collect data on. The building seemed like a long-lost friend. Bryan looked it over with me, thoughtfully sharing the moment, and the guide laughed, recognizing how much this rusty old building meant to me.

✵ ✵ ✵

The next morning, we had breakfast at the tented camp and then headed back to Kigoma on the boat. Imani sat at the bow, studying his signed postcard, and fellow guide Sixtus talked of his family, which lived hundreds of miles away. Sixtus hoped to one day work for the National Wildlife Authority in conservation, a job that would allow him to be closer to his family, with a better salary, and, equally important, to make a difference in preserving wild Tanzania.

As we motored along, the park border was all too evident, denuded by villagers scavenging firewood. Kate's allergies were unleashed by the smoky air, reminding us of forest fire days at home and their smell of ash. I wondered whether someone was carefully managing the fisheries and protecting the lake's water quality, and even more important, if the problems we had seen here and in Uganda were emblematic of those in other African countries.

It was hard to leave Gombe that day. So much had happened in this place that had forever changed my life. I wanted to be here, to make sure Gombe continued, to protect the next generations of the chimps I had known so well. I wanted to save the forests of their less well-protected chimp neighbors and to solve the puzzle of how chimps and people can co-exist. I needed to know that it would go on, and that these chimps would be here forever.

CHAPTER 5

FACADE AND SURVIVAL

As we left, I thought about how easily we had gotten off so far. Each day of our trip had been perfect. We had made friends along the way, carried chimps through the forest, drunk Scotch whiskey, and talked about the old days with Jane. But I knew better from having lived here in the past. East Africa is a place of two extremes—and, as of yet, we had experienced only one of them. I thought about Bryan's skepticism—his sense that so much of our interaction with the Africans was just a facade, that we had bought these experiences and they were false. Now, here we were back in Kigoma.

✦ ✦ ✦ ✦ ✦ ✦

"Real" East Africa lay just at the other end of the lengthy Hilltop driveway. We were headed to the Jane Goodall Institute's office, planning to meet with the staff there and hoping to catch up with Tony. As we walked the dirt road, we passed the jail campus, the antiquated power plant, the shops and vendors. The streets were filled with men on bicycles and with women carrying wood on their heads while their *kitenga*-swaddled babies slept on their backs. We greeted young people in school uniforms as they passed, speaking just as casually as we might have done while out for a walk at home.

An archaic gray-steel ferry lay anchored in the harbor, and we knew just what its purpose was. It would load two hundred refugees before the end of the day and begin the short journey to deliver them back to their homes in the Democratic Republic of the Congo (DRC). Several days per week throughout the coming months, this boat, and others, would load up to two hundred souls who had little idea of what they were returning to. On arrival at their destination, they would be given three months' provisions and the support of the United Nations High Commission on Refugees (UNHCR) as they attempted to reclaim their lands and lives in their former communities. But given the many concerns Jane had expressed about the repatriation of these Congolese refugees, that boat seemed spoiled, for there was too much uncertainty surrounding it. Too many recent clashes had occurred in the areas the refugees were returning to, and there was too little rule of law and reason.

These people were part of Kigoma's continuing sad legacy as a refugee capital. It had acquired this solemn responsibility by virtue of its location on the western border of Tanzania. Kigoma Region lies on the shores of Lake Tanganyika, with Burundi just thirty miles away to the northwest, the DRC thirty miles across the lake to the west, and Zambia 220 miles to the south. Rwanda, the site of genocide that killed more than one million people in 1994, lies to the north. Because of years of tumult and war in the region, Kigoma had become one of the world's most critical centers for refugees and international relief organizations.

Most of those being repatriated now were refugees who had entered Tanzania between 1994 and 1998.[1] Tanzania and the UNHCR were attempting to peacefully and safely return these refugees to their homes within a reasonable period in hopes they would still be able to reclaim their lands and reassimilate into their former communities. But there were also some refugees in Tanzania who had been allowed to stay far longer: the "1972 Burundians."[2] These were the refugees I had once seen struggling across Gombe's beaches as they fled the first wave of Burundian genocide, and, just as it had been thirty-six years since I had lived in Tanzania, so it had been thirty-six years since they had fled their homes in Burundi, almost a lifetime ago.

✦ ✦ ✦

I have never been traumatized in any significant way, yet I am unmistakably fragile when it comes to the refugees of East Africa. "I can't watch that film," I told my daughter's eighth-grade teacher during a visit to the Museum of Tolerance, in Los Angeles, years ago. I was an adult chaperone, yet it was me the teacher was tending to, not the eighth graders.

"Better you should stay outside," advised the Holocaust survivor leading our tour.

Ultimately, I did go in briefly to see the start of the film on Hutu-Tutsi genocide in Burundi and Rwanda. If a Holocaust survivor could do it, I told myself, then I certainly had no excuse. But I proved ridiculously fragile during even modest discussions of the atrocities, as I imagined what those 1972 Burundians had endured. The genocide they had escaped had killed two hundred thousand people and maimed countless others.

The result of tribal warfare between the Hutu and Tutsi peoples, it was the first of the Great Lakes genocides that would later also consume the DRC and Rwanda. The refugees' stories had been shocking and difficult to deal with: cases of rape and torture. Soldiers brutalizing whole schools, maiming children with one slice of their *panga*s, assaulting teachers, and sometimes killing everyone in the school. Some parents had been forced by their assailants to kill their own children, and onetime neighbors had inexplicably become predator and prey.

The atrocities had understandably caused an estimated 150,000 Burundians, mostly Hutus, to seek refuge, the majority fleeing to the Kigoma area. From there, they had been moved to three camps in the western interior of Tanzania to protect against possible border incursions by rival factions intent on murdering them. The camps saved thousands of lives, but the refugees' stories left difficult memories in my mind that resurfaced each time there was a new wave of regional genocide.

Given all I knew about Burundi's history of atrocities, I was little prepared to hear, when traveling with a friend in 1985, that she had booked us a three-day stay there. We were traveling from Dian Fossey's Karisoke Research Center, in Rwanda, en route to Gombe in Tanzania, and the easiest route was via Bujumbura, Burundi's capital. An old German boat, the *Liemba*, could deliver us from Bujumbura to Kigoma, near Gombe. First, however, we would spend three days of rest and relaxation at a Bujumbura resort.

It was frightening to think of going to Burundi, but I went anyway, knowing that this was a time of "peace." Much to my relief, we arrived to find Hutus and Tutsis working side by side wherever we traveled. The Burundian government included ministers from each group, and curiously, there was no sign whatsoever of the atrocities and hatred of 1972.

We spent our days at a lakeside Bujumbura resort. While there, we enjoyed lunch with a young Joe Wilson, the deputy chief of mission at the US Embassy there at the time, years before his wife, Valerie Plame, was exposed as a CIA covert operative by newspaper columnist Robert Novak. We also became friends with an African woman named Felicity, a chauffeur—thirty-nine years old and the mother of two children—who offered to show us the city. Everything about her was quite Western, including her dress and her attitude. One day, when she invited us to lunch, we had the opportunity to finally ask.

"Isn't there still a lot of hatred between the Watutsi and the Bahutus?

I remember people being killed in 1972. Aren't you afraid it will happen again?"

Felicity looked momentarily astonished, and then she stared closely into my eyes as though she was about to expunge these thoughts. "No, there's no hatred anymore," she assured me. "We all get along together. I don't know what you mean."

But in truth, Burundi was still secretly seething and would erupt once again in 1993, killing thousands more.

✦ ✦ ✦

We finally arrived at the Jane Goodall Institute's Kigoma office, walking yet another long, red driveway to a modest compound of buildings along the lake. Everyone there was skipping-lunch busy that day, because Jane had just departed for Uganda and left instructions for a host of new refugee programs. Augustino, our host, was buried with work, so he hurriedly introduced us to a French volunteer who would show us around until he was available.

"*Jambo*," said Julie with a sumptuous French accent. Adorned in a skirt and sandals, bits of long, brown hair draped behind her ears, she had a Spartan look fitting for a woman who had just returned from volunteering for a month at the Lugufu Refugee Camp. She was in the midst of organizing her photos, and she was keen to share them.

Her duties had focused on helping ready the refugees for repatriation. She had worked with some of Kigoma's newest refugees, those who had fled the DRC in the late 1990s at a time of new political uncertainty there. The camps had filled quickly: the five thousand refugees arriving weekly had quickly swamped the capacity of the existing refugee camps, forcing the creation of new camps like Lugufu. Yet even after the political crises had quieted in neighboring countries, refugees continued to pour in. Many were looking for a better life, some for schooling or food security, and others simply to be reunited with a loved one who had fled earlier. By early 2000, more than 650,000 refugees had entered the Kigoma region, accounting for one in three residents of the area and further straining the ability of Tanzania, the United Nations, and relief organizations to provide for them. But 2008 was a different time, one in which Tanzania was focused on emptying the camps. The Lugufu Refugee Camp was close to completing the return of its inhabitants to their homes in the DRC.

"It was amazing," Julie told us. "There is so much work to do. These people are being sent home not knowing if their lands have been appropriated by their neighbors who stayed behind. Many of the young people have been in the camp so long that they only speak Swahili. How will they communicate back in Congo? And the three months of supplies they're being given isn't anywhere near enough."

The UNHCR, she explained, was promising to help the refugees as they returned home, but she wondered how effective it could be in sorting out disputes as the refugees tried to reclaim any property they had abandoned years ago. And although those without a previous home had been promised refuge in newly constructed "peace villages," who knew what really lay ahead for them? Julie had worked in every imaginable capacity at Lugufu in her campaign to connect conservation and human welfare. She had been part of a troupe of actors, portraying for camp residents how to prevent AIDS and how to ensure the health of their children. She had taught classes on violence prevention and shown refugees how to sustain themselves by breeding chickens, building hatcheries, and living more sustainable lives. The work had been done alongside the Jane Goodall Institute's remarkable Lugufu Roots & Shoots coordinator, Shadrack Meschach, the third in a line of Tanzanians who had introduced the program to fifteen schools within the camp and taught skills that would be critical to survival.

As she showed us photos of her hosting Jane's visit to the camp, there was a strange relief that, at long last, I was finally reconnecting with that troubling flip side of East Africa. Until now, we had reveled in chimp walks and seeing old friends. But now, we were seeing true East Africa, rife with refugees, AIDS victims, and people racked by malnutrition and infectious disease. Here, once again, was real life in Africa, a place thoroughly tangled in the clutches of poverty. How could one possibly hope to solve the problems of the chimps without also addressing conservation's mortal enemy, poverty?

We headed back to the United States later that same day, and our eighteen-hour trip afforded plenty of opportunity to reflect on it all. I thought of refugees and genocides and fragmented forests. I thought, too, of Gombe, weighing the smoky skies and large settlements around the park that we had seen and wondering what they portended for the future of the chimps.

PART II

GOMBE EAST AND GOMBE WEST, 1972–1976

CHAPTER 6

THE PATH TO GOMBE STREAM

Our expectations for Gombe's future had been so different when I was nineteen. At the time, the entire world was enthralled by its newfound knowledge about the chimpanzees. Never before had we believed that animals could have such rich social lives or be so closely related to humans. We assumed that the chimps' novel notoriety would ensure their future, never imagining that they could one day be endangered.

Gombe was a thriving colony of European and American students and Tanzanian staff in 1972, and each week brought exciting new discoveries of the complexities of these intelligent creatures. It was a rare opportunity to not only be immersed in the lives of chimpanzees but also to work for the legendary Jane Goodall.

✦ ✦ ✦ ✦ ✦ ✦

"Today, class, we'll watch a film about a young woman scientist living with chimpanzees in Africa," Mr. Visser announced to our twelfth-grade social studies class. It was 1970, and about the only woman scientist I had ever heard of was Madame Curie. I tried to envision this new scientist, imagining a tough, thick-framed woman living on a tree branch next to a family of chimps. The boy next to me yawned, realizing he'd just been blessed with forty-five minutes of protected sleep time.

"Okay, hit the lights!" Mr. Visser shouted to the girl in the corner as he hunched over the projector. His nose was pressed against the motor as he threaded an inch of film onto the back reel. "Someone get the blinds."

The familiar clackety-clack of the projector began, and the screen flashed the National Geographic Society's logo and music. It was a new film, not one of the older ones that broke every ten minutes, causing the reels to spin and the end of the roll of film to flap. The opening credits completed, the film switched to an intriguing scene—a motorboat with a captivating woman seated at the bow arriving at a beautiful beach.

"It was 1960 when a young English woman arrived in Tanzania in search of wild apes," the film narrator announced. The shot focused on the willowy woman, her long, sun-streaked hair neatly pulled back into a graceful ponytail. She had doe-like brown eyes, a pert nose, and lips drawn into almost a heart shape. As the boat arrived at its destination, she pulled her binoculars to her eyes, hoping to sight the "elusive chimpanzee." She emerged from the boat looking adventurous, yet natural and feminine—hardly the jungle researcher I had imagined. Already, I was completely enamored.

The film told how Dr. Goodall began studying chimpanzees in 1960, aided initially by her mother and several African staff members. She had spent that first unheralded year living in a tent and doing everything possible to get close enough to the chimps to observe them. This often called for hiking to "the Peak" and listening for chimp calls in order to locate them. Once they were found, she would race down the hillside, hoping to get within range and to accustom them to her presence.

The film switched to a scene months later, as some of the chimps began coming into camp for bananas and losing their fear of humans. It was a cast of characters—elderly Flo, the matriarch, and her spirited daughter, Fifi; belligerent Hugo; and old Mr. Worzel. Their facial expressions, emotions, and surprising intelligence were unmistakable. And there in the midst of them was long, lanky Jane Goodall. As I sat watching, I was filled with the desire to be in this woman's place, studying wild chimpanzees.

I left for Stanford University in 1970 with that vision, and although freshman year was spent rather uneventfully, my second year began with astounding news—Dr. Jane Goodall would be a lecturer for the first month of introductory Human Biology classes. Hearing that, I instantly made plans to attend.

That first day of lecture was unforgettable. In a hall packed with three hundred students, Dr. Goodall walked to the speaker's podium, looking shy and even a little awkward. But all that changed instantly as she started in, letting loose with a piercing set of pant-hoots, the chimpanzee calls of excitement. As the calls echoed into the hallways, she confidently announced, "And that is how chimps call to one another." The entire auditorium lit up with an energy rarely seen in morning lecture.

She told us of a cadre of fascinating wild chimps, each with a name and their own unique personality. There was David Graybeard, the first chimp to befriend her, and Mike, the new leader of the community who had ascended to alpha status by tossing about a very loud empty gas can while looking aggressive and dangerous. There were Evered and Melissa, who had snuck away from the others for a week, enjoying a lovers' escape. It sounded almost like a soap opera, with chimps as caricatures of humans.

Now, fifty minutes into the lecture, I wondered how I could possibly get to work for this fabulous woman. That was the moment when Dr. David Hamburg, head of Stanford's Program in Human Biology, came to the podium for an announcement: A special program was beginning in which interested human biology majors could spend six months working with Dr. Goodall in Tanzania. Eight students a year would be selected. They would receive two quarters of college credit, and their expenses would be covered.

With that, the business of selecting my college major was instantly and wholly settled. I was determined to work for my idol, Dr. Jane Goodall, and surprisingly unfazed by the fact that just eight students per year would be so lucky. If sheer will and absurdly dependable good luck had anything to do with it, I knew my senior year would be spent in Tanzania, studying the wild chimpanzees.

✦ ✦ ✦

"Nancy, it's for you," my mother had said. "A Dr. Hamburg?"

It was the summer after sophomore year. I was home, working as a recreation leader, and not expecting a phone call from Stanford University.

"One of the students leaving for Tanzania in three weeks isn't able to go," he told me. "I wonder if you'd be interested in taking his place?"

There was not even a moment's hesitation. I accepted instantly, barely following the details he discussed, and thanking him four times before hanging up.

Gombe was on.

✦ ✦ ✦

The beginning of August was spent hunting for items like rain ponchos with duckbill hoods and a cheap guitar that would not be missed if destroyed by humidity and mildew. I memorized simple Swahili sentences out of a letter written by two Stanford students to new inductees like me. But, I wondered, how do you really pronounce "*Tafadhali, ninataka kufuata soko mtu sasa*" ("Please, I would like to follow a chimp now")? And why would you really want to say "*Wewe, unaweza kwenda chini*" ("You may go downstairs now")? I tried to imagine being in the wilds of Africa, out of contact with friends and family for the next six months, living in a remote area of Africa. I devoured the public library's copy of the CIA manual on Tanzania, which described the basics of life there, hoping to get an inkling of what lay ahead.

On the day of departure, my parents drove me to the airport. My mother and I were in tears, while my father was delighting at how he had rigged the guitar box so I could carry it on my back. He had emblazoned the embarrassing words "Chimp Chaser" across it, certain he would secure me many interesting new friends in the course of my travels. As it turned out, his efforts were effective, although not all the acquaintances seemed exactly what my father had had in mind. Nevertheless, it was a hit with a variety of weathered Arab porters at the Cairo airport, where fellow student Faye Benedict and I found ourselves overnighting en route. It was 1972, a year of war between Egypt and Israel, and a new airport was being built. We watched excavated sand being carried away, not by bulldozers but in baskets on the heads of long lines of workers.

"I think we're spending the night on these benches," Faye said, pulling out a deck of cards for the long hours ahead. Faye had Dutch-boy brown hair, glasses, a state-of-the-art backpack, and a Swahili dictionary. "How about some apple?" she asked, whipping out her Swiss Army knife and slicing it into pieces like a surgeon.

"Sure, I'd love some." We munched happily for a moment, not having eaten much since morning. "What do you think it will be like?" I probed.

"Gombe?"

"Yeah. Do you think it's like a jungle?" I asked.

"Oh, yeah . . . or forest. Probably lots of fruit trees. Lots of humidity. Probably lots of bugs and snakes," she added.

"Snakes? Really, do you think so?" I could barely believe she had suggested it, but I wasn't too worried. "Well, at least there won't be any poisonous ones," I said.

"What do you mean, there won't be? They have green and black mambas. They're as poisonous as you can find, and there aren't very good antidotes."

"No way," I said. "There's no way that Stanford could send us anywhere with poisonous snakes. They can't put students in any kind of danger. What if one of them got hurt?"

"They've got scorpions and centipedes, too."

"No way!"

"'Fraid so—and, obviously, malaria."

"Yeah, but there's no way that we could ever catch it. We've got malaria pills."

"Ah, come on. Those help, but there's no guarantee you won't get a pretty good case. I can't believe you didn't know this!"

I wasn't afraid of the outdoors, but the thought of deadly poisonous snakes and malaria was terrifying. I took solace in the fact that none of Dr. Goodall's former students had ever died of any of these things—to my knowledge. Surely, it must be okay. Until now, I had liked Faye a lot, but suddenly my affection was waning.

We became lifelong friends over the course of the following week as we experienced one unexpected event after another, a few of them unsettling even to my far-better-prepared friend. Together, we lived through a near airplane crash, missed flights, spent nights in seedy hostels atop bars with prostitutes and blaring music, and took a two-day journey on a steam train across Tanzania. We could only laugh at the improbable situations we continuously found ourselves in, having resigned ourselves to our ping-pong-ball-like existence.

It was one of the longest and most eventful weeks of my young life. But finally, the steam engine train delivered us to the western Tanzanian town of Kigoma, just a two-hour boat ride from Gombe National Park. We were about to meet our first Gombeites, those who would be delivering us to our final destination.

✦ ✦ ✦

There stood two *wazungu*—white people—the only two we had seen in several days. Although the man was tall and thin, the woman short and stout, they were dressed identically, wearing rumpled brown shorts, dull button-down khaki shirts dusted with dirt, and tacky plastic sandals unlike anything I had ever seen. They seemed disappointingly nonchalant, as though we were just two more people coming to Gombe. I assumed they had no idea of the week we had just lived through.

Jim and Toni had spent the night here in town, doing the week's shopping for food and supplies. Jim, quiet and with a sparse brown beard, was a Stanford student, one of five undergraduates at Gombe for the six-month assignment as field assistant to Dr. Goodall. Toni was more colorful, even in khakis, and somewhat of a curiosity. Her abrupt voice and coiffed hair seemed curiously out of place.

"Where have you guys been?" she asked. "Weren't you supposed to be here a week ago?"

Without giving us much time to answer, she continued, telling us that she would be leaving Gombe soon and that she was just visiting for a couple of weeks until her mentor, Louis Leakey, was able to finalize arrangements for her to study bonobos. Leakey, the anthropologist famous for establishing Africa as the source of humanity's origins, was responsible for Jane's field research, as well as that of Dian Fossey on gorillas and Birute Galdikas on orangutans. The last of the remaining unstudied great apes was the bonobo, a species similar in appearance to but separate from chimpanzees. Little was known about bonobos, particularly because they lived only in remote forests of the Congo Basin. And although we normally would have peppered her with questions, we let the conversation drop, hoping to hasten the last leg of our journey to Gombe Stream.

We began walking to the lake along Kigoma's main street, the only tarmac road in the entire city of thirty thousand. Simple storefronts lined the street, adorned with signs in English that advertised products from China. Outside some shops, Indian owners stood, looking bored. African tailors seated at foot-pedal sewing machines worked away in front of others. As we walked, we gathered a following of Africans, pointing and shouting "*Wazungu!*" as though we were part of a circus sideshow. It was a long ten minutes, but we finally arrived at the boat, where, stretched before us, was immense Lake Tanganyika, 410 miles long. The mountains of Zaire, some 30 miles across the water, were perfectly lit by the afternoon sun. We loaded the baskets of supplies onto the Gombe motorboat and departed at last.

Jim kept the boat close to shore as we motored. The lake was crystal blue, and just beyond its pebbled beaches rose the enormous peaks of the Great Rift Valley. The mountains were thick with vegetation, except for some wind-whispered grasslands atop the very highest peaks. The beaches featured an occasional small village, home to fifty or a hundred people, and there were a few fishermen's shacks with tiny silver fish laid out to dry in front of them. Our boat inched along, ignorant of how desperately Faye and I yearned to finally arrive. My stomach churned from the nasty fumes of the boat engine, or perhaps simply from nerves. Jim noticed Faye and me anxiously scanning the shore.

"See the ridgeline up top of those peaks?" he yelled over the noise of the engine, pointing skyward. "It's three-quarters of a mile high, and if you ever hike it, you'll feel every foot of it. These are some steep mountains."

As Faye gazed upward, her eyes grew big, reflecting both the beauty of the imposing mountains and the tough hiking that lay ahead of us.

"We're at the western edge of the Rift," he said, "and it runs for hundreds of miles, all the way up to the Dead Sea in Israel. Kilimanjaro, the Virunga volcanoes, the Rift Lakes—they're all part of it."

I had learned that the Great Rift Valley was formed at the edge of two tectonic plates, resulting in the enormous mountain ranges, lakes, and volcanoes—and its seismic activity. I had expected it to be impressive, but this was breathtaking. The range seemed to rise impossibly high and to extend forever.

"And see that sign?" Jim asked, pointing at a bent metal marker nearly hidden by overgrown shrubs. "That's the Gombe park boundary. Another ten minutes or so, and we'll be there."

Finally, the boat entered a cove that looked familiar. I had seen so many pictures and videos of this place that I recognized it. Just up the beach was the Commons, a rusty generator standing alongside. Down the beach was Jane's cement block home, its wire windows allowing the lake air free entry. In between was the wire "cage" that had been constructed to protect Jane's five-year-old son, Grub, from the baboons and chimps, and there was the pit toilet, fondly referred to by its Swahili name, *choo*. A path on the right led up a steep hill to we knew not where. The hillsides were verdant, almost an Eden.

As I studied the shore of this unspoiled place I was soon to call home, I saw movement. There, walking along the beach, were two chimps followed by a dark-bearded American man in khakis and a dark-skinned African field assistant. Faye and I exchanged glances of thrilled amazement, barely believing we were seeing chimps already. Jim and Toni, by contrast, acted as though it was nothing out of the ordinary.

We docked and unloaded the boat and followed Toni up the beach to the Commons. As we moved closer to the chimps and their entourage, the humans gave us a distracted wave. The chimps, for their part, paid absolutely no attention and continued grooming one another. Once we had passed, the chimps stood and started up the hill, one of them walking upright on his hind legs.

It was Faben, a chimp often featured in films about Gombe, and I felt as excited, as if I were seeing a Hollywood movie star up close. A victim of a local polio epidemic, he had overcome his paralyzed right arm by walking upright. His chest was thrust somewhat forward, and there was a certain swagger to his walk, giving him almost a John Wayne demeanor. Faben had improvised many solutions to his disability, even finding ways of climbing trees one-handed. He looked stunningly human as he strode across the beach.

Next to Faben was another familiar face—that of Figan, his brother, burly, thick trunked, and all muscle. He and his brother had formed a successful alliance within the chimp community that had allowed Figan to become the powerful alpha male. Now, seeing him up close, I could appreciate what a formidable fighter he must be. Faye and I watched in amazement as the chimps ambled off into the distance, researchers in tow.

Next, we entered the Commons, finding a small commissary and a first aid station. Through the doorway was a big room with a large dining table, a small library, and sofas and chairs. The room had a musty smell of mildew, and the cloth sofas felt the least bit damp from the constant humidity. As with Jane's house, the large windows were covered by wire mesh rather than glass, and the lake's fresh aroma was everywhere.

We met people a few at a time as they began to gather for supper. Each of the young researchers approached us, asking about our trip and welcoming us. It was clear that we were the new attraction and that people were curious to see who we were, what we looked like, and what kind of entertainment value we'd have. They sat with us, telling fantastic tales of close encounters with green mambas and angry baboon alphas, and of new primate discoveries being made. It had that first-day-of-school feel to it, fear and excitement all rolled into one.

It wasn't until dinner that we finally met Jane and her photographer husband, Baron Hugo van Lawick, as they arrived at the Commons. Jane greeted us with a cordial "Hello" and "Welcome," followed by a quizzical "Was it you who sent me an odd telegram recently?"

Faye and I flashed uncomfortable glances at each other.

"We were trying to save money," I stuttered, realizing that the excitement of my long-anticipated moment of meeting Jane was fast deteriorating into embarrassment.

Because of all the unanticipated delays en route, Faye and I had spent most of our available cash on train and plane fares, hotel rooms, and food. We had little left for the telegram, yet we felt certain that we needed to send word to Jane of our whereabouts, convinced she must be terribly worried about us. We selected the most inexpensive telegram possible, picking a standard greeting that read, "Congratulations on your new arrivals," and did not bother signing it. Our scrambled nineteen-year-old brains had thought this would convey that we were delayed but would be arriving soon—or at least that we were still alive. It made sense at the time.

Jane and Hugo gave us the benefit of the doubt and welcomed us, inviting us to join them for dinner. And with that, matters quickly improved. We launched into tales of our travels and hung on Jane's every "Oh, how horrible" and "I think you'll like it here." We peppered them with questions about the chimps and their years of work at Gombe, and of Hugo's study of wild dogs on the Serengeti. As we watched the sun set over the lake, Faye and I could hardly believe that, at long last, we were sitting at dinner with Jane and her husband, on the brink of months at Gombe with the wild chimpanzees.

CHAPTER 7

A DIFFERENT TIME

Looking back to 1972, it is hard to believe how the natural world has changed in just four decades. There were few thoughts of human encroachment on natural habitats, of endangered populations of chimpanzees, gorillas, and orangutans. Instead, we were excited and enamored by new observations of apes fashioning tools and having complex relationships and societies, and of their intelligent thought. The Gombe Stream Research Center was just twelve years old at the time.

✦ ✦ ✦ ✦ ✦ ✦

"Time to head out," I heard a voice calling into my hut. It was Peter Meic, one of the Stanford undergraduates. All was darkness outside except for a slight hint of pending daylight and Peter's shock of blond hair.

"Hold on," I whispered. "I'll be right there." I threw on my cutoff blue jeans and hurried out the door. It was good to see Peter after having spent the night in my tin hut, imagining its invasion by mice, snakes, geckos, and centipedes.

We hiked along a steep trail toward the research area. It smelled like a garden after rain, and the surroundings looked remarkably like California. I had expected an Amazonian jungle, so it was good news to instead find woodlands and fruit trees that seemed far more familiar and safe.

"We're going to observe Nova and her daughter Skosha. I followed them last night until they nested so we'd know where to find them this morning—that is, as long as we get there before they wake up." I stepped up my pace and tried to sort out Skosha's name, finally realizing it was Jane's play on words for Canada's Nova Scotia.

As we got to the research area known as Camp, we met up with the African field assistant accompanying us this morning. Helali was short and slight but obviously an expert in chimp following, and it was not surprising to learn that he had been one of the first Africans Jane had hired. He led the way, knowing far better than Peter just how to locate the sleeping chimps a half-mile away in an obscure and difficult-to-find fruit tree. We followed the path as far as we could, then began trekking cross-country through the brush. Sunlight was barely issuing through the tree branches as we arrived at the base of the tree in which Nova and Skosha were sleeping.

"Do you see the nest?" Peter whispered. He pointed to an obvious mass of branches, a four-foot-wide pile of hand-folded leafy vegetation that appeared to provide a comfortable and reasonably secure platform for a bed. I could see the nest just fine, but there was absolutely no indication of chimps in it, and I wondered whether we had gotten here too late. It was cold and ridiculously early, and so far, chimp following didn't seem very inviting.

After a couple of dull moments, we finally detected some movement. A moment later, a little head appeared. Bleary-eyed Skosha was sitting atop her sleeping mother, looking about the forest for what the morning might hold. As she yawned and stretched, my opinion of chimp following instantly improved. Her mother popped up shortly after, urinating over the side of the nest—which Peter promptly documented on his tape recorder. In fact, he continued to detail every bodily function, interaction, and movement the chimps made.

After sitting for a few moments, Skosha climbed onto her mother and held fast as Nova climbed down the tree some twenty yards from where we sat watching. Skosha looked quite comfortable and content as she rode on her mother's back. She was like a doll, her fur tousled from sleep, and she had a perpetually drowsy look. We quietly got up, following Helali's lead, and began to walk along behind the chimps, keeping a twenty- to thirty-foot distance. Still sleepy, Nova set a leisurely pace as she ambled, and it was a relief to finally feel the first rays of morning sun. Skosha's white tail tuft shone like a flag. Peter explained that the tuft, which lasts through most of childhood, protects the young by making it easier for the mother and others to spot and protect them.

After five minutes, Nova moved off the path to a large, brown termite mound that looked like a four-foot-high sand castle. I held my breath, amazed that on my very first follow, I was about to witness the extraordinary tool use that had put Jane and her chimpanzees on the anthropological map.

Nova began fishing for termites, expertly stripping a twig with her mouth and inserting it into the termite mound. The twig was covered with swarming termites as she extracted it. She then swiped it sideways through her lips, swallowing down the termites. Next to her sat Skosha, who mimicked her but ended up with more termites on her fur than in her tummy. She gave up and leaned up against her mother, looking skyward as though terribly bored.

We heard a sound in the brush behind us. It was Pallas, another female chimp, carrying her eighteen-month-old son, Plato, on her back. Plato bounded off Pallas's back, running to Skosha to play. Meanwhile, Nova moved matter-of-factly alongside Pallas without apparent greeting of any kind and began fashioning another tool for termite fishing. The two seemed relaxed and comfortable with one another, as though they were good friends.

The chimps' agility at making and using a tool was impressive. Prior to Jane's reporting of it, many scientists had considered humans to be the only living creature able to make and use tools. Years later, we know that many animals are, in fact, adept at it: gorillas and orangutans have been seen modifying sticks to gauge water depth, dolphins wrap sponge over their beaks to protect against abrasions as they forage on the ocean bottom, and elephants use rocks as hammers. We have also seen chimps use tools in untold numbers of ways, such as pounding seedpods open with rocks, employing sticks as weapons, and using leaves to scoop water into their mouths.

As Skosha and Plato wrestled and tugged at one another, it was obvious they were good friends, just as their mothers were. The two mother-infant pairs, I learned, frequently spent their days together. No doubt it made life better for each pair, since it allowed the mothers to feed in peace while their children played nearby. Unknown to us at the time, these friendships and close bonds were also important in dealing with the uncertainties of life in the forest. Just three years later, at the time of Nova's death, Pallas would adopt five-year-old Skosha. And when Pallas died five years after that, it would be Skosha who adopted Pallas's five-year-old daughter, Kristal.

It wasn't hard to distinguish Skosha and Plato. Skosha was slow moving and even a little clumsy compared to the quick and spirited Plato. Nova and Pallas were easily distinguishable, too—as much by their parenting as by their appearance. Pallas, sporting a V-shaped bald patch atop her head, loved to tickle and play with Plato. She was more at ease, allowing him to wander away from her without concern. Nova, in contrast, kept a constant vigil on the pair.

"How long do they stay with their mothers?" I asked.

"They're pretty much like humans," Peter responded. "Skosha will stay with her mother until she reaches sexual maturity, around age ten to twelve. And Plato will start moving off sooner, usually somewhere around age eight. They stay with their mothers for a long time because there is so much they have to learn just to survive. Females only give birth about every four years."

The youngsters were batting at one another, Plato dangling two feet off the ground while hanging from a tree branch and Skosha tugging on his foot. When Skosha stood up and grabbed both legs, Plato tumbled from the branch and landed squarely on top of her. The two were laughing like children, "Huh-huh-huh-huh," rolling over and over on the ground as they played.

We had been out following the chimps for three hours—a short follow, compared to the usual four to eight hours—but Peter had a research meeting to get back to. We returned to the path and on to Camp.

❧ ❧ ❧

Standing at the entrance to Camp was what looked like part of a movie crew. A tall, blonde woman with blunt-cut bangs was extending a microphone on a five-foot pole near a mother chimpanzee grooming her infant. The woman looked like a movie-set soundman, but in reality she was recording chimpanzee vocalizations. Next to her stood a man in his late twenties with a trimmed beard and horn-rimmed glasses, recording data about the chimps' activity.

"Frans and Hetty—meet Nancy!" Peter shouted out. "I'm off to a meeting. Can you help her get lunch when it's time?"

"Yah, suuuuure," Hetty hissed in a whisper, trying to minimize the damage to her recording in progress. Peter quickly disappeared, entirely ignorant of his faux pas, leaving me to watch the pair at work.

Peter had just introduced me to graduate student Hetty Vanderijt and her husband, Frans Plooij. The Dutch couple was nearing the end of their two-year stay at Gombe. Hetty's research focused on infant vocalizations and how young chimps learn to communicate, and Frans was studying infant development. The two appeared utterly and intensely fascinated by even the slightest whimpers of the young chimp.

When lunchtime arrived, we walked to the nearby kitchen to make ourselves sandwiches with bread baked in a wood-burning stove by Dominic, the cook. Ma Ling plum jam, a sign of China's new alliance with Tanzania, sat on the counter for us to slather onto the warm bread.

Over lunch, Frans and Hetty spun funny stories of their days at Gombe. I heard tales of fabled prior students and of the cast of chimp characters. A particular favorite was a male chimp named Hugo, with whom Frans had a history. The chimp had reached into his hut one day, grabbing a pair of underwear off the top of his pile of clean clothes. Frans had chased him up the slope, shouting at him and trying to scare him into dropping them. But the chimp defied him, slipping the underwear onto his head like a hat and then picking up some rocks. Hugo then stood up and began lobbing them at Frans, letting him know not to expect the underwear to be returned any time soon.

By now, all three of us were almost in tears, thinking of Hugo standing triumphant, decked out with underwear on his head. Frans finished the story, saying that he was never able to get the underwear back, instead having to take the teasing of his fellow researchers for the next three days. Hugo wore the underwear until they were in shreds, so torn that they literally fell off him.

"Those were the proudest three days of Hugo's life," said Hetty, "and some of the longest of Frans's."

❖ ❖ ❖

The Gombe Stream Research Center did, in fact, have an "upstairs" and a "downstairs." Downstairs, the low-lying area along the beach, was largely the domain of the baboon researchers. Although there were baboons throughout the park, a favorite troop, Beach Troop, the subject of much research, was easily found there. Downstairs was also where we gravitated to at the end of the day, coming together for an evening swim in Lake Tanganyika, and then dinner. Grub spent his days there, being schooled and mothered by Jane and watched over by a staffer at other times.

Most of the huts that housed students were upstairs, up a steep and lengthy forest path. Camp included the office for the Stanford undergraduates, the kitchen, and Pan Palace, which provided office space for the graduate students. The Palace was an essential part of a new banana-feeding strategy, revised because frequent feeding of bananas had altered the chimps' behavior by encouraging them to frequently return to camp. The new plan called for providing a small number of bananas not more than once a week to ensure that all the chimps could be located and studied yet minimize impact on their natural movement throughout their range.

Opening a special door inside Pan Palace allowed researchers to enter "the trench"—a twenty-foot tunnel dug into the hillside. At shoulder height along each side of the tunnel were bins in which researchers placed the bananas. The back of the bin was then closed up securely, and the observer released a catch so that the outer door of the bin fell open, revealing the bananas to the chimps sitting outside. Chimps entering camp quickly learned the new routine and moved hurriedly to the trench if they heard any movement suggesting bananas were on the way.

Faye and I were beginning to get to know the colorful bunch of human characters at Gombe. There were the African staff, most of whom had worked at Gombe for many years and who took great pride in their work as chimp and baboon research assistants, cooks, and general staffers. Hilali was the senior tracker, both by virtue of having been there the longest and by his splendid knowledge of the chimps. He knew perfectly where to find them, understanding how their foraging depended on the season and on which trees were laden with fruit. He also had an uncanny ability to keep up with the chimps, no matter how quickly they moved, how many vines there were to get tangled in, or how thick the thorns. He could spot fresh dung, discarded fruit rinds, and broken twigs—all evidence of nearby chimps. And he could hear chimp calls from across the valley and immediately pinpoint the likely location.

Another of my favorites was young Moshi, who worked upstairs with us. Round and shy and sweet, he looked like he couldn't have been more than sixteen years old. Even twenty years later, when I visited Gombe again, he still looked sixteen years old, even though he now had two wives and many children.

Gombe's other residents included Jane; her husband, Hugo, who divided his time between Gombe and the Serengeti; Grub; eight grad students, and five Stanford undergraduate students. As we walked into the dining area, we met Richard Wrangham, Anne Pusey, and Mitzi Hankey, a cadre of European graduate students. Richard was Gombe's current alpha male, with a lively personality and tremendous diplomatic skills. Studying male chimpanzees, he was respected for his ability to stay with a study chimp for days without losing him, an achievement requiring tremendous physical ability and tracking expertise.

My first task was to train as a research assistant. I needed to not only master the disciplined process of recording chimp behavior and the identities of a multitude of chimps but also demonstrate my proficiency at data collection before I could provide any substantial help. The start of my training had already been delayed for three days while I dealt with my first episode of whatever dreaded Gombe disease it is that causes vomiting, diarrhea, and a desire never to eat or drink again and prompts one to lay prostrate on the concrete floor of his or her metal hut, imagining that the end is near. By Gombe day five, however, the illness had passed, and it was time to jump in. I was to meet up again with Peter Meic, who would be teaching me all I needed to know.

We sat together in the undergraduate office, talking about the research and waiting for a study chimp to arrive in camp so we would follow it together.

"Here you go. This is your tape recorder, over-the-shoulder bag to carry it in, and clipboard for the check sheets."

Peter handed me the items forthrightly, as if hopeful I would leave immediately on a chimp follow and start reducing the backlog of data needed by the end of the month. "Be sure to carry extra pens, lunch, water, and a rain poncho, because you never know how long you'll be out there for."

My job, Peter instructed me, was to systematically record just about everything I witnessed for as many hours as possible. Our goal was to collect at least sixteen to twenty hours of observations on each of the study chimps per month. I was assigned to study four mother-infant pairs. For the month of September, I would be observing mother Nope and her seven-year-old son, Mustard; Pallas and her two-year-old son, Plato; Passion and one-year-old Prof (the name, short for *Professor*, was bestowed in honor of Dr. David Hamburg); and Melissa and her two-year-old daughter, Gremlin.

"Just wait until you have a follow that takes you up Sleeping Buffalo," Peter joked, referring to one of Gombe's most challenging slopes.

"Do they ever get sick of us following them?" I asked.

"No, they're pretty used to us," replied Peter. "Trust me—if they wanted to ditch us, they could do it, no sweat."

"Do you think they know who you are? Do you like some people and not others?" I asked.

"The adults don't pay much attention. But the babies do. They'll wander up sometimes and try to take my check sheet. Once, Plato tried to get me to play.

"It's tough when they do that," he continued. "We aren't supposed to respond, but it's hard not to."

About then, one of the graduate students called out, "Fifi's in Camp! Anybody need hours on Fifi?"

Like a firefighter hearing the alarm, Peter jumped up and started suiting up. He checked his shoulder bag, strapped it close to him with a belt, and headed directly out the door and up the slope to where Fifi and her infant, Freud, sat quietly. Freud was only a year old, too young to venture far from his mother. For now, he leaned sleepily against her, one hand holding on to her side.

I followed Peter to an area about fifteen feet away from the chimps and watched him enter information on his check sheet. He wrote in codes to show what the mother and infant were doing every sixty seconds and continuously reported how far apart they were. If they did something particularly interesting or interacted with others in any way, he recorded the details into the tape recorder.

Finding Camp fairly uninteresting, Fifi and Freud didn't stay long. After just a few minutes, Fifi pressed Freud to her chest, where he held himself tight as she moved away. We followed along behind.

"Hey, this isn't so bad," I told Peter, feeling relieved that I was keeping up with Fifi, Freud, Tanzanian tracker Juma, and Peter fairly well.

"Yeah, you're doing great," said Peter without much conviction.

I looked to see what lay ahead, feeling thankful that Fifi was sticking to the trail and not taking us through thickets and vines. But then I lost a breath, for there was Sleeping Buffalo. Luckily, there really was no time to stop and think about it. Fifi had just shifted into hyperspeed, practically running up the side of the mountain as though she were on a mission.

Juma and Peter were keeping up fairly well with the chimps, losing sight of them only occasionally. They were wearing khaki shorts and Tanzanian plastic sandals, and bushes along the side of the path repeatedly scratched their legs. I, on the other hand, quickly fell so far behind that I could no longer see chimps nor observers.

"Now what do I do?" I muttered out loud to myself, checking out one particularly large scratch across my knee. Just then, Juma sounded his distinctive call, something like the sound children make when playing Indians, to let me know they were nearby and in which direction. Feeling relieved that I wasn't entirely lost, I clambered up the mountainside as rapidly as I could. The path was steep, and by the time I arrived I was breathless and worn out—and very happy to see Peter and chimps seated on the ground, pausing for at least a few moments.

I bent over in exhaustion and put my hand up on a tree branch to steady myself, only to realize that I had placed my hand on top of someone else's. I looked up to apologize to Juma, assuming it was his, but instead found myself face-to-face with a young chimp named Pom, who was sitting in a low-lying tree. She gave me a curious look, implying, "Don't you know you aren't supposed to touch us?" I removed my hand as quietly and respectfully as possible and backed away.

We spent hours following the group. At times, it was fascinating and wonderful to watch, especially when the infants were playing nearby. Less interesting were the times when the chimps fed for long periods, doing nothing out of the ordinary. But the worst times were when the chimps were out of sight for minutes on end, often high in a tree. We circled below, trying to get even a glimpse of their activity, recording at perfect one-minute intervals the fact that we could see absolutely nothing. By now, I was feeling every rock through the soles of my shoes and frustration at going to such great lengths to document the fact that the chimps were unobservable.

As sunset neared, Peter leaned over and let me know that we were nearly done for the day. The chimps were building a nest in a tree ahead and lying down to sleep. I tried to immerse myself in the beauty of the sunset over Lake Tanganyika, but somehow it couldn't compensate for just how miserable I was feeling. I was exhausted and had mosquito bites in places I couldn't reach, blisters on both heels, and torn shorts. I thought of my Stanford roommate, whose overseas college experience involved living in an Italian villa in Florence with sixty party-hearty others.

Thankfully, within a few days, my endurance increased, and I began to enjoy the challenge of keeping up. I was getting better at recording observations, finally recognizing most of the chimps, and fascinated by the intricacies of chimpanzee lives. I was getting the hang of things, and an Italian villa was sounding dull and pampered.

❖ ❖ ❖

The chimp community of Kasekela Valley, the community that Jane had made so famous, included about sixty individuals, all part of what is called a fission-fusion society. The Kasekela chimps, like chimps everywhere, were constantly meeting with other community members and forming new subgroups for hours or days at a time. Mothers and infants often traveled with other mothers and their children, but at other times, they moved about their territory alone. Other days, they might join up with a large group of chimps who included males as well as females with large, pink bottoms—swellings that waxed and waned, indicating their fertility and their receptivity to mating. Whenever a female was in estrus, there was always enormous excitement and tension as the males jockeyed for the opportunity to mate without being pummeled by someone higher in the social hierarchy. The mothers generally rushed out of harm's way as soon as any excitement started, and the infants clutched them as they barked loudly and bowed so as to appease any nearby excited males who could potentially threaten them.

On one particularly eventful day, a large group of chimps became wildly agitated as they approached a waterfall. For some unknown reason, the cascade always excited the chimps, leading the males to perform splendid feats and outbursts. The group we were with had begun hooting loudly. The females ran to one another for hugs of reassurance, and the hair on the males went erect as they started to posture and grimace. The males finally became so stirred up that they erupted into running about the area, beating trees, swaggering upright on their legs, and demonstrating their machismo. These displays were a means of establishing or maintaining their rank in the social hierarchy. Thankfully, they never directed their actions toward us, but it was still sometimes frightening to be so close by.

On occasion, we would come upon chimps from one of the three other communities within the confines of Gombe National Park. A new group of chimps whose territory lay at the southern end of Kasekela was slowly separating itself from its former membership within the Kasekela community. Seven males and four females had slowly started moving their range to the south, interacting less and less over a period of years with the chimps of Kasekela. To the north was a third community, Mitumba, and to the south the Kalande community, groups that remained largely unstudied until the 1980s and later.

※ ※ ※

I had read the stories about every chimp who Jane had ever written about, and it was thrilling to now be meeting them firsthand. I was especially eager to meet the members of the Flo Family, a group consisting of ancient matriarch Flo; her adult sons, Figan and Faben, whom I had already met; her daughter, Fifi; and her youngest son, Flint. Featured in many of Jane's books, some members of the family had become celebrities in their own right. Flo was easy to distinguish in photos by her appearance as an ancient, sporting a torn ear and a thin build. Although she was elderly and flawed, she had a surprising charm. She was confident and intelligent, even high ranking, and in addition, she was a loving and capable mother. If infant Flint looked as though he might get into trouble teasing a baboon with a branch, she would tickle him and distract him until he all but forgot about the baboon. When the males displayed, she was rarely the target of their aggression, and it was clear that the males were drawn to her, even when she was not in estrus.

Just about everyone's favorite chimp, however, was Flo's daughter, Fifi. The world watched as Fifi grew from a young juvenile, consumed in playing with her pals and brothers, to a wonderful six-year-old who was fascinated by her new baby brother, Flint. She watched attentively at times as Flo cared for and babied him. Soon, she began picking him up when Flo wasn't looking and carrying him off, as though playing with a doll. Fifi, Flo, and Flint were constant companions during these years. Fifi remained at her mother's side even as she became an adult and then a mother herself.

Although Flo had been vigorous into her old age, she finally started to slow down as she became pregnant with yet another infant in 1968. Flint was now four years old, but he was exceptionally attached to his mother, even more so than most chimp offspring. Flo made efforts to wean Flint, but he fiercely resisted, even throwing tantrums when she would push him away from her breast. Compromised by fatigue and age, Flo uncharacteristically gave in to his tantrums and dependence.

The problems only seemed to worsen following the birth of new baby Flame. Flo still had not fully succeeded in weaning Flint, and he even tried to sleep in Flo's nest with her and the baby. When Flame was six months old, Flo developed a pneumonia-like illness that left her so weakened that she was unable to even climb into a tree at night to build a nest. It was at this time that Flame went missing. The cause of her death is unknown, but from here on out, Flo seemed to give up.

With the loss of his sibling, Flint's dependence on his old mother only worsened. Even three years later, at age eight and a half, he sometimes still insisted on being carried on her back, and he remained at her side long after the age at which most young males would have begun living apart. And yet, despite his dependence and demands, Flint's devotion to Flo seemed to also provide some comfort in her old age. She had become too frail to be able to keep up with other chimps in social groups, so she must have appreciated his presence at times.

Faye and I had fully expected to meet the legendary Flo on our arrival at Gombe in 1972, and so we were ill prepared to learn that she had died just two weeks before while crossing the stream, presumably of old age. Her passing, unbeknownst to us, had drawn international attention and had even been memorialized in an obituary, written by Jane, in Britain's *Sunday Times*. The obituary noted that Flo and her family, which had been the subject of an estimated forty thousand hours of observation, had taught us a great deal about animal—and human—behavior.

But that should not be the final word. It is true that her life was worthwhile because it enriched human understanding. But even if no one had studied the chimpanzees at Gombe, Flo's life, rich and full of vigour and love, would still have had a meaning and a significance in the pattern of things.

Flo's death proved devastating to Flint. In the first six days afterward, he remained close to where she had fallen. During this time, he spent some time with other chimps, particularly his brothers, Figan and Faben, but he inevitably returned to the site of his mother's death. During the next four days, he was not seen in the area, but by the time he returned on day 11, he had deteriorated markedly. He appeared vacant, weak, and depressed. Within a couple of days, he stopped eating completely.

Hearing about his condition one night at dinner, I invited myself along with Paul, whose job it was to study Flint. The next morning, we set off at dawn and found Flint exactly where Paul had left him the evening before. He lay on the dry rocks of the riverbed near where his mother had died. His eyes were sunken and vacant, and he barely moved.

Paul moved up to him slowly, speaking in a reassuring way as he approached. At first, Flint hardly registered Paul's approach, but he finally shifted his gaze without moving his head to briefly notice him. Paul peeled one of the bananas he had brought, hoping it would bring Flint to life again—but it wasn't to be. He remained as he was, lying lethargically on his side with his head propped on his hand. Soon, field assistant Rugema came alongside, certain that he could get Flint to eat, but once again, the chimp remained unresponsive and nearly lifeless.

There was little to do for Flint at this point, and so we sat, feeling quite helpless. But we stayed put, knowing that at the very least we could protect him from animals and other chimps and hoping that our presence was of some comfort. We spoke to him gently, soothingly. How odd it was to meet this special chimp here on his deathbed.

Flint died a few days later, just three and a half weeks after the death of his mother. An autopsy showed gastroenteritis and peritonitis—stomach and intestinal disease. But all of us who were there to see it could not help but believe that grief and depression were the primary causes of his demise. With his passing, the world was stunned to observe a new context in which chimps, like humans, experience deep emotional attachments to those they love.

CHAPTER 8

NEW DEVELOPMENTS

Gombe research included studies of mother-infant relationships, the natural ecology of chimpanzees, and behavioral studies. At the time, the world was learning that chimps share both the honorable aspects of humans and less desirable traits as well. The days of believing that only humans are capable of intelligent acts and complex social relationships were disappearing with each new revelation of just how much our chimpanzee cousins have in common with us.

✤ ✤ ✤ ✦ ✦ ✦

We had much on our minds as we almost ran down the hillside toward dinner. Richard, who had been running the slopes in his plastic sandals for years, was much faster than I. He ran with precision, leaping on his right leg and catching a crevice in the dirt that kept him from sliding, then launching on his left leg. Back and forth, back and forth, as fast as he could go, he moved gracefully while I did my best to keep up. There was something exhilarating about running that crumbly, steep path that had been shaped by rivers of rainwater, the feeling of being a seasoned adventurer—and one of a lucky few to experience it. As I looked at Richard, I could see he was not nearly as tired as I was. Perhaps some part of his incredible stamina was the result of the lengthy chimp follows required of a student studying male aggressive behavior. His male subjects traveled nearly five kilometers (more than three miles) daily, whereas my mothers and infants managed just three kilometers or so.

Our paths had crossed earlier in the day when the Kasekela males he followed joined up with Madam Bee, a female who had been little seen in Camp in recent months. The trackers had brought me to the group for my first sighting of her.

"Look there—in the bushes," Richard had said. The nervous barking of three female chimps helped me locate them in the thick brush. "It's Madam Bee and her adolescent daughter, Little Bee, and juvenile daughter, Honey Bee." Little Bee, with a deformed right foot, was easy to spot. It was good to finally be seeing these mysterious chimps who had once been an integral part of the Kasekela community, but it seemed odd that they had quit coming to Camp or interacting with my study chimps.

It was an exciting time to be at Gombe, for Richard and his colleagues were making surprising new observations. Until then, Jane and others had thought of the chimps as innocents—what humans might have been had they not had such big brains. But now, we were learning that chimps also share some of the dark behavior of human beings, and could be aggressive and brutal. We were learning how chimpanzees at Gombe differ from chimp communities elsewhere and appreciating their cultural differences. The importance of female hierarchies and relationships was emerging, the intricacies of how they cooperatively hunted animals for meat were well understood, and the wealth of information established by Jane had continued to expand.

As we arrived at the dining hall, I sank into a chair and watched the more energetic, ever-social Richard engage everyone in the room in a discussion of their day. Dinner was on its way, thanks to the Tanzanian cooks. Who knew what it would be tonight (though it was certain to involve rice and curry)? We joked about the food, but we knew that we were lucky to have such hearty meals, rather than the very bland and less nutritious *ughali* root, which most locals depended on.

The evenings seemed different with Jane gone to teach at Stanford and to raise funds. There was no jockeying for the opportunity to tell her about our day's events, no Dictionary Game after dinner, no one to dote over Crescent the serval (a midsize wildcat) when she prowled in from the forest late at night and meowed at the front door. But there was still the sunset swim in Lake Tanganyika before dinner—and thoughts of misbehavior not normally tolerated, such as a brief escapade of waterskiing behind the Gombe speedboat on some curious old skis whose presence no one could quite explain.

The Gombe Stream Research Center had changed substantially in recent years as more students and advisers had arrived. In Gombe's modest beginnings, Jane was the sole researcher, joined there by her mother, Vanne, and a few African staff. *National Geographic* photographer Hugo van Lawick arrived in 1962 to document Jane's work, and the two of them fell in love and were married in 1964. Her first student, Edna Koring, arrived soon after, helping expand the research.[1] At the time, studies focused on chimp behavior and ecology. The world learned that chimps are vastly more intelligent than we had imagined any animal to be, that they were tool-using beings with complex social relationships, that they are mostly fruit eaters but sometimes hunters and meat eaters, and that they share much in common with humans.

Many scientists took great interest in Jane's research. One of the most influential was Dr. Robert Hinde, of Cambridge University, who helped redesign the methods with which data were collected at Gombe and who helped her earn her PhD. Jane proved herself a capable scientist and resisted pressure from a faction of the scientific community to treat the chimps as subjects by assigning them numbers rather than names.[2] She revels to this day in having let common sense triumph over the scientific method taken to the extreme.

Dr. David Hamburg was a second powerful influence on Jane's life during this period. A psychiatrist interested in the biological basis of human aggression, he believed the chimps provided a natural model. When Gombe was struggling financially, he helped secure financial support to keep it open. Dr. Hamburg also arranged Jane's academic appointment at Stanford University and created the program of which I was a part. Faye and I were numbers seven and eight of a lucky group of undergraduates working at Gombe, continuing the long-term studies of chimps and baboons that Jane and others had initiated years before.

Meanwhile, Jane and her wild chimpanzees had vaulted onto the world stage, attracting the fascination of young and old, all captivated by poignant television specials and books portraying the personalities and real-life dramas of the Gombe chimpanzees. The world was changed forever, rocked by the startling notion that humanity's place among the creatures of the earth was not so astonishingly different after all.

The 1970s yielded yet more new revelations about the complex lives of chimpanzees. Shockingly, a "civil war" was documented at Gombe from 1974 to 1977 as an army of eight males of the Kasekela community gradually decimated the small Kahama community to the south, brutally killing them one at a time. On one occasion, Little Bee was present as the Kasekela Eight beat up her mother, Madam Bee, and left her to die five days later. Little Bee departed with the males, leaving her younger sister at Madam Bee's side.

By the late 1970s, we had learned much more about the lives of young female chimps like Little Bee. Her transfer from the Kahama community to the Kasekela community happened gradually, between 1972 and 1974. As she began to have her first sexual swellings, she was of little interest to the males of her own Kahama community but was of substantially more interest to those in Kasekela. The latter would recruit her, seemingly insisting on her traveling temporarily with them while in estrus. Afterward, she would return to Kahama to accompany her mother. Over time, the males increasingly forced her to accompany them and to mate until, at long last, she remained always with the Kasekela community. Her transfer to the adjacent community proved typical of many young chimp females, no doubt an evolutionary adaptation to minimize inbreeding.

The impact of disease acquired from humans had first become apparent in 1966 when a human polio epidemic spread to the Kasekela chimp community. At least fifteen chimps demonstrated clear evidence of polio, and six of them died. Although some of them regained the use of their paralyzed arms and legs, many suffered permanent deficits. Like Faben, Madam Bee lost use of one arm. Melissa was luckier, regaining the use of both of her arms, but she remained permanently unable to raise her chin normally or to turn her head. The severity of the outbreak caused Jane to intervene, successfully immunizing many of the chimps by providing bananas containing oral polio vaccine.[3]

Other disease outbreaks, including respiratory disease, intestinal parasites, and even mange, would affect the chimps over the years. Following an outbreak in 2000 of respiratory illness and the death of two chimps, important new guidelines would be established, putting an end to feeding bananas to the chimps, limiting exposure to tourists, banning any humans from being near the chimps if sick, and reducing the number of people living in the park.

We were also learning about chimp sexual behavior, reproduction, and evolutionary principles—such as what factors determine reproductive success and the number of offspring produced. Chimp females develop very obvious, large sexual swellings during estrus, signaling their receptiveness to mating. The swellings last about thirteen days, progressing from slight to complete swelling and back again, and the females have a menstrual cycle of about thirty-six days. Dr. Caroline Tutin, who arrived in fall 1972, was learning that females can mate more than one hundred times while sexually receptive, sometimes with all the adult males in the community.[4] The females usually become pregnant about every four years, when they stop breastfeeding, and gestation typically lasts eight months.

We had the impression that higher-ranking males often have an advantage at mating but that a clever lower-ranking male chimp could also be a successful breeder. On occasion, a male had been observed to guide a female in estrus away from the rest of the community for a period of days, becoming her only sex partner during that time. The males often co-erced the females to break away, waving branches or even attacking them if needed. But sometimes, after they had left the group, the female would willingly stay with the male, and the chimp couple would appear relaxed and content, leading us to refer to these episodes as honeymoons.

We wondered who the father was each time a new baby was born, but we had no way of knowing with certainty. Years later, new methods of ge-netic analysis would answer our questions of paternity and how the social hierarchy influences it. Based on analyses of hair, excrement, and even food chewed and spit out, researchers studied the paternity of fourteen Gombe chimps, substantiating our impression that higher rank translates into greater numbers of offspring. But the studies would also show that we had been correct—that other factors also play a role, including being sneaky at having sex undetected by higher-ranking males, as well as just plain sex appeal.

The findings also proved many of our guesses at who fathered whom to be on target. Belligerent Frodo was, in fact, the father of Titan, a young male who was beginning to demonstrate the same kind of bullying as his father. Wilkie, as alpha male, had successfully fathered Faustino, Gaia, Conoco, and Schweini. We also learned that inbreeding can occur, the results showing that Frodo had sired his brother, Fred, despite his efforts of his mother, Fifi, to avoid sexual relations with him.

Gombe researchers were reaching out to other chimp scientists to un-derstand whether chimp learned behavior varies by locale and community. If evidence of varying traditions was found, it would imply that chimpan-zees, like humans, have their own cultural characteristics that distinguish one group from another. It did not take long to start accumulating evi-dence of chimp cultural traits. One instance came from the nearby Mahale Mountain chimps, which clasped hands over their heads when two indi-viduals groomed one another, a behavior not seen at Gombe. Techniques for feeding on ants varied, with some chimp populations poking a long stick into the nest with the one hand and using the free hand to then sweep the ants into their mouths, whereas other communities used a short stick to collect a number of ants and then swept the stick through their mouths.

More than seventy behaviors would ultimately be found to vary among chimp groups in ways that cannot be explained simply by environment or genetics, implying societal differences passed from one generation to the next.[5]

The mother-infant research was showcasing the wide array of maternal parenting styles, some mothers being quite permissive and others demonstrating far less patience with their infants. The early years of mother-infant bonding were also proving to be as critical in chimpanzees as they are in humans in ensuring good mental health. Early learning was also essential, allowing young chimps to learn from their family and community how to groom, collect termites, hammer open an impenetrable nut or fruit, build a nest for sleep, and perform all the many other skills necessary for survival.

Overall, we were learning a vast array of scientific morsels that, when you inspect them, speak to how much chimps resemble humans. Their hypermuscular bodies, easily excitable natures, and poor impulse control almost seem to make them caricatures of humans, emulating both the best and worst of our behavior. But they are—along with humans, orangutans, bonobos, elephants, and dolphins—one of a handful of beings capable of recognizing themselves in a mirror, they are the only other creature besides humans that will search out and kill others of their kind militia-style, and they, along with the bonobos, are the animals whose genome so closely matches our own. They truly are our kin.

Jane's students would go on to comprise the lion's share of the world's most influential primatologists. Richard Wrangham would go on to Harvard University and conduct influential long-term studies of chimpanzees in Uganda, and Anne Pusey would devote much of her career to analyzing the long-term records from Gombe and establishing their contribution to our understanding of chimpanzee conservation, while also mentoring a prolific new group of Gombe students. One student with whom she worked, Lilian Pintea, would become world renowned for his work in applying geographic-information systems (GIS) to the job of conserving chimps by closely monitoring their habitats. Caroline Tutin would go on to become a champion for the gorillas and chimpanzees of West and Central Africa. Dr. Tony Collins is still at Gombe, overseeing its baboon research and enabling the Jane Goodall Institute's conservation efforts. Frans Plooij and Hetty Vanderijt became important figures in understanding infant behavior. The list of renowned and influential scientists goes on, including names like Tim Cluttonbrock, Mark Leighton, Elizabeth Lonsdorf, William McGrew, Jim Moore, Leanne Nash, Craig Packer, Barbara Smuts, Craig Stanford, Geza Teleki, and Janette Wallis.

❖ ❖ ❖

One of the most interesting characters to arrive at Gombe during this time was a pet mongoose named Minnie. He was given to Jane when the park warden that had pampered him left Tanzania. Now Minnie had to fend for himself at Gombe, and he was irritable and mean. We all dreaded his approach, as did the baboons and the chimps. His aggravating presence often drove the troop of baboons down the beach, as though Minnie was the alpha.

One day, a haggard-appearing Fifi and Freud arrived in camp, with Minnie on their heels. Mustard, a seven-year-old chimp, came to their defense, chasing and waving branches at Minnie. Finally, Mustard drove the mongoose into an open banana box and trapped him by closing the lid. Joined by his mother, the two opened and slammed the lid on the chattering mongoose for moments on end. When they finally allowed him to emerge, the mongoose quietly departed. Minnie had finally been defeated by chimpanzee problem solving, if only for a few moments, and all of Gombe's primates gave thanks.

CHAPTER 9

KOBI

*Those who carry out scientific experiments with animals, in order to apply
the knowledge gained to the alleviation of human ills, should never reassure
themselves with the generality that their cruel acts serve a useful purpose.
In each individual case, they must ask themselves whether there is a real
necessity for imposing such a sacrifice upon a living creature.*
ALBERT SCHWEITZER, *The Teaching of Reverence for Life*

What was a captive chimpanzee doing at a place like Gombe, famous
for its wild chimpanzees? Here was a one-year-old infant chimp wrapped
squarely around the waist of a woman he appeared to regard as his mother.
It was hard to know which was the more out of the ordinary—the beautiful baby chimp, Kobi, or his nonconformist mother, Jill. The woman
winced as the baby chimp combed through her long, blonde hair with his
fingers and pulled too hard.

Jill, a free spirit, had traveled across the Sahara in a truck with three
others and spent the next two years experiencing Africa. The foursome
had purchased an orphaned baby chimp from a marketplace in order to
save it from being sold as a pet. Jill and friends then headed to Gombe,
where they hoped Kobi could be released into the forest and adopted by
wild chimpanzees.

They were disappointed, however, when they arrived. For a number of
reasons, putting Kobi back into the wild was not possible. Not only did the
Gombe chimp communities need to remain as unperturbed as possible,
but at the time, efforts to reintroduce chimps to the wild had uniformly
failed. As with humans, successful survival depends on years of learning
necessary skills, and an infant like Kobi, separated from his mother, would
not know how to survive. Add to this the fact that chimps in the wild
do not readily accept new individuals into their community, and it was
clear that other arrangements for Kobi's future would need to be made.
While the search was on for a suitable sanctuary, Jill and Kobi remained at
Gombe. Jill's friends, in the meantime, went off in search of a few weeks
of adventure.

Jill spent her days as foster mother to Kobi, learning firsthand just how difficult it is to raise a chimp. It was fascinating to compare this human-reared chimp to the normal wild infants we followed each day. Kobi exhibited the same need for constant reassurance and embraces as the other infants, and his whimpers and facial expressions mirrored those of his wild cousins. However, he was growing faster and bigger, given his superior diet. And his exposure to humans was allowing him to develop intellectually in ways that seemed slightly more advanced. He was bolder than the wild babies at moving away from his mother to play, and more curious about human items like shoes and tools.

He was precocious, and we observed firsthand what studies have since confirmed—that chimps advance through a number of cognitive developmental milestones at a more rapid rate than human babies during the first months of life. They are more active and physically coordinated, more capable at grasping and manipulating objects.[1] Before the one-year mark, however, humans have acquired complex linguistic and abstract-reasoning abilities that outstrip those of chimps. They develop greater creativity, show far greater insight into what others are likely thinking, and become adept at deriving solutions simply by imagining them, rather than depending on trial and error, as the chimps do. But although chimps ultimately lose in these intelligence comparisons, it remains impressive that we begin our lives with a number of comparable cognitive abilities.

With the breaking of the genetic code, researchers have firmly established just how genetically similar chimps and humans are, finding that more than 98 to 99 percent of our genes are identical. But differences between chimps and humans ultimately stem less from the host of genes within that 2 percent and more from one key difference in fetal development: the fetal brains of humans undergo a larger number of rounds of cellular division, resulting in our having three times as many neurons as chimps have. It is not so much which neurons but the overall quantity that spells the difference. The presence of more neurons results in an exponentially greater number of connections that permit human intelligence. "With enough quantity," neuroscientist Robert Sapolsky tells us, "you invent quality."[2]

Scientists have been fascinated by chimp intelligence for more than one hundred years. Among the earliest to study them was Wolfgang Kohler.[3] In 1913, he began seven years of research on a group of eight chimpanzees housed on Tenerife, the largest of the Canary Islands. Many of his experiments involved placing bananas out of reach and observing how the chimps were able to problem solve to reach them. Their solutions included balancing on sticks or stacking boxes to reach them, or using long sticks to knock them down.

Other scientists focused more on early development, drawing comparisons between chimps and humans. Films from 1932 show W. N. Kellogg's experiment in which he reared a chimp alongside his infant son. Kellogg brought seven-month-old Gua from the Yerkes Primate Research Station to live in his home, raising her alongside his ten-month-old son. The chimp quickly began outpacing the boy, learning to walk upright and handle a cup and perform other tasks at a younger age. Although the chimp could not speak, she could understand human language. After nine months, Kellogg found that his son could understand sixty-eight words or phrases; the chimp, fifty-eight.[4]

Kellogg cut his experiment short after nine months, when he became concerned that his son was emulating the chimp, more so than the other way around. One can appreciate his growing concern as the boy began barking and making chimp noises when hungry and progressing slowly in language acquisition. The experiment ultimately proved tragic when the chimp was returned to the primate research center and died shortly thereafter. Although the reasons remain obscure, Kellogg's son committed suicide years later at age forty-one.

Other researchers picked up where Kellogg left off. In the 1940s, scientists Keith and Catherine Hayes raised a chimp named Vicki in their home for seven years. Interested in the chimp's capacity for language acquisition, they wanted to understand how chimp and human intelligence differ. Vicki learned to understand words but had very limited ability to produce speech, largely due to disparities in brain speech centers and wiring of the vocal cords. She did, however, manage to pronounce four words—*Mama*, *Papa*, *up*, and *cup*—with great difficulty. Films of Vicki show her using her hands to hold her lips together to produce the unvoiced "puh" sound required to say "Papa."

Probably the best-known chimp-language experiment involved the famous chimp Washoe, whom researchers Allen and Beatrix Gardner raised in their home for five years, teaching her American Sign Language. Given that chimps lack the vocal cord structure to produce speech, the Gardners believed that substituting sign language would allow a more accurate assessment of chimp language ability, and in fact, Washoe proved quite adept at ASL. Over a period of four years, she acquired 130 signs, and in later years, she had learned more than 200.

Dr. Roger Fouts, who continued studies of sign language with Washoe and other chimps, watched as Washoe became a foster mother to a young orphaned chimp, Loulis, and observed him learning sign language from her and the others. During play, they might sign "tickle" or "play," and in this way, Loulis became the first creature to learn human language from nonhumans, acquiring essentially a full vocabulary of signs.[5]

Washoe and the others found ways of using the words they knew to describe things for which they lacked signs. For example, when Washoe first saw a swan, she signed "water bird," combining two words into a new descriptor. After observing Alka-Seltzer effervescing in water, another chimp, Moja, signed "listen drink," an apt name. Dr. Fouts describes the chimps' enjoyment of picture books, relating how they pointed to pictures and made the signs for what they were looking at.

❖ ❖ ❖

My own brief experience with Kobi this particular afternoon had already convinced me that at age one, he not only understood quite a number of words but had also fully mastered the old bait-and-switch. As I approached Kobi and Jill, he held his arms out to me. But as soon as I went to touch him, he grabbed my clipboard.

Jill kept Kobi largely to herself at Gombe, trying to keep him from having too much contact with humans and doing her best to emulate a chimp mother. Research from the 1950s and 1960s had suggested that chimps raised from infancy as family members often come to identify more with humans than chimps. The Gardners tell a revealing story of this warped sense of identity: Chimp Vicki was given a deck of photos to sort into one of two piles, human or nonhuman, which she did perfectly—with one exception. Given a card with her picture on it, Vicki placed her card in the "human" pile.

Thankfully, a sanctuary home was found for Kobi in the United States, and by December, arrangements were made for the chimp to be transferred. He and Jill would fly to Nairobi and then on to the United States. Faye and I found ourselves along on the flight from Gombe, en route to Nairobi for a short break. Ramji Dharsi, a longtime friend of Jane's, drove us to the airport that day.

"Cover him up now," Ramji told Jill. In an effort to keep the airport officials from seizing Kobi or demanding a bribe, Jill wrapped him up in a blanket to look like a human baby. As we pulled into the parking lot, Jill held him up against her shoulder, as though burping a baby, and the gate sentry, peering inside the car, suspected nothing. We held our breath, hoping Kobi would be quiet and well behaved.

We slipped onto the plane without incident, closed all the doors, and awaited our last okay for takeoff. Soon, the airport officer came by for one last check. When he announced we were good to go, there was a collective sigh of relief. The little airplane rolled down the runway, picking up speed until, at last, we started to lift off from the tarmac.

Just then, the captain noticed that one of the plane's doors was ajar. Apparently, in the haste to get Kobi inside, we had overlooked fully securing the door. There was nothing to do except to circle low over the airport and drop back down onto the runway. As the plane briefly touched ground and continued rolling, two of us jerked the door closed, securely fastening it. Up the plane lifted, and off we flew toward Nairobi.

Kobi eventually made it to the Primate Foundation of Arizona and did manage to maintain his chimp identity, fathering ten progeny as part of a breeding colony funded by the National Institutes of Health. He was able to live most of his life among other chimps and without experimentation. After decades of life in Arizona, however, Kobi once again found himself at the mercy of humans. He and the other foundation chimps became the property of the M. D. Anderson Cancer Center and were gradually transferred to biomedical facilities at Bastrop, Texas, between 2007 and 2010. The transfer meant better outdoor access and being housed in a larger social group but also put him at some risk of being a biomedical research subject.

Fortunately, he has gotten yet another reprieve, as NIH announced its plans to retire the majority of its chimpanzees to sanctuary. Now forty-one, Kobi is at the end of his life, and unfortunately, progress in transferring him and other chimps has been delayed by difficulties securing funding and sufficient sanctuary space. But if the elderly Kobi can hold on, his retirement and well-being will, at long last, finally be ensured.

CHAPTER 10

KIGOMA BOUND

I realize, in retrospect, that our life at Gombe was somewhat isolated from the lives of Tanzanians. Although we befriended the Africans with whom we worked and supported the spirit of *ujamaa*—roughly translated "personhood through community"—and African pride, we nevertheless were living in a postcolonial world in which the staff cooked our dinners, carried water to our homes, and acted as field assistants but not researchers. Thankfully, the situation at Gombe and throughout East Africa has changed substantially, and Africans now lead the way. In 1972, however, our primary contact with the real world of East Africa was confined principally to our periodic boat trips to Kigoma.

✦ ✦ ✦ ✦ ✦ ✦

We took turns going to Kigoma—a two-hour boat ride away if one traveled on the center's speedboat when the lake was quiet—on the weekly shopping trip. Other times, we took the water taxi—a slow, oversized boat that crept along the lake, stopping at every small village it could find. The taxi was stuffed to the brim with people, parcels, and chickens, and sometimes we were the topic of conversation throughout the interminable trip. The fact that we women wore pants seemed to add to the onlookers' amusement.

Once in Kigoma, the shoppers purchased the week's food and necessities at the market, picked up the mail, spent the night at the local hotel, and enjoyed the "big city." If you timed it right, you might even be there for movie night—generally, involving a spaghetti western from the 1960s. Out in the cool night air, a slice of humanity gathered, all eyes focused on the well-worn movie as it was projected onto the back wall of a white cement building. Children slept in their mothers' arms or lay spread-eagled on the dirt, while adults perched on any available landing or wall. Periodically, the old film would break, leading to unexpected intermissions in which six-year-olds leaped up to entertain the crowd.

It was the White Fathers, a group of Catholic priests, who taught Faye and me about the refugees we were seeing daily at Gombe. In recent weeks, the number of migrants had multiplied. As always, they were walking away from Burundi, the border of which was nearly thirty miles away, and heading toward Kigoma. They straggled along, looking tired as they carried their belongings, but they rarely discussed their circumstances as they passed. Yet the White Fathers knew their stories. These were the 1972 Burundians, 150,000 of them flooding into Tanzania. At the time, they were mostly Hutus who had avoided the fate of 200,000 others slaughtered during eight months of atrocities. It seemed inconceivable that the outside world knew so little about Burundi and this travesty. Meanwhile, the White Fathers bravely piloted their boats across the border at night, smuggling survivors out of Burundi despite the risk that they themselves might be killed.

And so it was in Kigoma where we saw the divergent nature of life in Tanzania. Walking down the main street, life looked peaceful. Neighbors helped neighbors; groups sat chatting and laughing. Young people in school uniforms sang as they marched by. Yet in this same city, we heard tales of a woman stoned to death for stealing food, of networks of thieves, of corruption and bribes. It was all here.

❦ ❦ ❦

Although Kigoma was the only "big city," many, many small communities dotted the shores of Lake Tanganyika. Faye, Tony, and I learned firsthand about some of them one evening as we drove the boat back to Gombe from Kigoma.

"The engine's stalled again," said Faye, walking back to see if she could help Tony diagnose the problem. We'd been on our way home for a mere thirty minutes, and the engine had already choked six times.

"It was fine yesterday," said Tony, looking puzzled. "I don't get it."

"I just wish we'd headed back a little earlier," I added, starting to feel a chill. We had eaten dinner before departing, and now twilight was on the horizon.

Tony primed the fuel line, then pulled the rope handle of the motor crank start. Again and again, he pulled it, but the engine only sputtered each time and sent up a strong gas odor.

"We're in trouble," he said. "I can't think of anything else to try."

Faye and I each tried the crank start a few times, but we quickly realized he was right. Not knowing what else to do, we pushed the supplies to either end of the boat and pulled out two paddles. With no way to lock the oars into place, we simply rowed as best as we could, trading paddlers from time to time.

It was dark now, and aside from the cold, the evening was gorgeous. Fishermen in fifty or more small boats were scattered about the lake, their lanterns lit to attract *dagaa* fish to the surface, where they could net them. The lights of the boats were arrayed just so, making it difficult to tell where the sky ended and the water began. Lanterns on the water, bright stars—it was all one night sky.

"Hmm—this could take forever," said Faye, sounding discouraged. "We're going to have to spend the night on the beach and figure out how to get the engine fixed tomorrow." We knew she was right.

We had purposefully stayed close to shore, so it was only a fifty-foot paddle to the beach. Once there, we jumped out of the boat and pulled it onto what appeared to be a deserted beach. It was covered with pebbles certain to be uncomfortable to sleep on.

"I suppose we can spoon," said Tony.

Tony was the charming new Scotsman, catnip to most women. "Okay," I said, a little too eagerly. Then, "What's spooning?" Not that it mattered, for whatever it was, I was probably willing.

Spooning in this case meant sleeping in the bottom of the boat, lying as close to one another as was humanly possible so as to conserve our body heat and stay warm. If one of us turned over, it meant all of us needed to turn over. Three sardines in a newly opened tin. I finally fell asleep, studying the stars, and wondering what tomorrow would bring.

Hours later, morning sunlight started to warm my forehead. Oddly, I thought I could hear the tinny sounds of African music played by cheap radios all around me. Opening my eyes, I woke to think I was lying in state. Tony, Faye, and I were on our backs in the boat bottom, surrounded by fishermen staring at us. We had beached our boat near their shacks and were proving to be quite a curiosity. As we finally came to and realized what had happened, we asked them for help, but none of them had a motorboat or knowledge of engine repair. Perhaps the next village would be able to help.

We took off, paddling in the direction of Gombe, passing another village unable to help. Finally, however, we spotted children in the distance, splashing and playing in the water. On a nearby hillside were earthen homes, and villagers out chitchatting with one another. Picking up our pace, we arrived to find that the naked children had been retrieved by two cautious young mothers and were lined up like a meerkat chorus line.

"*Jambo!*" we yelled in greeting.

The children chirped, "*Jambo wazungu*" as they pointed and laughed. It was clear we were some of a very few white people they had encountered in their young lifetimes.

Speaking broken Swahili, we asked for help and were directed toward the village. The children skipped happily alongside, as though they had just captured the biggest quarry of them all and were marching us to camp. When we got to the community pergola, we once again asked for help. Thankfully, this time there was a gentleman willing to transport one of us back to Kigoma, where the motor could be repaired. We did some quick negotiations and decided Tony would go. Faye would catch a water taxi to deliver the much-needed supplies to Gombe, and I would remain in the village with the boat until Tony returned.

Tony and Faye departed in their opposite directions, and I hunkered down, knowing I was in a safe place with good people and that I might just as well relax. I walked to the boat to grab the mail, then moved to a spot on the hillside to start browsing through it. Soon, however, I looked up to find the children once again in their long-line formation. They were grinning from ear to ear, as though they knew something I didn't. Finally, they pushed one of the boys forward. He was doubled over with laughter.

"*Kwa nini unafuraha?*" I asked, wondering what he was laughing about. Knowing he probably did not understand my Swahili, I also did a charade of looking puzzled with a questioning gesture.

"Mama?" he asked, holding fists up against his chest in a way that made the line of boys giggle harder. "*Bwana?*" he queried, now looking tough.

I laughed along with the boys while I tried to think what they were asking. Then it came to me: they wanted to know whether I was a man or a woman. Of course! I was wearing pants, unlike any woman they had ever seen, and I definitely did not have the build of an African woman. I was thin and straight and not nearly so well endowed as many women of the region. "Mama," I told them, feeling just a little bit like the missing link.

Eventually, Tony turned up with a working boat motor. We reinstalled the engine, thanked our new friends for their assistance, and headed home. We arrived home in time for dinner and were welcomed by friends who were curious as to what had happened. After thoroughly exaggerating all our adventures, we headed upstairs to bed, exhausted by our trip and more appreciative of life in Tanzania.

That same night, Jane sat working on her correspondence down the beach in her home. Little did I know that a letter to my mother was part of her evening's work—nor could I have imagined how she possibly found time. She had briefly met my mother at one of her recent lectures, and my mother had offered her a place to stay in Pasadena should it ever be of help. The gracious Jane wrote,

7 February, 1973

Dear Mrs. Merrick,

This is partly to say how nice it was to meet you at Pasadena, and partly to say how well Nancy is doing. There is the very nicest group of students here at present, and it was a real joy to get back to them. I wish I had more time to be with them—so much of each day is taken up with pure administration. And I am trying to teach Grub, also.

However, let me assure you that Nancy is doing very good things. She has shown initiative and diligence, and been a real asset in the mother-infant study. We shall certainly miss her when she goes.

She had an enforced night out on the lake with Faye and Anthony— about which she will no doubt write, giving graphic details. I should warn you also that she has fallen madly in love with a small ginger kitten, so check her luggage for smuggled fauna when she returns from Africa!

I hope to see you again when I am next in California. And thank you for letting us borrow Nancy for a while.

Yours sincerely,
Jane Goodall, PhD

My parents were not rich and lacked a grand home to offer—but this was Jane reaching out, even if it meant a long night of correspondence ahead. As for me, I was out like a light, dreaming of floating in a boat amid a constellation of lights on the water.

CHAPTER 11

AFTER GOMBE

These had been tough months for the Gombe Stream Research Center. Money was scarce, the food lean some days, and the boat engines and the generator were out of order more often than they were working. Although we were aware of the many concerns, we somehow failed to fully grasp how hard both Jane and David Hamburg were working to keep the center thriving. They lectured, wrote grants, sought pledges from donors, all the while overseeing the research, mentoring students, and dealing frequently with the Tanzanian government and the parks administration. We had little idea how minuscule our day-to-day challenges were compared to theirs.

❖ ❖ ❖ ❖ ❖ ❖

As the months passed, I began to savor those hours spent with chimps, knowing that all too soon, my stay would be over. I had grown enormously attached to the mothers and youngsters and knew them inside out. In fact, it appeared to be a two-way street. One day, I arrived in camp wearing long pants rather than my usual khaki shorts. Seeing this, Mustard came romping over to inspect the cuff of my pants with his finger. I pretended to ignore him, as protocol dictated, but it was good to know he had registered my existence all these months.

Jane herself had come and gone from Gombe as errands demanded. There were meetings in Dar es Salaam with government officials, trips to conferences, and a journey home when Grub was hospitalized in England with pneumonia. But late January brought a nearly uninterrupted month in which Jane was able to finally resume her Gombe life. Here was my opportunity to get to know this woman I so admired.

During the first few days after her arrival, each of us jockeyed for the opportunity to spend time with her, whether to discuss our own special concerns or simply to talk about the chimps. There were questions from the camp manager about new expenditures and requests from students to extend their stay or change a plane ticket. Poor Jane must have always felt overwhelmed those first few days by our constant needs. Most of us were confident we had been privileged to witness some never-before-seen chimpanzee action and could hardly wait to see her expression when she learned of it. But the astounding Jane always knew instantly what we were describing and could teach us far more about it than we ever could have imagined—what year it had first been seen, what had been learned subsequently, and what it revealed about the nature of chimps.

Jane has a wry sense of humor and a great sense of adventure, and so it was fitting when she arrived at dinner one night carrying a jar of termites and a reed. She stood at the front of the table and gave a brilliant delivery of the challenge she was presenting: if chimps are adept at catching termites on reeds and eating them, she said, then surely we could be as well, whereupon she fished out several termites and resolutely ate them. She then rounded the table, one student at a time, challenging us to do the same. Faye gulped two of them down with her eyes closed, thoroughly delighting Jane. Many of the others also managed to choke down a termite or two, all without being bitten. Nevertheless, I waved her off when it came my turn, unable to equal her daring spirit.

It was wonderful having Jane back. We had so much to share with her, seeking her approval for changes to the research and tapping her years of experience. And although she always was down to earth, I never stopped being dazzled by her, as if she were a rock star or a queen.

As the end of February approached, Jane departed again for meetings in Dar es Salaam and for a week in the Serengeti with husband Hugo. She had set herself yet another herculean task to accomplish there—this time, writing the majority of a manuscript she had promised. Spending her days in the tented camp writing from dawn until dusk, she did, in fact, manage to complete the manuscript.

❦ ❦ ❦

I had been charged with assigning morning duties to the Tanzanian field staff and was learning important life lessons in the process. One morning, I arrived with the assignments, only to have tall, quiet Juma tell me that he could not work that day.

Perturbed by his last-minute notice, I indignantly asked, "Why can't you work?"

"I go home," he told me.

"*Kwa nini?*" I asked, wondering why. He responded, but my Swahili was too limited. Finally, after several repetitions, it registered. This man had lost his two-year-old son to a case of diarrhea. His beautiful boy had died without him there because of a disease that, in the United States, would have been readily treatable—and even preventable by a decent water supply. There were no words for my sorrow at having verbally wrangled with a man devastated by his young son's death.

With each such error, I tried to learn some modicum of dignity-preserving humility and responsibility. Perhaps the world did not know of life in village areas of Tanzania, but I could become an advocate. Perhaps Americans did not register the two hundred thousand people killed in genocide in Burundi, but I could be a witness to each survivor who stumbled across the Gombe beach. I was feeling, full force, just how much my fairy-tale world of living among chimpanzees contrasted with the poverty and genocide the local Africans suffered, and I was beginning to wonder whether there was a way that I could possibly play a role in both worlds in the future.

❖ ❖ ❖

Mid-March arrived all too soon, and I realized that it was nearly time to leave Gombe. Trying to ease the pain, I began enumerating the things I definitely would not miss about Africa, especially the daily misadventures. By now, however, I had become so accustomed to them that they sometimes seemed more amusing than frightening. Just a few days before, I had been out swimming with my friend Emilie when a hippopotamus surfaced. We quickly made it to shore but could not help feeling puzzled by this inexplicable event. Gombe is not hippo habitat, but this one had wandered from a distant river, something that happened on occasion.

Thankfully, I had encountered the dreaded mamba snakes just twice, and always from a safe distance. I had grown accustomed to finding four-inch centipedes and had avoided the stinging *siafu*. I had been chased by bushpigs and nearly stung by a scorpion. An infected cut had led to pustules all over my body and had been cause for heavy antibiotics. Brief hostilities with Uganda and a border incursion by Idi Amin's army had aroused grave concern, but, fortunately, these issues had been resolved. I had been in a near plane crash, had had all my money seized at the border during travel to Kenya, and had escaped from a would-be assailant. I was one tough woman by now.

So here, in March, having finally mastered the art of taking difficulties in stride, it seemed wrong for me to be leaving so soon. But it was time, and my departure was only a couple of weeks away. I started to try to drink in every gorgeous day, every wonderful encounter with the chimps, each sunset swim in Lake Tanganyika. I mentally prepared to say good-bye to the exotic and wonderful life I'd been living here, completely absorbed in studying chimps.

One particularly perfect day, I hiked alone. I was gazing at the sky, exalting in being in this amazing paradise. I tucked my T-shirt up into my bra, exposing my belly, and walked along with my hands on my head through a gorgeous grass meadow. Just then, there was a sound ahead. There, at the edge of the meadow, appeared nine-year-old Goblin. He hadn't yet noticed me, and to my amusement, he was walking along, looking at the sky, engaged in the same type of reverie that I had been indulging in. As he glanced ahead on the trail and saw me, he did a double-take. Obviously, he had felt as alone in this forest as I had.

We both kept walking along the path, and as we met in the middle, we briefly exchanged looks of surprise and curiosity but kept walking in our opposite directions. After another thirty feet, I looked over my shoulder, enjoying the entire event. And just as I did so, Goblin did the same. We were in perfect synchrony, even up to each detail of our expressions and, likely, our emotions. Skeptics could dissect that scene, finding other explanations for the bond I felt with Goblin that afternoon. But to me it was a perfect, if humorous, moment of brotherhood between us, chimp and human, brother and sister, two souls sharing a meadow.

❧ ❧ ❧

When the departure date arrived, I flew with Jane to the Serengeti to spend two nights before flying on to Nairobi to catch my flight home. Ndutu was a mecca for a number of gifted young wildlife photographers who were rapidly becoming well known for their work, particularly in producing images for *National Geographic* articles and television specials.[1] The camp had been created in 1967 by George Dove, a commanding gentleman with a waxed mustache of enormous proportions and few but usually meaningful words.[2]

We arrived at Ndutu to find Jane's husband, Hugo, there, as well as his photographer rivals, Alan and Joan Root. Hugo's short stature and intense demeanor contrasted sharply with the taller Alan, who sported glasses and a head of thick, brown hair and was rarely quiet. Always beside Alan was

Joan, blonde and articulate, the levelheaded one of the husband-and-wife pair.

The Roots invited me along as they flew in their small plane to Olduvai Gorge to pick up a manuscript. Olduvai Gorge is the famous home of Mary Leakey and the site of the discovery of *Homo habilis*, a two-million-year-old human ancestor that at the time of its discovery in the 1970s was the earliest known tool user. It was exciting to see this river-cut gorge and the place where Mary, her husband, Louis, and their son, Richard, had conducted excavations.

After landing, we walked toward a small house in the distance that stood atop the parched savannah. Mary Leakey's house was the only building or hint of civilization visible. We walked in the heat, finally arriving at the house. I stopped at the doorstep, waiting for Alan to knock on the door, but instead, he simply opened it and entered. The house was dark and empty. He walked to the bookcase, where he found Mary's manuscript, showed it to Joan, and led us quietly out of the house. I hoped I hadn't just been an unwitting burglary accomplice.

The Roots told of misadventures in a hot-air balloon while capturing bird's-eye-view photos of the migration of wildebeests. They were using the balloon to capture time-lapse sequences of the migration, of which the world at that time knew relatively little. Alan had played an important part in creating Serengeti National Park years ago, documenting the perimeters of the park with his photos to ensure that sufficient land was protected to accommodate the whole of the great migration. He was full of stories, and he reeled off puns like, "Before we were married, she wore a monocle, and so did I. Together, we made quite a spectacle."

That evening's dinner was a celebration of Jane's and George Dove's birthdays, and we sat down to a table setting more elegant than any I had ever seen. At each place were three glasses—one for burgundy, one for wine, and one for champagne—and three knives, four forks, and two spoons. There were butter bowls, finger bowls, and appetizer and salad plates. The dinnerware was silver and china, and the number of servers seemed to multiply throughout the evening. Toasts were made to birthdays and new accomplishments. Course after course of food appeared in what must have been the grandest dinner I will ever eat. It was a fitting last night in East Africa and an extraordinary glimpse of a period in Africa that was fast disappearing in those postcolonial times.

❊ ❊ ❊

I returned home to a summer job studying a captive group of chimps temporarily housed on an island at Lion Country Safari, in Southern California. The chimps, together from early childhood, were to be here for just a few months until the opening of Gombe West, the Stanford Outdoor Primate Facility (SOPF). I would join a team that was collecting observations of their behavior, and although it was a blow to go from researching in Africa to working at a California theme park in a zebra-striped jeep, I was thrilled to still be in the business of chimp research.

On my first day, we drove through the park to the lion section and parked our jeep across a moat from two one-acre islands of chimpanzees. There, on the nearest island, were seven chimps, wildly excited to see us, standing on all fours and hooting. The alpha male's hair went on end all over his body, signaling his excitement, and he began a display. Shadow, another male, began chasing one of the females across the island. Curiously, however, the third-lowest-ranking male ran to the alpha female, seeking a hug for reassurance. Once things calmed down, he ran up and put an arm around Shadow. His head was bobbing in an amusing way, as though he couldn't decide between needing reassurance and wanting to play.

"Who's that one with the dark coloring around his eyes?" I asked my new supervisors, Pal Midgett and Dr. Patrick McGinnis.

"That's Bandit," Pal said, smiling. "He's a clown." It was obvious that he was Pal's favorite.

There were three young-adult females on the island. Robust Gigi, the alpha female, had a young infant named Delta. Bido, whose name was short for *libido*, was even tempered but apparently notorious for her precocious interest in sex. By contrast, Polly seemed somewhat neurotic, not having adapted as well as the others. All had been captured in Africa as infants and brought to Tulane University's Delta Regional Primate Research Center (later renamed the Tulane National Primate Research Center) as orphans. There, they were grouped together, and their development and their social behavior were studied in great detail.

Like the orphans of Ngamba Island, they had nurtured one another past their early trauma and developed in surprisingly normal ways. Pal, their caretaker, loved to tell stories of their early years at Delta. His best tale was of their escape from their one-acre enclosure: the chimps had used a lengthy branch to vault their way up the side of their enclosure, allowing them to reach small holes in the metal fencing near the top. They then used two smaller sticks as pitons, securing one and then moving the other up to a slightly higher spot and gradually making their way up and over the fence to freedom. Their jailbreak was short lived, but it was a glorious moment for the chimps.

✦ ✦ ✦

One day, one of Lion Country Safari's hungry lionesses did the unthinkable and walked into the moat, eyeing the chimpanzees. We watched nervously, hoping she would go back and join the other lions, but instead, she began swimming out to their island. Horrified, all we could do was watch and alert the park veterinarian by walkie-talkie of what was unfolding.

The chimps were chaotic as the lion approached. They hooted, hugged one another, and swaggered on their hind legs, trying to dissuade the determined lion. The calls of the chimps could be heard throughout the park. As the lion emerged from the water onto the island, the chimps got behind an old log, eighteen inches across, and continued to holler at her. The lion prowled cautiously at first, but then, as she began to move more aggressively toward them, the chimps found a solution. First one, and then several, of them began to slowly push the log forward, rolling it toward the lion so that she was forced to back away toward the water. Their stunt bought them the time they needed for a ranger to arrive to dart and tranquilize the lion and spared their lives.

Months later, we moved the group to the SOPF, yet another brainchild of Dr. Hamburg: a facility to allow scientists to correlate hormone levels and patterns with chimp behavior. By rewarding the chimpanzees with food and encouragement, they would accustom them to cooperating when the researchers needed to draw blood to determine hormone levels. This would provide a more humane and less disruptive approach than the usual practice of pinning chimps in a squeeze cage or anesthetizing them.

Each of the two chimp groups had their own two-acre enclosure, and their behavior and personalities were as fascinating as those of wild chimps. Among the favorites was CJ, an adolescent nearing maturity who spent hours observing the older males from a cautious distance, sizing them up and learning their moves for his eventual takeover of the alpha position. Even neurotic Polly proved endearing as she mastered motherhood despite having been separated from her own mother in infancy. We watched her daughter, Palita, grow from a totally dependent and sleepy infant to a boisterous youngster, always ready to play.

But my favorite chimp of all time was Bandit. He was gentle, intelligent, fascinated by people, and always mischievous. He never tried to be dominant in the group. He settled, instead, for being its clown, often playfully baiting the other males for the sheer fun of it. If a screwdriver dropped into the enclosure, he immediately took it to one of the enclosure doors and tried to remove a bolt. He was the first to willingly extend his arm and allow us to draw blood. He was the grown chimp who loved to play chase with the babies and the one that was always thinking. He observed us as much as we observed him, and he often sat directly below the observation deck, trying to get even a glimpse. How often I wished we could sit down for a long talk in order to know what thoughts went through his head, for Bandit was wise beyond expectation.

One day, as I stood at one of the enclosure wire windows, Bandit came to sit with me. My friend Debbie, who I worked with at the facility, was dying of cancer, and it was comforting to have him there. He extended his hand through the bars, as though trying to touch my tears. Perhaps he was curious about them, since chimps do not cry. But after a brief moment, his focus shifted to me. He sat quietly, seeming to sense my sadness, and rocked just a bit as though sharing my upset. He remained there next to me for minutes on end until my crying passed, providing what was probably the most extraordinary moment I have ever shared with a chimpanzee. In that instant, Bandit became my David Graybeard, an extraordinary chimpanzee, intuitively reaching across species in a moment of compassion.

❦ ❦ ❦

In May 1975, everything changed overnight at Gombe when four of Jane's students were kidnapped and taken across the lake by guerrillas critical of Mobutu Sese Seko, president of Zaire. (Mobutu had given the Democratic Republic of the Congo that name several years earlier.) The guerrillas had hoped to capture Jane herself to draw media attention to their cause and to win a large ransom, but ultimately they took the other four when they could not find her. Eventually, all four students were released, but the kidnapping forever changed Gombe. For now, it was no longer safe for European and American students, or even Jane herself, to work at Gombe.

The research would be passed entirely to the African staff to bravely carry it forward.

Even for me, safely back at Stanford, the kidnapping was life changing. It seemed too hazardous to consider graduate work that would require a return to the region, at least for the foreseeable future. My friends had been kidnapped, and all of us who were a part of the Gombe community had spent three months worrying that the guerrillas might kill them. It bonded us for a lifetime as only such a traumatic event can. But in its aftermath, it was clear that East Africa would remain a dangerous place for chimp studies in the near future.

Medicine and public health now loomed larger in my thoughts for the future, and in August 1976 I headed to medical school in Cleveland, hoping to someday return to Africa to combine health care with conservation. Four years of medical school were followed by three years of internal-medicine residency at a public hospital, and then by medical research and public health school. By now, I was thirty-three and tethered to a conventional life. In 1987, I married, and fifteen months later, I became a mother. Meanwhile, my parents were entering their seventies, and East Africa seemed an impossibility, at least for now.

It was a wonderful time, this new life with husband and children—the path that many of us choose—but I remained determined not to lose sight of chimpanzee concerns. While I was living in Washington, DC, my path crossed Jane's once again as she moved the offices of the Jane Goodall Institute to the area. It was a cherished moment to place my infant daughter in her arms to admire and exciting to once again flank her in advocating for chimps. Washington was ripe with opportunities to promote chimpanzee welfare through connections to major advocacy groups, and Jane introduced me to many of them. During these same years, I received the disturbing news that not only had SOPF closed but also many of "my" chimpanzees had been sent to become breeding stock at a research center. There were painful rumors, too, that some of the younger chimps were now subjects in biomedical research.

When we moved to California in 1989 to raise our family, we continued as chimp advocates and supporters of Jane's work. Soon after she launched her international youth initiative, Roots & Shoots, we organized a group to spread the word about Dr. Goodall's work and about chimpanzees and conservation. We attended her lectures, were part of periodic

Gombe reunions, and belonged to numerous advocacy groups. Over the years, we learned from Jane's talks that the forests around Gombe had become denuded due to locals cutting trees for fuel wood. But even with all this, I never came anywhere close to understanding that chimps throughout Equatorial Africa were under siege. It was only in 2008, when I saw Gombe with my own eyes again, that I finally began to suspect.

PART III

GREAT APE ADVOCATES/
WHAT WE LEARNED, 2008–2011

CHAPTER 12

SOUNDING THE ALARM

Back from Africa, we learned that our suspicions were right—chimps clearly are in jeopardy throughout their range. It seemed inconceivable that, in my lifetime, humans had first come to appreciate how remarkable and intelligent chimps are, only to push them toward extinction. The most extraordinary animal on Earth, the being most like us—I wondered how there could be any hope for the human species if we were not able to save even our next of kin.

It was difficult to keep delving further, because the news seemed so grim, but a photo of a six-month-old Gombe chimp that I had posted as my screensaver proved helpful, providing a daily reminder of why it was important. And there, beside my computer, was the photo of Jane, sitting on the steps at Gombe with my family, reminding me of my long-standing obligation.

And so began a journey to discover what, if anything, can be done. The journey would lead directly to two chimpanzee champions, the enigmatic Ian Redmond, who provided a road map to the issues, and once again, the grande dame herself, Dr. Jane Goodall.

✣ ✣ ✣ ✣ ✣ ✣

Summer 2008: We returned to the United States, inspired by all we had seen. We could picture Stany passionately lecturing high school students at Ngamba Island, invoking them to become stewards in the fight to protect chimps. We imagined Lilly Ajarova, the sanctuary's executive director, walking the Ugandan villages, educating people to protect their forests. We marveled at Dr. Goodall's strength, traveling nonstop to get the word out about how endangered chimps and their forest have become. And we remembered the African people who had powerfully reminded us of the poverty and human conflict that so complicate the fates of apes and humans alike.

We returned home with questions, too—in fact, far more questions than answers: Was the rapid increase in the number of Ugandan chimps needing sanctuary care unusual, or was it emblematic of problems chimps were facing in other parts of Africa? Was our impression that the number of chimpanzees at Gombe was declining correct? Had they transferred to other communities? Had they died of disease introduced by human visitors? Were there other explanations?

Some of the answers would prove decipherable from data sheets sitting in filing cabinets in Minnesota. Dr. Anne Pusey, a Gombe graduate student when I first met her in 1972, was now director of the Jane Goodall Institute's Center for Primate Studies at the University of Minnesota and a professor with graduate students of her own. (She has since become professor and chair of evolutionary anthropology at Duke University.)

Years before, Pusey had visited Jane's home in Dar es Salaam, finding Gombe journals and photos sitting on open shelves. Knowing the value of this information, she worked with Donald Buford, then director of the institute, to create a new center at the university in which to archive these materials. From these meager beginnings sprang today's research center, which has become a leader in chimpanzee research. Investigators there had broken new ground by coupling satellite information on forest-vegetation trends with years of data on chimp behavior to understand how chimpanzee survival relates to healthy forests.

Gary and I visited the center in 2003 while attending an international reunion of Jane's former students. During our tour, we saw some of the digitized photos, listened to lectures, and met the scholars who were now at the forefront of chimp research. It had been a stimulating day, but of all the day's events, the heart-palpitating moment came when I opened a filing cabinet marked "Original Check Sheets."

Fingering through the folders, I found them—my check sheets. They were yellow, marred by rain that had blown through the office grille windows at Gombe so many years ago. But they were a direct connection back to 1972, when we had wondered what the future of these data would be.

During 11 min. of interaction with the mongoose, the following occurred. MU [Mustard] branch waves, chases mong. MU sits watching mong, whimpers; NP [Nope] approaches; MU follows her away from mong. MU approaches mong, slaps, stamps on tree, branch waves, chases, closes it in banana box. NP sits in contact with MU, and they open and close b-box containing mong.

Now, just returned from our African trip, I found myself reading a recently published article showing that our data had proven not only useful but also important. Pusey and colleagues of hers had analyzed the more than forty years' worth of data to understand exactly how the local chimp communities had fared over time, identifying which factors posed the biggest threats to them.[1]

Their findings showed that habitat loss and human encroachment were isolating the various chimp communities from one another and that diseases such as polio and respiratory illness had also taken a toll. Overall, the chimp population had declined at a rate of 0.56 chimps per year since the 1960s and now numbered about one hundred. The small population size, along with the fact that three communities of Gombe chimps were now isolated within an area barely large enough for one, meant that they had become extremely vulnerable. The chimps in the middle, the Kasekela chimps, were best situated, since their range was entirely protected within the national park boundaries. But the communities on either side were now competing with humans who were cutting down trees for fuel along the park perimeter. I thought back to how obvious the park borders had appeared on our recent boat ride, the surrounding areas stripped of trees and vegetation.

The report was disturbing, for here was evidence that the community of chimps I had worked with and loved are, in fact, in trouble. I had heard at the Gombe reunion in 2003 of the need for a chimp corridor linking the Gombe chimps to adjacent communities. This would allow interbreeding among the communities and help ensure a more robust genetic pool. But I had assumed back then that there was still plenty of time for such interventions. Now, with this new report, I couldn't help being concerned.

I hoped that the Gombe chimps were an isolated case of a local population in trouble. Gombe National Park is an unusually small park, and perhaps chimps were faring better in less densely populated areas of Tanzania. E-mails to knowledgeable friends, however, soon suggested that chimp populations in all of Tanzania now numbered somewhere between 1,000 and 2,600, not very numerous at all. Learning this, my next hope was that chimps were faring better in other parts of Africa, but web-based information compiled by the Great Ape Survival Partnership was about to provide the most shocking news of all.

GRASP is an innovative project of the United Nations Environment Programme (UNEP) and the United Nations Educational, Scientific, and Cultural Organization (UNESCO) with an immediate goal of lifting the threat of imminent extinction faced by gorillas (*Gorilla beringei beringei* and *G. gorilla gorilla*), chimpanzees (*Pan troglodytes*), bonobos (*Pan panis-cus*), and orangutans (*Pongo abelii* and *P. pygmaeus*) across the twenty-three countries in which they range. In establishing itself, the group compiled stacks of information for all the great apes and made it widely accessible, work it continues to this day. Taking advantage of its base within the United Nations, GRASP was also using its links with governments to foster agreements promoting conservation of the great apes. Much of the work was being led by Ian Redmond, cofounder of GRASP in 2002 and now its chief consultant.

I opened the GRASP pamphlet on chimpanzees, guessing I had finally found the information I was after.[2] Colored red on a map of Equatorial Africa was the range in which chimpanzees survive today. Looking at it, I assumed chimps must be widely distributed within the Central African area and paid less attention to the relatively small red shadows in West Africa.

But as I read on, I learned that chimpanzees are now extinct in four African countries (Benin, Burkina Faso, Gambia, and Togo) and nearly extinct in five others (Angola, Equatorial Guinea, Mali, Senegal, and Sudan). Their populations in another five countries (Burundi, Ghana, Guinea-Bissau, Nigeria, and Rwanda) are described as "extremely depleted," meaning that they survive in very confined areas and in numbers inconsistent with long-term viability. Even the large yellow circle on the map was somewhat misleading, for chimps were not uniformly distributed over that wide swatch, but rather were simply confined to select areas within the yellow border. Overall, it was clear that the Gombe chimps are only one of far too many chimp communities in Africa facing catastrophe—something I found completely unimaginable—unless drastic action is taken. Years ago, the world was enthralled by the wild chimpanzees. Yet now, less than forty years later, these same wonderful creatures were endangered. The news struck hard and left me feeling completely defeated. That is, until I met Ian Redmond.

✦ ✦ ✦

One October day in 2009, he came walking into the foyer at the annual expo of the Wildlife Conservation Network. Although I had never met him, I instantly knew who he was. Ian Redmond looked unchanged from the photos of his days in the 1970s, when he worked with Dian Fossey. He sported a thick brown beard and looked almost like an admiral in his khaki shorts and a safari shirt with epaulets. I had only recently discovered the wealth of information available at GRASP and was eager to meet this legendary man who had played such a vital part in its founding. I went to shake his hand, but he reflexively pulled it away.

"I'm afraid my knuckles are still smarting from the Gorilla Run," he said, wincing.

Redmond had just participated in a fund-raiser in London for the Gorilla Organization, in which 640 participants, sporting gorilla suits and running shoes, had run a 5K to raise awareness about Africa's gorillas. Unlike the other participants, Redmond had insisted on traveling barefoot, his feet painted black to match his gorilla suit. He had knuckle-walked on all fours for the majority of the run, quickly being left behind by the 639 others, who elected to run upright. This apparently failed to affect Redmond in the least. He sauntered the entire distance, periodically hanging from railings, running between starry-eyed lovers, giving children a ride on his back, and even jumping onto a milk truck.

And so, at long last, I was meeting the legendary Redmond, a lifelong tropical field biologist and conservationist renowned for his work with elephants, rhinos, and mountain gorillas. Mirroring Dian Fossey's experience, his life changed when poachers murdered a favorite gorilla named Digit years ago, and he subsequently became a key player in organizations like the Gorilla Organization, as well as the Born Free Foundation and the International Fund for Animal Welfare. He also helped found GRASP, the Ape Alliance, and other groups.

When I met him, he was in the midst of his observance of the International Year of the Gorilla, a conservation campaign backed by the UN. He had recently returned from a five-week tour of eight African countries, drawing attention through his blogs and lectures to the loss of gorilla populations through Africa. Now, he was beginning a lecture tour that would take him across the United States, traveling by bus so as to minimize his carbon footprint, just as he had done while traveling in Africa. He was on tour to help support GRASP's work and to do whatever he could to raise awareness here and in Africa about the critically endangered gorillas.

As luck had it, Redmond was planning a lecture at the Los Angeles Zoo a week later, and I quickly purchased tickets.[3] He would be speaking about his beloved gorillas, the great ape with which chimpanzees often share forests, and providing an overview of what it will take to save Africa's great apes.

❦ ❦ ❦

"I can see why he is ambassador for the Year of the Gorilla," my husband whispers as he, my mother, and I sit in the front row for Redmond's talk. "He has got to be the world's most likable guy."

He warms up the crowd, noting how much enjoyment he has gotten out of being called "Your Excellency" several times since becoming the ambassador to the gorillas.

"There are actually two species of gorillas, the eastern and the western, each of these groupings being split into two subspecies," Redmond says. "One of the biggest differences between them is the exaggerated hyper-prognathism of the eastern gorillas, producing a very elongated head."

"And the importance of this," he adds, "is that if you're ever in a bar and an eastern gorilla walks in, you won't need to ask, 'Why the long face?'"

Once the crowd has stopped groaning, Redmond launches into his talk in earnest, giving us a road map of all that can be done to save the gorilla and other African apes. He tells of the lessons successfully learned from past conservation work to protect the mountain gorillas: the importance of tourism to fund conservation work and to improve the local economy, and effective monitoring of the apes within their reserves by veterinarians, biologists, and antipoaching patrols.

Redmond had recently visited the African forests of the Cross River gorillas, a subspecies of which only 250 individuals survive. There, he met a chief's son who had killed a gorilla that had raided his family's crops. The man was acclaimed by his family for his brave actions, and the meat and body parts were sold, bringing money to the family. But he was shaken by the dignity of the animal he had killed and disturbed to learn from Redmond how endangered gorillas are. It proved life changing, and the man is now working to bring ecotourism to his community. He has also created a snail farm to raise giant snails as a food source. The five-inch snails grow rapidly in an outdoor cage, and snail farmers can reap about $400 annually, compared to the $70 they would get from killing a gorilla for bushmeat. We can see the benefit of supporting organizations like the Wildlife Conservation Society that are sponsoring patrols and offering alternative livelihoods so as to help bring these gorillas back from the brink.

Next, Redmond tells us about the impact of the bushmeat trade. Bushmeat, the meat of native forest animals such as antelopes, elephants, monkeys, and apes, provides the principal source of protein to Africans living in rural areas, where the average family consumes the meat of local animals about twice a week. But consumption is far higher in areas where log-ging has been introduced, and many of the animals killed are now being shipped to the cities, where bushmeat has become popular. One million metric tons of bushmeat—the equivalent of almost four million cattle—is taken annually in the Congo Basin, and hunting and trapping for bush-meat is now posing an even greater threat to some species than deforesta-tion. Although relatively little killing of chimps for bushmeat occurs in countries like Uganda and Tanzania, it is a major risk for the chimp populations of central and western Africa.

A number of approaches to thwarting the bushmeat trade are being attempted, according to Redmond. City markets, for example, are in-creasingly being monitored so that laws against killing of apes are bet-ter enforced. Even DNA methods are beginning to be used to determine the species of some bushmeat that might otherwise be falsely passed off as other legal meats like antelope. Governments are increasingly trying to identify bushmeat rings; one such investigation in Cameroon recently netted fifteen illegal traders in a sting. The Forest Stewardship Council is calling for multinational logging companies to harvest trees more sus-tainably and asking consumers worldwide to purchase only products made with certified timber. Consumer power is beginning to have real impact, he tells us, particularly in Europe.

Next, Redmond shows us a video of a public-service announcement airing in Cameroon that encourages people to "eat other meat." Soccer star Geremi, a national hero in Cameroon, agreed to record the message to encourage his fans to avoid endangered species bushmeat—an effective countermeasure, since televisions are widely available in public places like bars and restaurants. The spots, created by WildAid's Active Conservation Awareness Program, carry the slogan "When the buying stops, the killing stops too." Even where televisions and electricity are nonexistent, another group, the Great Apes Film Initiative, is finding novel ways to ensure that those living adjacent to the great apes know what magnificent creatures they are.

I find it hard to believe when Redmond mentions a group of gorillas in Gabon that have been essentially wiped out by the slow spread of Ebola vi-rus through the forests of that region. Ebola, a much-dreaded viral disease that causes severe hemorrhaging and death in a majority of those who con-tract it, has killed more than a thousand people since its discovery in the 1970s. Until Redmond spoke, I had mistakenly believed it is a disease that affects only humans. But no matter how devastating Ebola is to humans, it appears to be having an even greater impact on chimps and gorillas. In the mid-1990s, more than 90 percent of the ape population in Minkébé National Park, in northern Gabon, died during an outbreak. There were also major deaths due to Ebola in Odzala National Park, in the northwest of the Republic of the Congo, from 2003 to 2005. (The Republic of the Congo is a nation distinct from—but neighboring—the Democratic Republic of the Congo.) Gorillas in other, smaller parks have been similarly affected, and it is estimated that a third of the world's gorilla population living under protection in national parks has died in the last fifteen years. The impact of the deadly virus has resulted in the upgrading of the western gorilla's status to critically endangered as of 2007, and efforts are being initiated to vaccinate gorillas against Ebola by darting individuals under the supervision of skilled wildlife veterinarians.

With Redmond's next litany, we are surprised to learn that even cell phones, computers, and other electronics are contributing to loss of Africa's great apes. Our phones and other devices contain a mineral called coltan, which is extracted from poorly regulated mines. Coltan, the name of which is an abbreviation of *columbite-tantalite*, is a metallic ore capable of holding a high electrical charge, making it an ideal substance for use as a capacitor in cell phones, laptop computers, and other electronics. It is a rare commodity, and 80 percent of the world's supply lies in the DRC. Impoverished miners there stand to earn four to twenty times more than average Congolese workers, and as a result, an estimated ten thousand poor Africans are zealously mining coltan, using destructive techniques and clearing large chunks of forest—even in national parks. Those same miners are also hunting local animals, such as endangered elephants and gorillas, for food.

Redmond offers yet another possible step to stemming the problem. If component makers like Intel and General Electric would insist that capacitor producers use only certified coltan in their products, this requirement could have an overnight impact not only in reducing habitat destruction by the miners but also in dealing a huge blow to control of the profitable "conflict mineral" trade. Forces from the DRC, as well as neighboring Rwanda, Uganda, and Burundi, are smuggling uncertified coltan out of the eastern part of the DRC and using the millions of dollars of revenues generated from the high price for coltan to sustain their war efforts in the region. Few of us buying new cell phones and laptops have an inkling of the situation, or of the consumer power we could exert, so it is an added relief to hear that advocacy groups are aggressively pushing for legislation to bar import of the DRC's conflict minerals. (In August 2010, the United States Securities and Exchange Commission enacted regulations requiring US companies to publicly disclose use of minerals originating in the DRC, and many companies now ensure that their products contain no Congolese coltan.)

Redmond speaks passionately as he describes why continued deforestation spells disaster not just for the great apes and other animals but for humans as well. He reminds us that Africa has already lost more than two-thirds of its original forest, particularly in areas with explosive population growth.[4] The result in Equatorial Africa has been to create remnant forest stands in populated areas, leaving unperturbed forest only in Africa's Congo Basin. The basin remains the second-largest tropical forest in the world, surpassed only by the Amazon, and its health is integral to preventing a sinkhole of biodiversity loss, desertification, and climate change not just in Africa but even here in the United States. Predictions have been made that deforestation of the Congo Basin would decrease precipitation in the Great Lakes area of the United States by 5 to 15 percent and by 17 percent in West Africa and would have an impact on southern Africa's rainfall as well.[5]

These forests, which have been referred to as the lungs of the Earth, are critical to reducing atmospheric carbon load. Their loss would not only rob us of some of the Earth's wonders and diversity but also cause a 20 percent increase in greenhouse gases. When forests are burned to clear them for agriculture, enormous amounts of greenhouse gases are emitted, making Indonesia and Brazil the third- and fourth-largest carbon emitters in the world, behind China and the United States. Loss of forests, coupled with global warming, could also produce widespread drought and affect the lives of millions of Africans.

Redmond tells us that initiatives like the UN's REDD+ (Reducing Emissions from Deforestation and Forest Degradation) are under way to counter these threats by providing financial incentives and funding to less developed nations to conserve forests and to encourage sustainability. (The plus sign was added to REDD's acronym to address a number of concerns, chief among them being those of indigenous people who worried that they were being left out of the program, that it did not require rich nations to take responsibility for their carbon emissions, and that it could incentivize governmental seizure of lands they have fought hard to obtain. As the program morphed from REDD to REDD+, new emphasis was placed on going beyond deforestation and forest degradation, and including the role of conservation, sustainable management of forests, and enhancement of forest carbon stocks.)

The Congo Basin forests provide a massive carbon sink, locking in twenty-five to thirty billion tons of carbon, and REDD+ programs are launching as fast as pilot projects and infrastructure can be established. The UN hopes that such projects will help local communities improve their economies while helping them better manage the natural resources on which their futures so heavily depend.

Applause signals the end of Dr. Redmond's lecture, and he launches into his one-on-one campaign afterward, shaking hands and engaging audience members that come to congratulate him. But we, deep in thought, are slow to get up and leave the auditorium. Hearing about chimp extinction in so many African countries was a wake-up call about the dire circumstances of great apes, and Ian's lecture now seems to be signaling the road back. The problems he outlined are numerous, but it appears that with sufficient funding and effort, every one of them has potential solutions. Here is a conservation hero who isn't overwhelmed by the challenges, one so well grounded that he is still willing to ride buses in rural Africa or run 5Ks on his knuckles if that is what is called for. He reminds me of yet another larger-than-life hero I know.

❋ ❋ ❋

We had seen Jane at that same San Francisco conference where we first encountered Ian, and it was our first meet-up with her since our family visit to Gombe.[6] She casually strolled into the exhibit area, adorned in her customary Dockers pants and an earth-toned wool shawl. She visited the various exhibits, likely enjoying the fact that the crowds hadn't yet noticed her. After a while, her assistant escorted a patron over for a photo, and we joined them. The minute she recognized us, she smiled and raised her arm over her head, demonstrating that her previously dislocated shoulder was back in working order.

She told us about her latest world travels and her initiatives to save chimps and forests. We were impressed, fully realizing just how strenuous a schedule she keeps. Once, we had tried to keep up with her for two days while she was visiting our area as she gave lectures and attended fund-raisers and meetings with patrons. There was even an unplanned foray with a high school student to visit an industrial hazard the young woman was fighting against. By the end of the two days, we were exhausted, having little or no idea how she manages it.

Later that day, Jane shared treasured photos she had recently taken at Gombe, particularly excited by the image of a young bushbuck as it drank from Lake Tanganyika. After showing them to us on her computer, an old model in disrepair, she let us know that she wouldn't dream of wasting money on a new computer when hers was still functional, no matter how slow it was. It felt ever so good to be there with her, such a matchless character, the only person on Earth who greets me with a pant-hoot, this woman of such infinite spirit.

The greatest highlight of that San Francisco day was the pairing of Jane and Ian—almost like lightning striking twice in one place. Here stood the two ultimate champions for great apes, embracing one another and drawing inspiration. It was a rare moment that somehow offered a distant hope that it might not be too late to save great apes after all.

❊ ❊ ❊

I now knew for certain that chimpanzees and other great apes are endangered, and Ian Redmond had briefly outlined a number of the problems they face, even suggesting possible solutions to some of them. It was time to start delving further into the issues, examining each one in order to better understand the future for chimpanzees. Along the way, I would find people I knew who were playing key roles in ensuring a future for great apes, and I would meet other newcomers. There would be a field trip to East Africa, interviews, and travel to conferences in order to learn the fundamentals of the issues. It would take understanding the plight of not just wild chimpanzees but also of chimpanzees living in captivity in the United States, and of the other great apes. But it promised to be a worthwhile journey, and one that was long past due.

CHAPTER 13

IN THE NICK OF TIME

Knowing that ecotourism has been important in saving some great ape populations, it seemed a natural starting place for my investigation, and one that might have applications for other great ape communities. In today's world, dollars spent by travelers to East Africa to trek among mountain gorillas and chimpanzees have become vital to protecting these great apes by funding patrols and benefiting the local economy.

Years ago, I visited the first and most highly credited ecotourism effort, having little idea at the time that it would not only provide a prototype for decades to come but would also be pivotal in sparing mountain gorillas from outright extinction. An awkward visit to Dr. Dian Fossey's nearby Karisoke Research Center contributed a memorable experience.

❧ ❧ ❧ ❧ ❧ ❧

Base of Volcan Visoke, Rwanda, May 11, 1985. Our entourage came to a sudden stop. My friend Susan, four Rwandans, and I were about to embark on the long hike to the Karisoke Research Center, a gorilla-research station in the sad, gray saddle of two volcanoes, when an African man in a green jumpsuit emerged from the wall of mist in the distance. A patch on his jumpsuit read "Karisoke Research Center," and he was carrying a small envelope, his gaze fixed on us. After a short conversation with our guides, he handed the letter to me. Inside was a terse message: "Visitors are not allowed at Karisoke. The letter I sent you made that clear. You are not authorized to visit. —D. Fossey."

"She never told us anything," I told Susan after she had read it. "I never received a reply to my letter."

We looked at one another, wondering what to do. Dian, who had befriended her and offered constant encouragement, had been our friend Debbie's only hope as she struggled with breast cancer at the age of twenty-three. Knowing of Debbie's dream to study gorillas, she promised her a research position just as soon as her treatments were over. Sadly, Debbie did not survive to work with Dian, but the hope of doing so had helped her through her ordeal.

Now, years later, we had traveled half the world to get here, to see what Debbie's dream might have looked like had she lived, and to see the place where her ashes had been spread. Shortly after Debbie's death, Dian had seemed open to the visit, and I hadn't felt any hesitation about writing to Dian shortly before our trip to ask permission. After fifteen minutes of difficult deliberation, we asked our guides to lead on, hoping to reason with Dian once we arrived. We took off on a long, slow climb in rain and mud, up the mountain toward Karisoke.

Dian had gone to Africa in 1966 with the help of Louis Leakey. Studying mountain gorillas required moving to the remote Virunga Mountains, located along the politically volatile borders of Uganda, Rwanda, and the Democratic Republic of the Congo. She had left her job as an occupational therapist in Kentucky, intent on studying the gorillas. Knowing what an isolated area she would be living in, she had even taken the drastic step of having her appendix removed before moving to east Africa, something Leakey later confessed he had suggested in order to test her determination.[1]

She spent years studying and protecting the mountain gorillas, and worried as the number in the Virungas fell to an estimated 250.[2] She became entrenched in keeping poachers and other intruders out of the protected area, and when five gorillas were murdered, she worked with Ian Redmond, her friend, to establish the Digit Fund (later called the Dian Fossey Gorilla Fund International) to ensure more effective patrolling and antipoaching efforts. She also fought fervently against initiatives she believed might endanger her Karisoke gorillas. Her ardent opposition to the work of several former students put her squarely into controversy, particularly regarding their proposals for ecotourism. To Dian, it constituted exploitation of the innocent gorillas, and she feared it would put them at risk of disease and ill-advised exposure to tourists. In contrast, students Amy Vedder and Bill Weber thought ecotourism offered a means of developing funding for much-needed conservation, educational, and social programs.

❧ ❧ ❧

It was an exhausting hike to Karisoke that day. Not only were we still reeling from the troubling letter, but the air was thin at this high altitude as well. It was slow going, given the steep slope and the weight of the equipment. We had insisted on carrying most of our things ourselves, and were beginning to regret it. Susan's hiking boots kept sticking in the mud, making a loud sucking sound each time she lifted one out.

The higher we climbed, the more eerie it became. Our guides told us it was perpetually cold and overcast, with rain ten months each year. The camp was located at ten thousand feet, and a climb up to the volcanoes would take one as high as twelve thousand feet. Many of the trees were dead, suffocated by the Spanish moss that dangled from them. Stinging nettles penetrated our clothes, leaving us feeling fairly miserable.

Just days before, we had enjoyed a wonderful day in the sunshine, observing a gorilla group that included a large male silverback, two fuzzy juveniles, several females, and even a week-old infant. We'd seen what peaceful creatures the gorillas are, far less aggressive and volatile, compared to the chimps. The gorilla adults spent the day feeding, mostly on bamboo, and the silverback was so accustomed to people that he passed by closely enough that his hair brushed my arm. The juveniles played much of the day, their thick fur and dark eyes making them irresistible.

We had started getting hints that things were not well with Dian just as soon as we had arrived in the small city of Gisenyi. Our guide the previous day had looked concerned when we mentioned our intention to visit her camp. While visiting the offices of the Mountain Gorilla Project, we first heard about a number of students having departed early from Karisoke. We knew that the past several years had been very difficult, starting with the gruesome murder of Dian's favorite gorilla, Digit, in 1977. His death had been followed by those of others of Dian's favorites, including Macho, Uncle Bert, and Kweli.

✦ ✦ ✦

One of Dian's African staff came to meet us as we entered the Karisoke camp, letting us know that we were not allowed. We felt like interlopers, but there was little to do at this point. We were there, exhausted—and hopeful of at least getting the opportunity to explain ourselves. The man went into a nearby cabin and returned with a young American, David Watts, a spectacled, easygoing young man who today is a Yale University anthropology professor. After brief introductions, he quickly herded us into his cabin.

"We'll talk and see what we can figure out," he reassured us. "It'll be OK, but I'd stay out of sight." He seemed intrigued by visitors who had been students at Gombe, and he appeared happy to see new faces. Watts, from the University of Chicago, and Peter Clay, a zookeeper at Chicago's Lincoln Park Zoo, were the only two graduate students there.

We spent the afternoon hearing stories of the gorillas: about young Maggie, who liked to sit in people's laps and chew on their collars; of a gorilla threatening a water buffalo while another was giving birth; of Group 5, where four females had recently been transferred. There had been no gorilla poaching in the past two years, thanks to the Digit Fund and the Mountain Gorilla Project.

We also heard many stories about Dian. In her desperation to protect the gorillas, she had become severe in her handling of poachers, threatening them in hopes of getting the word out to all in the area that poaching was a bad idea. But her health had spiraled downward with the deaths of Digit and the others. She was dealing with emphysema so severe that by 1984 she could no longer trek to Karisoke without oxygen, and stress and isolation were taking a toll. Overall, it was clear that she was facing daunting health issues but that her mission was, in whatever time she had left, to protect the gorillas.

"There's one other thing I have to tell you . . . ," said Watts.

"What's that?"

"Dian doesn't want you to visit Debbie's memorial. She's told the staff she'll fire them if you go near it." We knew that she meant it.

Susan and I had hoped for all these years to make the trek Debbie had been unable to manage, but now it was clear that seeing the plaque in her honor was not worth risking the jobs of the Africans; besides, it seemed less important now, knowing that this austere place wasn't all that Debbie had hoped. We had no desire to add to the misery it appeared Dian had descended to. We left early the next morning, sorry to have caused Dian's distress.

Just eight months later, Dian was found murdered in her cabin soon after receiving a new visa that permitted her to remain in Rwanda for at least two more years. Most people guessed that it was a local who killed her, possibly a poacher, given that she had made numerous enemies with her unconventional actions against them. But there were others who also might have had cause, including those who hoped to make money from tourism in the area. Reading the news of her murder, I felt heartbroken and wondered whether her strategy had backfired. Would her death mean the certain extinction of the mountain gorillas?

❖ ❖ ❖

Thankfully, others had laid additional groundwork for important conservation programs. Amy Vedder and Bill Weber, who had updated gorilla census data and done ecological studies in the late 1970s, concluded that the Virunga mountain gorillas would survive only if poaching and habitat loss could be stemmed. Current tactics of park protection were not working and were breeding resentment among locals. The people of the region were calling for one-third of the park, 12,400 acres, to be turned over to cattle raising, a proposal that would mean the loss of the remaining bamboo habitat, which was essential to the gorillas.[3]

Vedder and Weber, who had fostered relationships with government and park officials, were allowed to submit a counterproposal, and they crafted a plan for hiking tours to observe the now world-famous gorillas. By encouraging tourism, they hoped that income would provide funding for park patrols, habitat preservation, education, and even programs to benefit the two hundred thousand people of the region living in poverty.

Their plan was adopted and implemented under the auspices of the organization they established with others, the Mountain Gorilla Project (now the International Gorilla Conservation Program), and their efforts were successful. They accustomed two groups of gorillas to the presence of humans and developed a team of Africans to lead the new ecotourism program. Almost as soon as it was up and running, the program was in big demand. By charging tourists several hundred dollars to see the gorillas, the ecotourism program was able to remain small and well controlled yet still produce significant sums for conservation. By the 1980s, the program was attracting ten thousand tourists a year and providing revenues of $5 million. Things looked hopeful—that is, until Rwanda's political stability began to disintegrate into genocide in the 1990s.

As fighting erupted outside Virunga National Park in 1991, tourism came to almost a complete halt. It was to be a lengthy interruption, as one of the worst genocides of our time broke out in 1994, resulting in the deaths of more than one million Rwandans. Some refugees fled to the park, posing an immediate threat to the gorillas from poaching, disease, and deforestation. With the country consumed by ethnic violence, there were fewer government resources for the Virunga gorillas. For many years to come, nongovernmental organizations would provide the supplemental funds and knowledge needed to protect the gorillas. They trained and funded patrols, purchased state-of-the-art equipment, and maintained oversight, preventing any major killing of the gorillas and chimpanzees and protecting the parklands from being appropriated by farmers and loggers. Wildlife areas lacking NGO support did not fare as well, however. The Gishwati Forest Preserve, for example, lost 90 percent of its fifty-eight square miles to farmers, and Akagera National Park lost 580 square miles of critical savannah habitat to cattle raising.

Fortunately, peace and political stability have returned to Rwanda over the past decade, and the government has once again been able to manage and develop its gorilla-conservation programs. Today, about twenty thousand tourists visit the gorillas annually in Rwanda, bringing revenues of $10 million for the national park service. Of this amount, 5 percent goes directly to benefit local communities by building schools and clinics. Many observers tout the Virunga ecotourism as a model conservation program and one of the most successful in decades. Similarly successful ecotourism programs are operating at Mgahinga Gorilla National Park and Bwindi Impenetrable National Park, in Uganda. Unfortunately, an estimated one hundred mountain gorillas in the adjacent Democratic Republic of the Congo frequently find themselves in jeopardy due to political instability that prevents effective ecotourism programs there.

☙ ☙ ☙

I had followed news of the mountain gorillas for many years, worrying each time that I heard of new political turmoil in the Democratic Republic of the Congo, Rwanda, or Uganda. I remembered how dismal the predictions had been for their survival, and without their champion, Dian, how could they possibly survive? It was a welcome surprise in 2008 at Ngamba Island to hear an update on the mountain gorillas over dinner conversation.

"We went on two mountain gorilla treks." The taller of the two new overnight guests had just come from visiting the mountain gorillas of Bwindi Impenetrable National Park. "It was amazing to see them. One of the females had a new baby. They are so beautiful."

"Was it worth the hundreds of dollars they charge?" asked another guest at the table.

"Yes, absolutely. They are indescribable, and most of the money goes to protect the gorillas. We were told that they are actually increasing in numbers because there is enough money from tourist visits that the government can hire extra rangers and guards to protect them from poachers."

I thought of Dian at that moment, remembering how, when she died in 1985, the number of mountain gorillas was fewer than five hundred, and their extinction by 2010 was viewed as an absolute certainty. With the influx of refugees into the forest in the early 1990s, an estimated sixteen gorillas were murdered, and several rangers died protecting the others. But the entire Virunga population might have been wiped out had it not been for the accomplishments of Dian years before in bringing mountain gorillas to international attention, as well as the conservation work of her and others such as Amy Vedder, Bill Weber, and Ian Redmond. In hearing the welcome news of gorilla survival and resurgence, I felt that Dian's work had not been in vain. She and others had saved the mountain gorillas from extinction, at least for now.

New heroes are needed now to protect the other gorilla species and subspecies, all of whom are suffering the same threats as the mountain gorillas: plundering of the forests, tremendous political uncertainty, and the bushmeat trade. Reports in 2009 for one area in West Africa, Kouilou, revealed that gorillas were being killed at a rate of 4 percent of the region's population each month and sold as bushmeat, decimating the local population, which had dwindled to just two hundred.[4]

It is ironic that the mountain gorillas now have a more secure future than most other African gorillas and that they are the only species of great ape to actually be increasing in numbers. Although their current population is still small—on the order of nine hundred individuals—their remaining habitats are protected by reasonably effective conservation programs that provide economic benefits to local communities.[5] Now, it is the gorillas in areas without successful ecotourism and conservation programs whose threat of extinction is rapidly growing.[6] For many great apes, ecotourism is not a plausible approach, both because of the political situation in the areas where they survive and because it would expose these last critical individuals to human disease and other hunters. But it is clear that where ecotourism can be implemented, it can help both great apes and locals, and that it has saved the last remaining populations of mountain gorillas.

CHAPTER 14

LINKING DESTINIES IN UGANDA: 2011

When one tugs at a single thing in nature,
he finds it attached to the rest of the world.
JOHN MUIR

❧ ❧ ❧ ❧ ❧ ❧

Trying to learn about cutting-edge conservation programs via the Internet is helpful—but really understanding them requires a personal visit. It was time to head back to East Africa to begin learning in earnest what, beyond ecotourism, can be done to solve these critical conservation issues. So, in 2011, we returned to Uganda.

We learned that saving chimpanzees in impoverished rural areas is complicated beyond measure by the competing needs of humans with whom they must try to coexist. It was evident that long-term conservation is not possible without engaging local people as partners and addressing their basic needs and that the well-being of both people and great apes depends on protection of the forest. We met some astute conservationists who are implementing ingenious approaches to save both ape and human lives.

❧ ❧ ❧ ❧ ❧ ❧

An oversized man in safari gear pardoned himself as he stumbled over us in hopes of getting even the vaguest glimpse of a chimp. It was hot, and we'd been here for almost an hour. The man and his family were struggling to keep up with their field guides, who had moved to the other side of the enormous fig tree where four male chimps were feeding. These were the only chimps the field guides had been able to locate, so twenty of us stood here drenched in sweat, straining to see them. Yet a perfect azure sky backlit the tree branches, and a balmy breeze blew in the leaves. Somehow, it all seemed worthwhile.

Our guides, Richard and Shem, told us of the 120 individuals who were part of this chimpanzee community and of how dispersed the group had become these past weeks, due, in part, to less rain than usual and thus less fruit. We'd purposely planned our trip to Uganda during the summer dry season so as to avoid the more usual daily drenching rains, which produced an average of sixty-three inches of rainfall each year. The terrain was reminiscent of Gombe—hardly surprising, given that both lie in the Albertine Rift, the western branch of the Great Rift Valley. I jockeyed for a new position and nearly landed on Bryan, who lay sprawled on the grass, looking amused.

This trip was the sequel to our 2008 visit, and its purpose was to visit cutting-edge programs that not only defend chimps and mountain gorillas but also couple that effort with promoting the well-being of local people. We knew that great ape conservation is doomed to failure if it doesn't also address human need, particularly if locals are living in extreme poverty. Uganda would be the perfect place to visit some exemplary projects as well as to see wild chimps and mountain gorillas, and even to revisit the Ngamba Island Chimpanzee Sanctuary.

Currently, we were at Kibale National Park, research site of Dr. Richard Wrangham, a former Gombeite who was now professor of human evolutionary biology at Harvard University. He had become renowned for his long-term studies of chimpanzee behavior and ecology and had directed the Kibale Chimpanzee Project since 1987 at the Makerere University Biological Field Station, in western Uganda. He and colleagues had conducted more than thirty years of study there, producing a massive amount of scientific literature on critical aspects of protecting a forest under siege from a growing human community. Between 1996 and 2006, Kibale National Park had managed to maintain its forest cover and primate populations, whereas neighboring forest patches had shrunk by half and lost much of their wildlife.[1]

Wrangham's studies have focused on a community of about fifty chimpanzees. Although the group is accustomed to human presence, it is observed only by members of the research team. However, by 1988, it was apparent to Wrangham that a separate ecotourism project was likely in the best interest of the park's overall wild chimpanzee population of about 1,200 individuals.[2] Such a program could potentially benefit conservation and local people through its financial impacts while also increasing sentiment for the chimps and their forest at both the local and international levels. Consequently, the chimp community we were visiting today had been successfully habituated to humans, and an ecotourism program had been established. The program proved highly successful, earning revenues to help fund critical wildlife protection and providing tourists with rich observations of wild chimpanzees. And although we had timed our visit poorly, it was fascinating to see what his work had wrought and to see a wild-chimpanzee community other than Gombe's.

＊ ＊ ＊

Our next stop was to the Kasiisi Project, yet another important outcome of Wrangham's presence in Uganda. The project grew out of a visit Wrangham's wife, Dr. Elizabeth Ross, and his sister, Kate Wrangham-Briggs, had made in 1997 to the sorry-looking primary school near Kibale National Park. They arrived to find a school in such disrepair that the classrooms had to be evacuated in high winds for fear that the walls would collapse. Some classes had upwards of 150 students, most lacked books and blackboards, and the premises were without potable water or enough pit toilets. As if conditions weren't bad enough, the school was further overwhelmed by a flood of new pupils when the Ugandan government instituted mandatory primary education.

The school visit led Ross and Wrangham to establish the Kasiisi Project to support education, health, and conservation education in local primary schools. Its first order of business was to improve the local school, not only by constructing new classrooms but also by providing water tanks and bathrooms. Efforts broadened to include creation of scholarships, construction of libraries and staff rooms, and provision of health- and conservation-education programs. The project has since expanded its activities into thirteen other schools, creating boarding facilities for students who otherwise would have to travel prohibitively long distances, building a preschool, offering teacher training and computer education, and even providing electrical power.

The programs have raised academic standards, not only increasing the number of students going on to secondary schools and universities but even leading to one graduate's recent admission to Harvard University. The program has a strong emphasis on conservation education and on educating girls. Today, students are continuing their education and, in the process, helping secure the promise of better-paying jobs in the future. And the community knows that finding a way to coexist with the chimpanzees and maintain the forest is important and benefits the human community.[3]

✦ ✦ ✦

The Kasiisi Project has benefited not only the education of its students but also their health and nutrition. One of its essential programs, the Kasiisi Porridge Project (KPP), works to combat the high rate of hunger and, like the Kasiisi Project, was prompted by a momentous school visit, this one in 2005.[4] As Kate Wrangham-Briggs tells the story:

> I asked Lydia, the Headmistress, if I could visit one of the class-rooms, to which she agreed though warning me that it was lunch time. "Fine," I say. "Where do they have lunch?"
>
> "I said lunch 'TIME,'" laughs Lydia. "They don't actually HAVE lunch!"—alluding to the fact that many students' families are too poor to afford a midday meal.
>
> And so one thing led to another, and now 1,250 school children are getting daily porridge.[5]

Wrangham-Briggs left the school that day, promising the headmistress that she would help fix the situation. She and others quickly located funding to create a school-lunch program to provide maize-flour porridge to hungry students. The project grew so quickly that, within five years, it had created two school kitchens, hired cooks, built latrines and water tanks, and found donations to provide porridge for upper-division students at two primary schools located within five kilometers of Kibale National Park.

Few places in the world have a greater need for KPP's services than Kabarole District, where the schools are located. Uganda's children have one of the highest rates of malnutrition in all of sub-Saharan Africa—and Kabarole District has an even higher rate. Among children ages six to fifty-nine months, 43 percent have stunted growth as a result of poor diet and/or disease, and many local children suffer malnutrition based on an insufficient number of calories in their diet and a deficiency of critical proteins.[6] Although the area is one of the most fertile areas of Uganda, high rates of undernourishment result from the region's immense poverty and limited educational status.[7]

The KPP initially focused on providing a daily cup of maize-flour porridge to students at lunchtime. The porridge immediately proved a godsend to students who were so poor that many ate only a single daily meal, usually in the evening, after a long day of school, chores, and walking to and from school. It seemed to not only help students concentrate better on their studies but also to encourage their families to let them stay in school. Soon, as a result, the schools were seeing children who were taller and whose weight was closer to normal.

❧ ❧ ❧

So far, KPP was making life better for students at two schools—but how could it grow further and continue into the future? Wrangham-Briggs and others went to work on phase two, the creation of an innovative twenty-acre multipurpose farm that is now well under way. Two newly graduated British architects volunteered their sweat and inspiration to design a self-supporting school farm able to cater to four thousand children in five local schools, complete with an education center, an eco-camp site for tourists, farm animals and crops, and an indigenous forest for timber and medicine. The completed farm would not only improve school nutrition but also teach effective farming methods, model the use of earth-friendly local construction methods, and make KPP sustainable in the long term by creating a steady stream of income.

One of the biggest challenges for architects Matt Parker and Rob Mawson was to master the art of traditional rammed-earth construction. In this simple technology, earth is mixed with equal proportions of small stones, sandy material, and clay and then rammed into wooden forms to provide a strong, low-cost wall material able to withstand the region's frequent earthquakes. Because it is eco-friendly, the architects were keen to reintroduce the method to the community, but they encountered fierce resistance from locals who regarded rammed-earth construction as being for "the poor" and considered concrete "modern" and therefore superior.

The farm now includes crops for chicken feed and to supplement the porridge provided at the schools, *matooke* (cooking bananas), a fruit orchard, and even an indigenous forest that will provide fuel and timber, replenish endangered species of indigenous trees, and act as a valuable resource for the local community by providing materials, medicine, and opportunities for education. The local botanical garden has been sharing its expertise, and already, tracts of a fast-growing native tree have been planted.

Each of six rooms in the chicken house will hold six hundred chickens, and all the farm buildings have been designed to withstand local hazards, such as annual rainfall of thirty to forty inches, relatively frequent earthquakes, and the presence of soil pests such as termites. The chickens' eggs are already creating a stream of income, and carpenters have created special containers so that a single motorcycle can deliver up to sixteen trays of eggs to the city for sale. Additional profits are expected soon from sales of pigs and honey.

Back in the United Kingdom, KPP founder Kate Wrangham-Briggs, busy checking the books and preparing for upcoming fund-raisers, is hopeful that the KPP mission to turn the programs over to local Ugandans in one to two years can be kept on track. Accomplishing the construction of such an ambitious farm isn't an easy task. There are funds to raise, and there's always an unanticipated wrench in the works. But it is clear that she plans to see it through.

In Kasiisi, schoolchildren are rising for 5:30 a.m. chores and only a cup of tea to sustain them for the day. That porridge, that farm, can't come soon enough.

❧ ❧ ❧

We were learning about poverty in far clearer terms than we had understood it in our previous travels. Seeing the lives of locals through the lens of our friends, we finally were appreciating the severe poverty that surrounded us. How easily we might have otherwise passed children on the street, never suspecting how little they had to eat, or that their short stature was more than merely genetic. Of course, it wasn't just the children who were hungry, something we were about to learn during the next leg of our trip, when we traveled to Bwindi Impenetrable National Park.

En route, we pulled over to the side of the road to eat our lunches atop a breathtaking valley below. Staff at the hotel we had stayed at the previous night had packed us each a lunch that contained far more than we could ever have eaten. Below us, a few young men harvesting saplings stopped what they were doing, as if taking a break for lunch. The first of them, balancing a newly felled piece of young eucalyptus on his head, walked past us slowly but then inexplicably lingered nearby. It seemed odd—until our driver walked over and handed him the food left over from his lunch. The young man took the food gratefully and without hesitation. With that, we gathered up our surpluses and delivered the food to the other hungry young men farther off. It was the first of what became a regular occurrence. We shared our food often and tried to eat only what we needed so as to have more leftovers to contribute.

✦ ✦ ✦

We were headed to Bwindi Impenetrable National Park to visit a unique project linking the well-being of mountain gorillas to humans' health. First, however, we planned to go on a mountain gorilla trek, one of the most thrilling experiences the natural world offers, and something I had done years before in Rwanda. Because we had been late planning our trip and obtaining a permit, we had been assigned to a fairly remote site for our mountain gorilla visit, tucked atop what had to be the tallest of all the impossibly tall mountaintops of the region. Our safari vehicle tiptoed through unimaginable passes, twisted around hairpin turns, and charged directly up the mountainsides on narrow dirt roads.

We were finally nearing the lodge when another vehicle approached us from the opposite direction along a very long drop-off. Our driver backed into a pocket in the hillside, allowing the other safari vehicle to cautiously pass, and as it did, a sixtyish, well-coiffed American in the backseat called out to us, "You might just as well not bother going, because it is absolutely impossible hiking to get to the gorillas." But it did not matter. We had traveled to Uganda's far southwest corner, where it borders the Democratic Republic of the Congo and Rwanda, excited about this rare opportunity. The trekking fee of five hundred dollars per person only bolstered our intent.

By now, we were wondering where the national park and its impenetrable forest could possibly be. Every square inch of mountainside for miles on end, regardless of how steep or how high, appeared to be cultivated. It wasn't until we got to our lodge that we finally spotted a small stand of native forest, and even there, at seven thousand feet, people and farms were everywhere.

The next morning, we set off to meet with the rangers and the other tourists we would spend the morning with. The chief ranger divvied us up, assigning us to find the Mishaya Group, a band of twelve gorillas named for its silverback male. We then drove several miles to our takeoff point to meet the rest of our group: two park rangers, two porters, and a Canadian family of five. From there, we started the first portion of our hike atop a mountain ridge. Farmers, young children, and goats dotted the landscape as we hiked through farmland and small villages.

Soon, however, the hike became distinctly more intense, and we began to think of the woman's warning the day before. We clambered up treacherous clay hillsides, eyeing crops that reached so high up the mountainside that they must have depended solely on rainstorms for irrigation. We struggled on until we arrived at a grassy clearing near what had to be the edge of the Bwindi Impenetrable Forest. Crops grew even here, right to the forest perimeter. The sun shone on the grass and fields, yet the adjacent forest was dark. A pit sawyer's platform for sawing timber lay disconcertingly close to this protected area.

Imagine Hansel and Gretel's black forest, or a prehistoric jungle that was home to tyrannosauruses, and perhaps you can imagine the sensation we felt as we entered the forest and left sunlight behind. Our beret-attired ranger, complete with Che Guevara guerrilla backpack, had contacted other rangers by walkie-talkie and was trying to navigate us to their location. So far, this forest was proving to be far more treacherous and difficult than chimp terrain, fraught with long vines that caught us, sheer mountainsides that tested our stamina, and fallen logs. We wondered whether we would make it and wished we had been assigned a less daunting trek. But it all finally proved worthwhile as we inched our way toward a hilltop where sun was inching through.

"On your right," the ranger whispered.

I turned my head to find myself facing the magnificent Mishaya himself, fifteen feet away. Leaning against the mountain as though in a lounge chair, he was not the least bit perturbed by our presence. Below him stretched the entirety of a huge valley, and he seemed to be soaking up both the sun and the view. Kate and Bryan both looked as though they barely believed they could be standing so close to such a titan.

Mishaya was a gorgeous, furry hulk, spoiled only slightly by a gash over his left eye. An unusually testy silverback, he had incurred the injury two months previously when he initiated a fight with another gorilla group. As a result, a juvenile in his group had been severely injured and Mishaya had received cuts to his upper lip, an eyebrow, and some of his extremities. The rangers had considered removing him from the group for medical care, but fortunately, that had not proven necessary.

When a female carrying a baby, and a mischievous juvenile, passed by, the 450-pound Mishaya got up and slowly lumbered a few yards down the hill, carefully keeping himself between us and his family. We watched the group feed peacefully, and we snapped what must have been a thousand photos. Our permitted hour with the gorillas flew by as we sat awestruck, witnesses to a day in the life of mountain gorillas. Woolly juveniles careened on tree branches, females nursed their babies and fed on tubers, and Mishaya sat majestically surveying it all. Once the all-too-brief hour was over, the rangers herded us away, knowing it would be difficult for us to leave on our own. We straggled back through that same obstacle-filled forest, but this time we were elated at having just experienced something so profound that we were unable to find words for it.

❧ ❧ ❧

The next day, we hiked down a massive mountainside to our next destination, a welcome alternative to the circuitous six-hour drive our safari driver was enduring on the region's narrow roads. We followed the river, sighting monkeys, birds, and butterflies, and finally arrived at the Buhoma Guest Camp, a community-run lodge that lay just a few feet from the forest. The camp was unpretentious, a place where monkeys left evidence of their nightly visits on our porches and cottage names were misspelled. Each night at dinner, we could pick out the guests that had just returned from their gorilla trek by their unquenchable desire to tell us every detail.

It was time now to meet some of the people ensuring the future of those magnificent gorillas. We were to spend two days with Conservation Through Public Health, a group created by a brilliant Ugandan veterinarian, Dr. Gladys Kalema-Zikusoka.[8] While working for the Uganda Wildlife Authority, she had seen how the growth of the local human population was causing locals to farm even the areas immediately adjacent to the national park. This, in turn, was leading to a huge increase in ape-versus-human conflict and disease transmission.

She and her team set out to find solutions as to how humans, wildlife, and livestock could successfully coexist, quickly identifying a number of important issues that would need to be addressed. Gorillas sometimes raided the crops of locals, putting themselves at serious risk of injury by farmers and of acquiring infectious diseases that can be transmitted by humans, such as tuberculosis, scabies, and dysentery. Local people had little access to safe water sources, and 89 percent were living in unsanitary conditions, putting people at high risk of disease and child mortality. The areas surrounding Bwindi Impenetrable National Park are among the most densely populated rural areas in all of Africa; the local population had swelled not only because of large family sizes but also because of an influx of immigrants from the DRC and Rwanda.

When we arrived at CTPH, Dr. Kalema-Zikusoka was away, receiving yet another international accolade, so her team welcomed us. The group included David Matsiko, the field director, and Alex Ngabirano, director of field activities to improve human health. Following a briefing, we walked through Buhoma toward farms that bordered directly on the national park. There, we found one-room clay houses that were home to the poorest of the poor, as well as the farms, called *shamba*s, of some of the region's more well-heeled residents. We soon arrived at the *shamba* of a local shaman and his influential wife, who was a volunteer with CTPH.

The shaman took us into his office, donning a cowhide sorcerer's hat and passing around local herbs he uses to treat locals. But soon his wife, Miriam, emerged through the door, cutting short his presentation. She was here to demonstrate some of her work as one of CTPH's volunteers. The organization, we were about to learn, had been clever in finding twenty-five esteemed local leaders to volunteer as community health monitors by asking the local communities to nominate their most influential members. The monitors were proving to be remarkable foot soldiers in not only mitigating human and gorilla conflict but also providing family-planning, hygiene, and nutrition education and helping improve local health.

It took little persuasion to get Miriam to demonstrate one of the many lectures she gives to local people. Choosing to give us the lesson on the benefits of family planning, she prefaced it by telling us that the average local family has at least six to ten children and has difficulty finding food enough for all. She then began her talk, speaking eloquently and using a flip board of drawings to illustrate her points:

> If you have but two or three children instead of many, there will be more to eat, your children can go to school, and your man will not leave you each day to get away.

Her talk went on from there, but each point was illustrated by two drawings, the first showing the stress of a large family and the second contrasting it with the situation of a smaller one. Other flip boards and lessons covered a wide array of topics such as the importance of clean hands, how to wash dishes and utensils, and what to do if diarrheal disease develops.

Miriam then took us to tour her *shamba*, where we saw goats in the raised pen CTPH had helped her build. The enclosure allowed her family to collect goat manure for fertilizer and kept the goats from wandering into the forest, thus reducing the likelihood of their transmitting disease to the gorillas and other forest animals. The organization had helped her secure medication to cure the goats of parasites, and Miriam was delighted by how much healthier and robust her animals were as a result.

She then walked us to a small grove of banana trees at the back of the farm. We could see they were poorly located, since they were close to the forest, where they could easily be raided by gorillas and other creatures. In fact, the family had become fairly used to wild invaders. Yet they had also learned how to safely encourage the gorillas back into the forest and, in the process, had become an important resource to their neighbors in dealing with the situation.

We headed back to the CTPH offices for lunch and then took a tour of the premises, visiting the lodging they offer to tourists in Bwindi, and saw plans for a new guest lodge closer to the forest. Next, we visited their impressive laboratory, where technicians checked gorilla dung and other specimens for parasites and other infectious diseases. CTPH could even intervene on the rare occasions when a gorilla developed a potentially life-threatening illness. In these instances, the gorilla was darted with a seda-tive so that a veterinarian could provide the needed medical intervention right there in the field.

Later that afternoon, they drove us through the local mountains to one of the district health clinics. Although the clinic was only a few miles away, it took a long time because of the steep and winding dirt roads. Alex took advantage of the downtime to start preparing me for my role as "honored guest" at the meeting. I was to learn not only how to greet the health workers in their tribal language but also how to introduce myself by using the formal phrasing required of such a meeting. More important, I was to do it by heart, not reading off the back of a note card. I had ten minutes to get it right.

"*Webele munonga*" means "Thank you all." I knew I could master that. But it was "*Amazina gange niban nyeta*" that Alex assured me would make me friends for life with everyone in the room. Prior "honored guests" had rarely had the good taste to speak this formal means of saying "My name is" that locals considered an act of respect. "Think of the Amazon and the Ganges," I thought to myself, not having a clue of how to concoct a similar mnemonic for "*niban nyeta*." Ten minutes didn't seem nearly long enough to memorize the phrase.

It was Sunday, and the clinic was officially closed, but here, arriv-ing in the backs of small trucks, was the full complement of twenty-five community-health volunteers assembling for a three-hour meeting in our honor. We were seated at the front, next to those in charge, and the entire meeting was translated into English for us. I tried to appear relaxed and confident, and all the while, I kept *"Webele munonga, amazina gange niban nyeta"* continuously rolling through my mind.

The community leaders were evenly divided between men and women, middle-aged and young, all seated on wooden benches in a worn concrete building. Health posters were plastered on the back wall, and other walls bore painted messages such as "Sex is for marriage," "Do not give your body for favors," and "Wash hands to eat." The workers exhibited great pride in their work, and several had worked for organizations such as UNICEF. Others were teachers, and many were simply farmers.

Among them, they had accomplished 351 household visits that month, met with 118 individuals privately to offer or discuss family planning, and identified 37 people needing evaluation, and possibly treatment, for symptoms that might indicate tuberculosis. They had addressed community groups about health and hygiene, reaching an estimated 1,200 people—all in a month—and had provided birth-control pills or long-acting contraceptive injections to several hundred. In fact, they constituted one of the few groups in Uganda we had seen that was willing to not only openly discuss contraception but also provide it on the spot. These workers had also talked with households about the importance of clean water sources and hand washing to reduce diarrheal deaths. And in the course of this work, they were greatly augmenting the efforts of the local health clinic, which had vacancies for ten of its nineteen positions.

The meeting went on for two solid hours, much of it led by Alex, who tested their knowledge of hygiene and of indicators of tuberculosis and badgered them with bad jokes that prompted belly laughs. We heard from a long line of community leaders, each one offering a brief speech of welcome and a summary of their work. Those that could speak English did so to honor us, and the testimony of the others was faithfully translated line by line, adding substantially to the length of the meeting.

When the meeting had finally run its course, it was my turn. Trying to invoke the persona of Princess Diana, I rose to deliver those all-important six words. By now, the group, looking a little uncomfortable, seemed ready for this meeting to be over. No doubt they had suffered some pretty awful gracious-tourist speeches in the past.

"Webele munonga," I said with all the gusto I could muster. A few people with raised eyebrows slowly looked up, making eye contact and appearing somewhat hopeful.

"Amazine gange . . . niban nyeta," I spouted, feeling as though I had just landed a perfect dismount at the Olympics. The room erupted into laughter, with a few declarations in the native language, signaling how significant my effort had been. Alex smiled approvingly, as though I hadn't let him down.

❧ ❧ ❧

We finally met Dr. Kalema-Zikusoka herself a week later in Entebbe, Uganda.[9] She had left her two young children with her husband to come talk about gorillas and public health with us, and it was immediately evident what a remarkable presence she is. She shared her story with us over dinner, telling us of having trained at the University of London's Royal Veterinary College before returning to organize the first veterinary unit for the Uganda Wildlife Authority (UWA). An early experience in her new job proved pivotal. An outbreak of scabies was menacing Bwindi's mountain gorillas, and she was sent to investigate what could be done. Her analysis showed that the outbreak was the result of gorillas coming into contact with the discarded clothes of an infected person, and it forever impressed her with the potentially devastating impact of disease transmission among humans, gorillas, and livestock.

The incident ultimately prompted her, along with her husband, Lawrence Zikusoka, and coworker Stephen Rubanga to create CTPH. By founding a nongovernmental organization, they would be able to augment the work of the UWA and to develop their own resources. The organization proved so effective and groundbreaking that she soon was receiving accolades, including the prestigious Whitley Gold Award, presented for achievement in nature conservation, in 2009. Dr. Kalema-Zikusoka was now being sought after to replicate the program elsewhere, being elected or appointed to prestigious boards and national commissions, and being called on for international lectures and awards. That such a woman would take time from her family and work to have dinner with us not only seemed extraordinary but also spoke to her humility and purpose.

It was inspiring to sit with her and to be caught up in her energy. This gifted woman had fully realized the importance of augmenting the work of the UWA and ensuring the long-term health of the gorillas. Her organization had also dared to tackle head-on the issue of family planning in this largely Catholic country, where contraception is little discussed in public. Given her accomplishments, we were little surprised to learn of her distinguished parents: Her father had been a highly respected government official, one of the first to be murdered by Idi Amin's soldiers in the 1970s. Her mother, the remarkable Rhoda Kalema, is widely known as "the Mother of the Ugandan Parliament" for her years as one of its members and for her courage in coaxing women to become involved in politics in order to bring change. Rhoda Kalema ingrained in her daughter that those who pursue their dreams wholeheartedly will conquer adversity.

And so it is that Dr. Gladys, as she allows us to call her, has created a program that is protecting one of the two last precarious populations of mountain gorillas in the world while simultaneously benefiting some of the world's poorest people. Her program—like the Kasiisi Project—is bringing hope to the people whose daily lives are so interconnected with the great apes and other forest dwellers. It is critical work, and Dr. Elizabeth Ross and Dr. Gladys are tireless in their efforts to find the funding needed to keep their projects up and thriving.

Dr. Gladys's message is consistent: Supporting conservation can promote human health and reduce poverty. "My greatest joy," she tells us, "is seeing improvements in animal health and change in the way communities relate to wildlife, moving from being competitors to protectors." Our joy, we tell her, is in seeing projects like hers working successfully at the interface between bettering the lives of Uganda's people and protecting its wildlife.

CHAPTER 15

AFRICA'S SANCTUARIES
AND FRAGMENTED FORESTS

We returned to the Ngamba Island Chimpanzee Sanctuary in 2011 to learn what had become of our chimp and human friends there. This time, we would spend just a couple of days, for our friend Lilly Ajarova had bigger plans for us. She was taking us to see where these chimp orphans were coming from and why their numbers were escalating. Who could have believed that tobacco companies could play a major role?

The forests we were to visit were those located near burgeoning human communities, not the less accessible forests deep in the heart of the Congo Basin. We were to see the situation chimpanzees face in many well-populated rural areas of East and West Africa.

✤ ✤ ✤ ✦ ✦ ✦

Here we were, back on Lake Victoria and en route once again to Ngamba Island for a two-night stay, just long enough to see our friends from three years before and to learn what had become of the chimps. We wondered whether Mika was still alpha, how Afrika must be, and whether the sanctuary was still thriving. We knew little Mac would be missing, for he had died two years earlier. Although his integration into the group had been going smoothly, things went terribly wrong one night. All the chimps were in the holding facility during an evening storm that had them on edge when Mika began furiously displaying. A fight broke out between the males trapped in the room, and the surge of adrenaline led to tragedy. Mac was caught in the midst of it, suffering large bite wounds and bleeding that caused his death moments later.

Mac's death was devastating, and the sanctuary staff vowed it would not happen again. Afrika and another new arrival, Barron, were immediately moved out of the larger group to start the entire group-integration process all over again, but this time even more slowly and cautiously. Two years later, they were still in the process, spending their days with a group of young and mostly female chimps in a large outdoor enclosure.

The speedboat was rapidly approaching Ngamba Island. Several tiny figures in the distance were moving down to the dock, and so far, the island looked the same, except that the water level was lower due to years of waning rainfall, and some of the reeds and trees that had formerly been partially submerged were now exposed. We were starting to see people gathering on the dock, and it didn't take long to recognize our old friends Stany and Patrick.

We gathered our things as the boat arrived, eager to set foot again on Ngamba. A look of happy surprise swept Patrick's face as he recognized the four of us, and soon Stany was offering us a "Welcome back!" and a hug. They helped us haul our bags to the dining hall, and we sat down to catch up over some iced tea. The wind lent a gentle reminder of the gloriously warm day as we settled back into island paradise.

Stany and Patrick filled us in on life at Ngamba and all that had changed: Gerald had moved back to South Africa to be with his family, and Dr. Fred now worked for the Mountain Gorilla Veterinary Project. Rodney had fallen in love with the Dutch volunteer, and the two were to be married soon in the Netherlands. Thankfully, at least a few of our friends, like Philip and Mandy, were still here, still happily involved in helping chimps.

Barron had been the only new addition to the chimpanzee group since we had left. But all this was to change soon, as four new inhabitants were finishing their quarantine period and due to arrive at the sanctuary within the month. The four had been smuggled into South Sudan from the DRC by traffickers and would likely have ended up as pets in the Middle East had they not been rescued and sent instead to Ngamba.

Familiar pant-hoots signaled that the evening feeding was about to begin and that we needed to hurry. As we climbed the platform, it was like being reunited with old friends. We instantly recognized Mika, still the alpha, and Tumbo, still the peacemaker. Ikuru's hand had healed, and now she was higher ranking, presumably because she was physically better able to stand her ground. Sunday's love of carrots had passed, but he remained the tallest and skinniest chimp of all time. Bwambale was now a young adult, still staying at the edge of the enclosure during feeding—but he was handsome and full bodied and sure to start moving up the dominance hierarchy just as soon as he realized his own ability to do so.

The next morning, we went on the Forest Walk, this time for just a very brief excursion with many of the same chimps as on our first trip.

We walked for only five minutes before sitting down in a small clearing. Bili and her best friend, Namukisa, were chasing one another and laughing, and soon, Bili ran over to me, trying to get me to play and even play-biting my hand. She had grown even bigger since the last visit, and fearing getting knocked over, I stayed planted where I was. Rambo, now nearing adolescence, was sitting with Kate, all the while eyeing Bili and Namukisa. Occasionally, he got up to playfully shake his head and stamp his feet, but the females ignored him, so he gnawed on Kate's shoulder and began mischievously swiping at her rubber galoshes.

Sooner than I knew, Bili was back, this time waving her large, brown bottom at me in hopes that I would groom it. I was busy watching Kate trace her lifeline across her palm as Pasa watched carefully. When Kate got up to stretch, Pasa stayed put, brow furled, and briefly studied her own hand as though trying to discern her future. Meanwhile, Bili and Namukisa were back yet again, this time just a few feet above Bryan, playing aerial chase. Thinking of the array of possible disastrous outcomes he might be facing, he wasted no time in moving. Soon enough, it was time for the group to hike back for the morning feeding and the release of the other chimps so they could begin their day in the forest.

❈ ❈ ❈

With four new chimps soon to arrive, the sanctuary was fast reaching capacity. The staff's hope, until recently, had been to buy a bigger island that could better accommodate the growing population of rescued chimps. Unfortunately, however, tourism in Uganda was reeling from the dismal world economy, and financial support from donors had fallen. Now, instead, Chimpanzee Trust Uganda was exploring the possibility of one day releasing some of the chimps into undisturbed forests where they could once again live in the wild. From what we had seen of densely populated Uganda, it was hard to imagine that there could be any such forests, but we hoped, for the chimps' sake, that we were wrong.

The need for African sanctuaries had changed dramatically during the forty years since my work at Gombe. In 1972, the first and only sanctuary in West Africa, home to just a handful of chimps, had recently been established. But now there were twenty-one recognized sanctuaries in twelve African countries caring for more than three thousand primates among them. The sanctuaries, linked together by the Pan African Sanctuary Alliance (PASA), were all in similar straits, nearing capacity, and searching for solutions. The 750 chimps in those sanctuaries were clearly a fraction of those that would soon need rescue unless current trends were reversed.

By now, I knew enough about the sanctuaries to be certain that the people running them are among the planet's greatest heroes, each with an untold story of risking life and limb to help chimps. They live on shoe-string budgets and often have sacrificed their personal lives to care for primate orphans. Many are foreigners who arrived in Africa with no intention whatsoever of running a chimp refuge; they simply were on an African safari and came across a baby chimp in the marketplace in need of rescue. Others were ranchers in Africa who rescued a chimp, soon began receiving others, and eventually converted a portion of their land into a sanctuary. Still others came as volunteers and never left.

Attending some primate-conservation meetings in 2010, I had found myself giving one saintly sanctuary manager, Liza Gadsby, of the Pandril-lus Foundation, a ride to the airport. Liza was in the United States for the meetings and to visit her aging parents in Oregon; issues of elder care had overtaken the daily grind of keeping her primate orphans fed. As we drove, she told me how she and boyfriend Peter Jenkins had arrived in Af-rica twenty-two years ago as tourists, never suspecting that so many years later, they would still be there.

Now they found themselves immersed in the work of protecting chimps, drill monkeys, and the Cross River gorillas, the latter now numbering fewer than 250 individuals. They had established not only the Afi Moun-tain Wildlife Sanctuary, a critical habitat for the endangered primates, but also two other sanctuaries, the Limbe Wildlife Centre, in Cameroon, and the Pandrillus Foundation's Drill Ranch, with its Nigerian Chimpanzee Center. After years of exemplary work, their reputation had won Gadsby a prestigious Whitley Award, and Jenkins had fostered a trusted relation-ship with government officials. In fact, he had been so successful that the government had promised a two-year moratorium on timber harvesting in critical forests, providing him with soldiers and police officers to enforce the ban on logging. (The moratorium has continued, and Jenkins is now chairman of the local governor's task force on antideforestation.)

During the early years of their work, they had encountered back-lash from the logging industry and the local people it employed. Tires had been slashed and threats made, but they persevered, writing grants, seeking donors, finding partner organizations, and thinking about their elderly parents back home in the United States. More recently, they also began studying how to successfully release some of their drills into the wild. They, like other sanctuary directors, knew it would be important in dealing with a steady influx of new orphans. And, of late, a new area of urgency had emerged: to protect forests from being cleared for agriculture.

The sanctuaries have proven to be more than simply orphanages. Their presence has enabled local police to enforce a country's laws against trafficking in endangered animals by ensuring that there is a place to turn the confiscated animals over to for subsequent care. The JACK Sanctuary, in the DRC, for example, was created specifically to allow local law-enforcement officials to begin confronting a well-known local pet-trafficking ring. In addition, sanctuaries have become a mainstay in influencing local Africans by allowing them to visit and appreciate their local wildlife. The Limbe Wildlife Centre, for example, hosts 45,000 visitors annually, many of who are changed by their firsthand experience of the chimps and drills. In order to fund this work, sanctuaries are increasingly reaching out internationally through Facebook and other websites, sharing stories and updates of their chimpanzees, and seeking support. Many accept volunteers, and all can be accessed through the website for PASA (www .pasaprimates.org).

❖ ❖ ❖

Our Ngamba Island visit was short because our friend Lilly, the director, wanted us to visit a region in northwest Uganda to better understand the exponential growth in chimps needing sanctuary. Here, some three hundred chimps live in a densely populated fifty-kilometer corridor— unprotected lands that are either privately or communally owned—that stretches between Bugoma and Budongo Forest Reserves. The human population of the region, like populations throughout Uganda, is growing explosively. Hoima District's population had reached 345,000 in 2002 and more than 500,000 by 2012 and is expected to triple by midcentury. As a result, chimps are encountering people every day, putting both at risk of calamity.

We are little prepared for what we are about to see on our all-day drive, most of it on dusty dirt roads that toss the Land Rover like a ship on tortured seas. One settlement after another of dirty brown buildings stretches to infinity, home to people eking out an existence as subsistence farmers. We pass a sea of people walking the roads, biking sackfuls of rice or charcoal to market, men carrying tender, newly harvested trees on their heads, chickens and toddlers milling in front yards. Small stands of young eucalyptus are almost the only forest we see, aside from one hilly region in which other nonnatives, pine trees, have been planted as a source of fast-growing wood. The stands are nowhere large enough to supply a small village, let alone the cities through which we are passing, and even the occasional native forest is only the size of an elementary school yard.

We ask David, our driver, why there is not more effort to replant trees and to enforce laws against illegal extraction, especially of native species, and although we hear about corruption and the absence of sufficient numbers of forest monitors to enforce bans throughout the country, we know in our hearts that it all comes down to the enormous need in Africa. How can you convince a starving farmer not to harvest timber for the cash, fuel, and housing he needs to ensure the survival of his family?

David points out two unprotected forests that are home to small bands of chimps essentially trapped in what little forest has not yet been converted to sugarcane or tobacco or cut down for charcoal and timber. The chimps are surviving in these limited spaces, sometimes living on an unnatural diet of sugarcane and human crop food in place of their more normal diet of native tree fruits and the meat of small animals. Most of the groups number between thirteen and fifty chimps, and the smallest bands tend to stay together more than is typical of usual fission-fusion chimp communities. Here, the adult males have taken on extra responsibility for protecting the group, and often a male leads the chimps in line formation, while another brings up the rear. It is a tenuous existence, one that is exposing chimps to risk of human disease, poaching, genetic inbreeding, and serious injuries from snares and traps set by locals to catch small animals.

We pass long swaths of land converted to maize, rice, and especially tobacco. In one area, we even pass acres of roses, all of which will be shipped to Europe and the United States by the multinational corporation that has bought this critical land. Seventy percent of Uganda's total forestland, we learn, is privately held and largely unregulated, while only 15 percent of it is under management of the National Forest Authority; some 27 percent of Uganda's forest cover was lost between 1999 and 2005.[1]

· Locals have tolerated the chimps' stealing food reasonably well in the past, especially if only native fruits like bananas and jackfruit are taken. But farmers have viewed crop raiding as far more egregious when it has involved cash crops like sugarcane and cocoa. In those instances, farmers have set ferocious steel traps called mantraps and injured or killed chimps outright.[2] Chimps, too, have naturally become increasingly aggressive as the stakes for survival have risen. Frightened and aggressive chimps have injured people on occasion; small children are particularly vulnerable to vicious attack. All in all, it appears that chimps and people in Hoima are increasingly headed toward catastrophe, and humans are certain to prevail.

Deforestation is playing out throughout Africa, and it is a high-stakes game. Western Uganda is a particularly important battleground because of its importance to the world's biodiversity.[3] Although Uganda accounts for only 0.18 percent of the world's terrestrial and freshwater surface, it is home to 7.5 percent of the world's mammal species and 10.2 percent of the bird species, and more species of primates are found here than anywhere else on Earth within a similar range.[4] The majority of Uganda's five thousand chimps live in forest reserves or national parks, but about five hundred live in unprotected areas. Worse still, even the chimps in the so-called protected forest reserves are at risk because of corruption among some local leaders who are key to safeguarding the areas.

❖ ❖ ❖

The next morning, we grab a quick breakfast while watching the Al Jazeera newscast, then load up into the Chimpanzee Trust Uganda safari vehicle with Jovann, our guide for today. A local Ugandan, Jovann has a master's degree in conservation biology and a passion for chimps. We are headed to the Ithoya Forest, home to a group of about forty chimps. Their 518-hectare patch of forest (a little over a thousand square acres) is an island of vegetation that has survived only because the local vocational college, to which it belongs, has kept most would-be squatters away. The closest protected area is many kilometers away at the Bugoma Forest Reserve, home to about six hundred chimpanzees.

The Chimpanzee Trust Uganda newsletter we are reading tells of a Hoima man who was bitten by a chimpanzee as he chased it from his garden. The chimp, a female, had become separated from her baby by passing schoolchildren, and when the young chimp screamed, the female threatened the children. Seeing this, the children's grandfather tried to scare the chimps away but was bitten in the process. When we ask Jovann about the incident, he tells us that the man received medical care for the bite and made a good recovery, but he returned frequently to the Chimpanzee Trust Uganda offices in Hoima, demanding large sums of money incommensurate to the extent of his injury. Word traveled quickly of the man's bitter complaints, and the incident had set people on edge.

As we drive down the long driveway into the vocational college's grounds, Jovann says we will be meeting two of the twenty-five youth monitors Chimpanzee Trust Uganda has hired from the local community to patrol the remaining chimp forests. The youths patrol twelve local sites, where they document the mammals living there, conduct a census of the chimp population based on nest counting, track the movements of the chimps, and, perhaps most important, act as ambassadors within the local community to reduce human-wildlife conflict. "Every day," Jovann tells us, "they show the community that we must live harmoniously with the chimpanzee."

Bosco and Livas are fresh faced and handsome in their dark-green eco-guard uniforms and matching rubber galoshes. We ease into their thick accents gradually and find ourselves catching the excitement they have for their work, a prestigious job for which they competed with a sizeable number of others. They escort us into the forest, teaching us how to count chimp nests and explaining why identifying new nests is helpful in estimating the number of chimps still surviving in the forest. Evidence of heavy rains is everywhere, and our shoes get drenched as we hike through a bog that tries to suck them off our feet with each step. We search for tree roots and broken limbs on which to land, trying to keep from sinking into the muck. I am just through the worst of it when we hear pant-hoots ahead. Jovann and Bosco have stopped suddenly, earnestly studying something in the distance.

There, gazing at us from a hundred feet away, is an exquisite black chimp, a male with hair on end. He stares intensely at us, not even flinching, as we gather together in a group. Behind him arrives a burly brown male, and we can hear the calls of a few other chimps beyond. The agitated black male is starting to rock back and forth now, the beginnings of a pant-hoot on his lips. I presume he is getting ready to charge at some of the chimps in his group, and not at us. After all, these are wild chimps, unaccustomed to humans. I know from experience that they will be quick to disappear if we approach.

Jovann and Bosco inexplicably decide that we need to turn back to avoid them, something that seems silly to me at the time. But I instantly change my opinion as the wisdom of their decision becomes apparent. Both chimp males are aggressively following us, starting to pant-hoot with the distinct demeanor that they might give chase and possibly even throw us from the path. This is a first for me, being chased by a chimp, and it is dreadful and frightening—and puzzling. What can possibly account for this unnatural behavior?

Finally, the chimps quiet down and leave us alone as we make our way out of their forest, but their advance has made clear that these chimps are hardened, hostile, fighting for their lives in this forest. These are chimps unwittingly pitted by circumstance against Africans living in poverty— as well as against business interests that foster the growing of damaging crops like sugarcane and tobacco, and against corrupt individuals who have cleared entire forests for timber, pocketing all the profits.

❧ ❧ ❧

A brief break allows us to absorb what we're told was a very rare chimp encounter. By now, Lilly has joined the group, and while we wolf down our sandwiches, she gathers us up to talk about plans for the afternoon. We'll be returning to the forest to learn about an international initiative to save these forests by paying local landowners not to harvest old-growth trees on their lands. Chimpanzee Trust Uganda is playing a central role in the project, surveying the critical forest corridor between the Bugoma and Budongo Forest Reserves and enrolling landowners to participate in the study. The project, on behalf of the United Nations Environment Programme (UNEP), is being conducted by Chimpanzee Trust Uganda, the Ugandan government, and other groups, and the international community is watching it with great interest. The hope of participants and observers alike is that the critical corridors of forest between Budongo and Buhoma can be maintained in the interests of both the people and animals that depend on them. This is the first project of its kind that UNEP-GEF (Global Environment Facility) has undertaken.[5]

We go out into a different area of the forest with a tape measure and a GPS device to learn some of the ins and outs of the study. First, we pace the forest to estimate a one-hectare plot of forest and place a strand of yellow hazard tape to mark the area we are about to survey. Next, we map all the large native trees on the plot and size the diameter of their trunks to ensure they are sufficiently large to merit mapping. These are the trees that farmers will be paid to maintain and that will be monitored each year before paying the landowners their annual incentive payments. And although farmers will be allowed to harvest a tree for every four such trees found on a plot, we find little likelihood of harvesting in this forest. Of the four parcels we have mapped, only one of them contains more than a single large-diameter tree. Much of the remaining local forest has already been degraded through timber harvesting, and the great majority of forest now consists of young trees.

Lilly tells us that regional landowners who are randomly selected to participate in the study will receive an annual incentive payment of $35 per hectare to maintain the mapped trees. Experts have selected this payment as a reasonably strong incentive, given that the average household in the region spent just $460 each year (in 2006) to cover expenses.[6] The group of approximately four hundred landowners from forty local villages will be compared to similar numbers of randomly selected landowners and villages who receive no such financial incentives over a period of three years to determine whether incentive payments can save the day for chimps and forests. Having seen illegal timber harvesting everywhere we have traveled, it is hard not to feel skeptical as to whether these incentive payments and the study can save the forest. (As of January 2012, Chimpanzee Trust Uganda had recruited 262 landowners to conserve 1,260 hectares of land, but 219 of 764 plots of land that were originally candidates for the study no longer had standing forests. Similar trends were reported as of January 2013.)

Dr. Matthew McLennan has been studying the situation in Hoima District since 2006, and his doctoral thesis tells of unregulated forests under heavy pressure from timber concessions and cash crops, and includes his own observations of rapid loss of forests. His survey of the area provides further evidence that local forests lack any substantial government monitoring or enforcement of existing laws that prohibit cutting trees with chain saws or without a permit, a situation common in many of Uganda's forest reserves.[7]

People of the region have long coexisted with the chimpanzees, and as is true in most of East Africa, they do not hunt them. But the situation has changed as the population has more than quadrupled over the past fifty years, during which time farmers have increasingly grown cash crops like tobacco and sugarcane and timber cutting has begun in earnest. Not surprisingly, conflicts are beginning to emerge between people and chimps as they encounter one another. In fact, McLennan reports that chimps have almost daily contacts with humans, sometimes nonconfrontational but more often threatening as chimps are chased away from crops and property.[8]

It is clear from the survey that locals have little awareness of the impact deforestation is having on the chimps. Because they see the chimps more as they increasingly leave the forest to get to food and water, people wrongly assume that their populations are thriving. Although older people used to peacefully existing with the chimps are less worried, many younger people are afraid of the chimps and less tolerant. Some are concerned that the government will take their lands from them to make them into protected areas for the chimps. Their worries have caused some to clear-cut their lands, hoping it will make them less attractive to government and conservation groups.

The survey also points to common knowledge of local corruption. Some influential leaders are making considerable profits from clearing forests and selling the timber for illegal export to Kenya and elsewhere. Although bans exist against use of chain saws to fell trees, they are increasingly being used. Two of the forests that were most critical to the chimps had been devastated almost overnight, and by the time of our visit, only one last stand of large forest remained in the region, atop a hillside, which has made it harder to get to. Even so, we still saw smoke and activity atop that hill and knew exactly what it meant.

Clearing of forest for cash crops like sugarcane and cotton has been a problem in the past, but since the late 1980s, a new and more troubling crop has been devastating the forests: tobacco. It is now one of Uganda's biggest exports, and the British-American Tobacco Company and its Ugandan unit accounts for the majority of all tobacco production in Uganda. The company contracts with more than twenty thousand farmers in Uganda, paying them at a rate substantially lower than the average world price. Some contend that the company has not strictly enforced its policies against child labor or its requirement that farmers replant two hundred trees annually.[9]

Tobacco degrades the forest area because it quickly depletes the soil and requires wood harvesting for drying, storage, and curing of some varieties.[10] Tobacco can be grown only for a few cycles before the soil becomes damaged and less productive, so it is common for farmers and sharecroppers to advance into virgin areas, leaving the depleted soils in their wake.[11] The number of tobacco farmers and sharecroppers has swelled over the past twenty years.

Clearly, tobacco is important to Uganda's economy; tobacco companies buy harvests from thousands of farmers, pay taxes, and provide one of

Uganda's most financially significant exports. But because of it, Ugandans are increasingly beginning to smoke, resulting in health issues only too well known to the Western world.[12] And on a larger scale, one wonders what will happen to locals when the forests are entirely gone and they find themselves without timber and fuel and face devastated water supplies and desertification.

There are other emerging threats to Hoima's forest, particularly the recent discovery of huge amounts of untapped oil reserves at Lake Albert, part of the region addressed by a Payment for Ecosystem Services project. This has led to controversial approval of a project in oil exploration and development between Tullow Oil Uganda and Uganda's Ministry of Energy. Oil exploration appears to be driving the development of a new hydroelectric plant at Lake Albert and other developments that, unless coupled with comprehensive conservation programs, are sure to lead to further deforestation and greater pressure on the remaining chimpanzees of the region.

❧ ❧ ❧

Lilly spends the next twenty-four hours demonstrating the public relations campaign she is waging to save Hoima's chimpanzees. We visit a school to see a conservation-education program that is sensitizing children to the critical role that forests and biodiversity play. We visit other schools and student homes and see how Chimpanzee Trust Uganda's programs have fostered use of fuel-efficient stoves to minimize the amount of wood fuel burned. We lunch with a women's cooperative, learning how the organization is helping them find markets for their jewelry and baskets. We visit tree nurseries where native tree starts are being fostered and speak with an influential farmer who is promoting reforestation throughout the region, including through a regional farmers' cooperative. Lilly is working feverishly to win the support of the king of the Bunyoro people and his kingdom, within which Hoima lies, and to get financial backing from oil and energy companies of increasing prominence in the area. We wonder how she and her team can juggle so many programs and are thankful that they have a presence there, calling out the local corruption and greed that is devastating these local people, the poorest of the poor.

We know Lilly's programs are an essential start, but we can see that other major efforts are needed on a larger scale. We turn to Dr. McLennan for answers, knowing that there are no simple ones. Still, he outlines a number of important actions: Better forest management of trees that are food sources for people as well as chimps and other animals would be beneficial to all and would decrease crop raiding by animals, reducing human-wildlife conflict. Fast-growing indigenous species of trees need to be planted to reforest the area and to provide a sustainable source of fuel and timber. Mantraps must be banned, locals must be taught nonlethal forms of crop-raiding deterrence, and it seems critical that organizations step in to purchase key corridor lands that would ensure the survival of the hundreds of chimps in jeopardy on private lands. Tobacco and sugarcane companies should be required to conduct environmental-impact assessments performed by independent agencies. Even just enforcing existing protections of riverine areas and wetlands would go a long way toward protecting the remaining chimp habitat. Instead, in most cases, Hoima farmers are clearing the land right up to the streams and papyrus swamps so they can grow tobacco.

❖ ❖ ❖

Uganda is only one of many countries in which unsustainable cash crops such as tobacco and cotton are taking a toll on wildlife by rapidly depleting the soil. These crops are key cultivars in many African countries and grown by thousands of farmers, making it seem nearly impossible to make meaningful change. But a number of programs sponsored by governments and NGOs are pushing to promote sounder agricultural practices with higher yields and helping farmers improve their profits by accessing key markets.

One noteworthy program is Community Markets for Conservation (COMACO), an initiative of the Wildlife Conservation Society. Established in a region of Zambia that has been experiencing rapid deforestation, loss of its large mammal populations, and expansion of crops like tobacco and cotton, the program preserves biodiversity by focusing on improving livelihoods and food security. Early results suggest that it is saving wildlife, protecting forests, and fighting poverty in Zambia.[13]

The program began informally in 2001, targeting areas plagued not only by extreme poverty and hunger but also by high rates of poaching and deforestation for charcoal production. Initially, villagers were taught sustainable-farming techniques. Poachers were trained in alternative livelihood skills like carpentry or beekeeping, and food-insecure families were taught sustainable-agriculture practices involving crops that could be grown organically and could improve food security through their resilience to climate variation. (The crops also needed to have marketability so that families would be able to sell any surplus, increasing their personal incomes.)

Helping farmers market their products, the COMACO program, officially established in 2003, has been growing exponentially ever since. After six years, it had trained more than forty thousand farmers who bring their excess crops to community trading depots for grading, weighing, and selling to COMACO. The organization's trucks then transport the goods to regional trading centers, where they are bulked for further sale and in some cases processed into higher-value products (for example, processing peanuts into peanut butter). The community trading centers function collectively as a single company.

The results have been refreshingly hopeful. Populations of elands, elephants, hartebeests, kudus, roans, waterbucks, wildebeests, and zebras that had been in decline in the 1990s have stabilized with introduction of COMACO's programs. As a result of better crop yields and healthier soils, fewer people now hunt, and during the 2008–2009 season, there was a marked reduction of food-assistance requests to the Zambian district-government authorities from the communities where COMACO operates. In addition, among the seventeen thousand farmers that reported their crop yields in 2009–10, there was a 44 percent increase in the percentage that had grain stock sufficient to last through March, when new crops would be available from their current year's planting.

❖ ❖ ❖

Roughly two-thirds of the world's remaining wild chimpanzees are living in unprotected or minimally protected forests.[14] Thousands are facing the same day-to-day existence as the chimps we encountered in Ithoya Forest, compelled to leave the forest to get to a water source, having to raid crops when forest fruits are not enough, and being threatened on a regular basis with getting caught and killed by mantraps set by locals. The problem reaches far beyond western Uganda and is occurring in countries such as Cameroon, the Republic of the Congo, Guinea, Rwanda, and Tanzania— in fact, throughout Africa wherever human populations are pushing up against forests.

Change has to happen soon if we are going to save chimpanzees—and the many other species we love. We are in the midst of an extinction crisis, experiencing the biggest spate of die-offs since the dinosaurs disappeared sixty-five million years ago. One in four of the world's 5,487 species of mammals is facing extinction—and the numbers are significantly greater for the large mammals that humans most identify with: primates, ocean mammals, big cats, and others.[15] Unless we stop treating forests as commodities and start protecting critical habitat, we will lose not only these animals but also the forests. And with the loss of forests will come desertification and drought, killing millions of humans as well.

Professor John F. Oates, of Hunter College, City University of New York, has contentiously argued that chimps do not face any immediate risk of extinction, believing that they will survive in well-protected national parks past 2100, but even that best-case scenario somehow gives me small comfort.[16] Perhaps several thousand chimps will survive in the most well-protected national parks or landscapes, but 100,000 to 200,000 or more will have died. Writing about chimpanzees and gorillas of the Congo Basin forests in 2001, Dr. Caroline Tutin predicted that up to 75,000 gorillas and as many or more chimpanzees would die in the ensuing twenty years from hunting and habitat loss, especially those living in timber concessions.[17] It is an estimate that is difficult to verify, particularly given the unstable political situation in the DRC, but reports suggest Tutin's prediction may well be playing itself out.[18]

Meanwhile, chimps in unprotected areas are at risk every day—especially chimps like those of western Uganda. Dr. McLennan reports that those last forests that are so critical to the chimps he studies are now almost entirely gone, and satellite images show that deforestation is now active in protected areas of the corridor. New murders of local chimps are occurring as people and wildlife come into increasing conflict. It is clear that far too many African chimpanzees are just one bad encounter away from death, from just one wrong step into a mantrap, from just one more clear-cutting of their last forest fragments. I think of them every day and wonder how they are holding on.

CHAPTER 16

ENDING BUSHMEAT

Only after the last tree has been cut down . . .
the last river has been poisoned . . . the last fish caught,
only then will you find that money cannot be eaten.
CREE INDIAN PROPHECY

✦ ✦ ✦ ✦ ✦ ✦

We had learned about chimps and forests in areas with high-density human populations. But what about chimpanzees in less accessible forests where there are fewer human settlements? These are the regions where the final great expanses of forest remain, home to the last large populations of chimpanzees.

Killing and eating bushmeat is still a way of life for people in these areas. But today, the bushmeat trade has become an exotic industry that is posing as serious a threat to Africa's wildlife as deforestation. The world is watching—and searching for new ways of countering both.

✦ ✦ ✦ ✦ ✦ ✦

The news photo features the glowing countenance of a high school student closely examining a piece of ostrich jerky as she prepares to analyze its DNA. What, I wonder, could DNA analysis of jerky have to do with protecting Africa's great apes? But it turns out that DNA analysis has absolutely everything to do with it. For this is a wired world in which high school students from San Diego can help rangers in East Africa better protect the animals in their parks from poachers.

The story began years ago, as San Diego high school teacher Jay Vavra began working with Oliver Ryder, of the San Diego Zoological Society, to create a conservation-forensics course. Vavra wanted his students to use lab science to solve real-world problems at the cutting edge. What better task than to protect endangered animals in Africa by providing law-enforcement officials with improved tools for incriminating poachers?

Students learned how to use DNA analysis to study animal remains and identify what species they represent. Lab analysis of a specific gene would allow them to precisely identify the type of meat being analyzed. Once they perfected their own ability at genetic bar coding, they could devise plans to share the technique with African game wardens, giving them a critical new tool for convicting poachers. Wardens would be able to prove beyond doubt that the poachers' bushmeat was from a protected animal and prevent the poachers from going free for lack of evidence.

The students fired up the Internet and started finding grants for their project, contacting game wardens, and befriending the company behind the expensive equipment they needed. By 2008, Vavra and his students were on their way to Tanzania to lay the groundwork for their project, and in 2009, a team returned to Tanzania, this time to convene a DNA bar coding workshop at the College of Wildlife Management, Mweka. Eighteen participants from Kenya, Sudan, Tanzania, and Uganda would spend four days learning the new technique and sharing it with their organizations. The workshop would be a critical first step in arming local law-enforcement personnel with the ability to use wildlife forensics to fight the illegal-bushmeat trade.

The four-day conference got off to an ambitious start, but then the students encountered a significant snafu: the critical piece of equipment—the thermocycler—would not power up, and no combination of electrical cords and power converters could make it. But Vavra developed a plan B—sequencing DNA using an outdated and less effective method of sequencing—while two students searched for a local hospital that might have a thermocycler. The conference was saved at the last minute by the help of the Kilimanjaro Christian Medical Centre's research laboratory, a helpful technician, and some excellent eleventh-hour strategizing by the student team. Ultimately, the students succeeded, not only passing along the barcoding technique but also finding resources to help create new wildlife-forensics labs.

❦ ❦ ❦

Eating bushmeat is a time-honored tradition for generations of Africans. Bushmeat, the meat of wild animals hunted for food, is considered a luxury in big cities but remains fairly cheap in rural areas, where it costs about a third as much as farmed animal meat like chickens and goats.[1] It often is the only affordable source of animal protein in impoverished rural areas, and some feel it is critical to preventing malnutrition.[2] It is not only a staple for some Africans but can also be part of important ceremonial events. In some parts of Africa, for example, it is traditional to serve green monkey at a wedding. Clearly, bushmeat is a deeply embedded element of African culture.

Some experts believe that if bushmeat consumption was restricted to people living near wisely managed forests, it might be possible to feed locals without devastating local animal populations. Unfortunately, however, the commercial bushmeat trade is now a $6 billion commercial industry supplying bushmeat to millions of city dwellers who view eating it as exotic and prestigious. The increase in the number of consumers has been explosive, growing to more than 800 million in 2000.[3] Although it is particularly popular in Africa, and despite bans on importing it, bushmeat can also be readily found in places such as Brussels, London, New York, and Los Angeles.

Much of the meat comes from antelopes and small mammals, but great apes are not exempt, particularly in West Africa and Central Africa. Ape meat accounts for about 1–2 percent of bushmeat, and it is not uncommon to see a baby ape being sold in the market next to the cut-up body of its mother.[4] The trade, which has produced hundreds of chimp orphans, has been a major factor in the explosive growth of sanctuaries in Africa. Its impact has been so pervasive that scientists have called it the leading cause of the catastrophic decline in West Africa's great ape populations.[5]

Animals of all kinds are being hunted at six times the rate that forests can sustain, and poachers are especially flourishing in areas with weak governance, armed conflict, and logging concessions.[6] Particularly problematic have been organized groups of hunters that have taken advantage of roads cut into previously untouched forests, allowing them to drive vehicles into these remote areas and haul out the carcasses of huge numbers of animals. The impact on great apes and large mammals like elephants is particularly devastating because they produce offspring only every few years, making it harder for their populations to bounce back.

Few issues in conservation are more contentious than bushmeat. For years, there has been bitter acrimony between those calling for drastic limits on hunting and those insisting that such a move is not only impossible but also disregards the rights and needs of native forest people. In 2009, such discord led to the dissolution of the Bush Meat Crisis Task Force, probably the most well-known group to have attempted to tackle this difficult issue.

Poachers are motivated by huge profits they can make from selling pelts, ivory, and other animal parts. The African elephant is among the animals that historically have suffered most; as a result of ivory poaching, its population was cut in half between 1979 and 1989. Dr. Iain Douglas-Hamilton was one of the first to alert the world to this disaster, and the result of his efforts was an international ban on ivory and some rebounding of elephant populations. But in recent years, the problem has worsened as China's improving economic status has resulted in a huge demand for ivory that could completely overwhelm the planet's recovering elephant populations. Conservation groups are scrambling to raise sentiment in Asia against ivory so as to avert the final extinction of elephants by poachers, but it is a nasty crisis that such groups are desperately trying to solve.

South Africa's last 21,000 black rhinos are also under siege, the result of a Vietnamese government official announcing to the world in 2008 that he had been cured of cancer by ingesting rhino horn given to him by a traditional Eastern healer. In doing so, he created a potential end-user market of three billion people with a sudden intense interest in acquiring rhino horn for medicinal purposes. A number of rhino conservationists predict the demise of the species within perhaps ten years, despite ferocious, cutting-edge efforts to protect them.[7]

Given the threat to both elephants and rhinos, conservationists, looking for an immediate means of conducting successful public-awareness campaigns, have found that one of the most effective routes has been to harness the passion of Hollywood and sports stars in delivering their message. A group known as WildAid has been particularly effective, enlisting movie stars like Leonardo Di Caprio and Jackie Chan in public-awareness campaigns that rail against the wildlife trade and marine degradation and call on people to stop buying products that threaten animal welfare. Spots shown throughout the world reach approximately one billion people weekly.[8] People living closest to the forests often lack electricity or a means of receiving such messages. But even these people are being reached, thanks to the outside-the-box efforts of the Great Apes Film Initiative (GAFI), which uses pedal power to show nature documentaries to people in remote communities that lack electricity. Power used to run the projector is generated by pedaling a stationary bicycle, and films are sent virtually anywhere it is possible to transport a bike to as well, including remote areas of the DRC, where the bike is transported along the Congo River by boat. GAFI has reached over 300 million people by broadcasting films on national television, and 110,000 people living in remote communities have seen films screened with the aid of pedal power.[9]

Another tactic for wooing Africans away from bushmeat has been to promote other sources of protein and calories. The Clinton Foundation, for example, is working in Rwanda to help farmers grow and benefit from vegetable-based protein sources like soybeans. Other initiatives, like the Jane Goodall Institute's Lake Tanganyika Catchment Reforestation and Education Project (TACARE), are demonstrating the sustainable use of domestic animals like chickens to provide egg proteins, and other groups have even promoted humane farming of natural alternatives, such as giant snails.

Unfortunately, the biggest obstacles to ending commercial bushmeat and illegal trafficking are international wildlife-smuggling rings that are extremely well organized, well funded, and dangerous. Traffickers have been essentially untouchable due to widespread corruption within African government enforcement agencies, both at local and national levels. The World Bank has estimated that tens of millions of dollars in bribes are paid annually in sub-Saharan Africa, and studies have shown that the more corruption within a government, the worse its enforcement of wildlife laws. This ugly problem has had a severe impact on the conservation community for years on end.

Thankfully, not everyone has given up.

❖ ❖ ❖

With his thin build, dark beard, and ponytail, Ofir Drori does not have the classic appearance of a superhero—but a superhero he is. This flamboyant Israeli photojournalist seems to be miraculously successful at prompting African countries to enforce their laws against poaching and at stemming internal corruption where entire NGOs have failed. In fact, the mere mention of NGOs makes him see red, so thoroughly disgusted is he with their innocuous track records. Pay a bribe? Ridiculous. Accept the status quo? Never!

As described in his colorful book *The Last Great Ape*, Drori was traveling throughout Africa in 2002 when, one day, he saw poachers trying to sell a baby chimp. He went to the local police, who not only wanted a bribe to go after the poachers but even offered a chimp of their own for sale. Undeterred, he returned to the poachers with the Cameroonian book of law in hand and bluffed them into believing that wildlife-enforcement officers were on their way to arrest them. But then he said he would cut a deal with them: if they immediately turned the chimp over to him and provided information about other traffickers, perhaps he could intervene on their behalf. Somehow, it worked, and as journalist Tom Clynes writes, Drori became "both a father and the sole enforcer of Cameroon's wildlife-trafficking laws."[10]

Using the poachers as informants, Drori began amassing a team of local people and wildlife-enforcement officers to stage stings of local traffickers and confront rampant corruption within the government. His new group, the Last Great Ape Organization, began provoking arrests. Soon enough, however, Drori encountered the next weak link in the chain. Jailers and judges were also easily won over by bribes, and criminals easily won release from jail without sentencing.

Drori, outraged once again, engaged a key figure on his team to publicize local arrests, even reaching out to international news organizations in order to pressure the Cameroonian government to pursue prosecutions. Finally, one trafficker was brought to trial—and the scrutiny of the international community helped Drori succeed. When the criminal was convicted, Drori made sure that key government officials received a flood of attention and congratulations, raising the profile of wildlife enforcement and securing the cooperation of national leaders in new efforts to fight trafficking.

He went on to create a team of legal advisers to monitor court proceedings, thus minimizing the corruption that his organization was encountering in more than 80 percent of court cases. The legal team also began strengthening the skills and knowledge of prosecutors, as well as visiting jails to ensure that prisoners served their full jail time. Today, just a short few years later, prosecutions are occurring weekly, and large-scale operations are being foiled. About 87 percent of suspects in Cameroon are denied bail after arrest and receive sentences of years in jail or large fines. One of his organization's biggest successes has been the prosecution of an international criminal syndicate that had been coordinating the killing of three hundred elephants for their ivory every two months for three decades, employing hundreds of poachers across several countries and transporting the ivory in secret compartments of freight cars to Hong Kong.[11]

Drori has been winning the attention of major organizations like the United States Fish and Wildlife Service and Interpol and working with advocates in other African countries to scale up his unique organization.

Similar programs in Gabon, Guinea-Conakry, the Republic of the Congo, the Central African Republic, and Togo have been working cooperatively with Drori's organization to take on increasingly bigger trafficking rings, and together they have formed a network known as Eco Activists for Governance and Law Enforcement (EAGLE).[12] Ofir is not interested in online monetary contributions, but he is always on the lookout for super-volunteers to be, as he says, "warriors in this fight," stipulating that they must have experience in both Africa and activism as well as strong character and great devotion to the cause.

Drori's kind of courage and defiance is rare—something he finds surprising. In fact, he appears to have little appreciation of the fact that most of us are completely cowed by danger, and he seems deeply disappointed when other advocates take more conventional and less passionate approaches. "We have to find a new activism, don't you think?" he asks me with a sincerity that only slightly masks his unyielding conviction about the truth of his contention. "We have to dump the old NGO model and make real change, and it has got to breed and grow exponentially. This is about our own existence.

"We all have the ability to bring about this kind of change," he tells me in his parting line, and I can tell that he believes it with every fiber of his being. As he departs, I find myself once again in that uncomfortable yet inspired place that only such a remarkable person as Drori can create. The inner skeptic and coward within me likely will never be persuaded to become a warrior—but thankfully there are people like Drori who seem not to understand the word *impossible*. From my vantage point, their lives are difficult and their sacrifice enormous. But they are the ones who are making change, and I pledge, as he departs, to become part of Ofir Drori's worthy army.

❧ ❧ ❧

Drori and others note that it is far easier to deter individual poachers—as they do the actual capturing and killing of the animals—than the middlemen and the cartels. When these poachers are apprehended, it is often within the national parks, since the parks have the best-funded protections and patrols. Even in the parks, however, poaching continues. It is particularly problematic in the less well-known and poorly funded parks of West Africa and Central Africa.[13] However, poaching also persists in the parks of East Africa, affecting gorillas and chimpanzees, as well as elephants and rhinos. Garamba National Park, in eastern DRC, for example, had been home to as many as 20,000 elephants, but the number dropped to just 2,800 by 2012, and rangers have been under siege from well-armed groups intent on profiting from the ivory trade.[14]

Park rangers and conservationists are continuously striving to patrol the parks more comprehensively. But even if they succeed in protecting the parks, the fact remains that healthy great ape populations need large swaths of protected forest bigger than most national parks. Many critical conservation areas overlap the borders of several countries, and a national park model fails to create a partnership with neighboring countries. Given these limitations, conservationists needed to think bigger and to find ways of preserving the millions of acres needed to maintain resilient animal populations and forests.

Thankfully, scientists began considering these critical issues years ago, conjecturing that if core protected areas like national parks were surrounded by carefully administered multiuse forests, it might be possible to thoughtfully manage and sustain them in the best interests of both local people and wildlife. For example, 40 percent of the two million square kilometers of Congo Basin forest are allocated to timber harvesting, and just 12 percent are protected, and more than 50 percent of the current range of chimps and western gorillas lies within areas set aside for logging.[15] Conservationists recognized the importance of looking for ways to partner with timber concessions and other forest stakeholders.[16] Soon, the concept of landscape conservation began to take shape, aided by the involvement of two key players: the World Wildlife Fund (WWF) and the United States Agency for International Development.[17]

The WWF started by bringing 150 experts together in 2000 to identify areas of unique ecological importance, identifying twelve key landscapes that cover about 38 percent of the Congo Basin's forests. Just two years later, the Congo Basin Forest Partnership was established, based on an investment from the United States of $53 million. The CBFP coordinates the activities of thirty-six governments, NGOs, and intergovernmental agencies to protect and promote these high-priority landscapes. Its landmark efforts have greatly improved the outlook for these forests, and the United States has remained a steadfast supporter; the US government contributed an additional $75 million for 2006–11 to continue the work. (The work has been coordinated by the Central African Regional Program for the Environment, an initiative of the United States Agency for International Development aimed at promoting sustainable natural-resource management in the Congo Basin. Phase III for the period 2012 to 2020 is under way.)

Groups like the Wildlife Conservation Society have worked for many years to protect the Sangha Tri-National Forest, one of the most successfully protected landscapes, which contains some of the most unspoiled remaining forests and animal populations in the world. The portion of the landscape that lies within the Republic of the Congo, the Ndoki-Likouala Conservation Landscape, has been particularly of interest. Its core protected area, Nouabale-Ndoki National Park, is surrounded by multiuse zones, including several timber concessions and a community-managed forest reserve.

The Wildlife Conservation Society, which worked cooperatively with several of the timber concessions to develop sustainable-management plans for timber harvesting and coupled them with strong antipoaching efforts, then evaluated the impact on local forest elephants, western lowland gorillas, and chimpanzees and were encouraged by the results.[18] The populations of all three species remained more abundant in the areas actively managed and protected compared to the other regions. In fact, elephant and gorilla populations in some of the managed timber concessions were similar to or even more populous than those in the national park. Population densities were lowest for all three species in timber concessions without antipoaching programs, but even patrolled concessions proved incapable of preventing poachers from using logging roads to kill elephants. Nevertheless, the overall results were encouraging, suggesting that carefully managed areas surrounding national parks can support biodiversity, and a team of scientists recently issued a framework for use by timber concessions on how to effectively protect ape populations in compliance with certification by the Forest Stewardship Council, a nongovernmental organization.

Evidence exists, however, that some poachers and many of those higher up in the trafficking chain are stepping up their game and that more aggressive deterrence will be essential. More and more, the killing is done not by individuals but by well-organized and more sophisticated groups of poachers. Traffickers, for example, have been devising new tactics, such as using hidden compartments in shipping containers, changing their smuggling routes, and making their operating locations more difficult to detect. Benefiting from these tactics, they are estimated to have killed tens of thousands of elephants in 2011 alone, and infiltrating and toppling international crime syndicates will be required to cause a substantial impact.

Law enforcement is responding by increasing the number of highly trained enforcement staff and by making wildlife crime the focus of a greater array of international enforcement agencies. The recent establishment of the International Consortium on Combating Wildlife Crime is a big step forward because it will coordinate the work of a number of major agencies, but it has a big job before it. To deter current trafficking, it will need to accomplish not only many interceptions but also ensure effective prosecutions and jail time for the offenders.

CHAPTER 17

CHIMPS, GUERRILLAS, AND DR. HAMBURG

The Democratic Republic of the Congo, home to many of the last major unexplored forests of the continent, is a critical reservoir for populations of chimps, gorillas, and bonobos. Sadly, these forests, among the most dangerous in the world, are being increasingly plundered for their timber and their cobalt, coltan, copper, diamonds, gold, tin, and zinc. Corruption is thriving, and there is little way to enforce treaties and protections despite the presence of twenty thousand United Nations peacekeeping troops.

Until a way is found to overcome the violence so common in many regions of Africa, the future of a number of species of apes, and even of the planet, lies in the balance. New methods of resolving human conflict are urgently needed. Enter Dr. David Hamburg, a Stanford University professor whose life was changed by the kidnapping of several of his students.

✤ ✤ ✤ ✤ ✤ ✤

The last great populations of chimpanzees and other great apes live in volatile regions of the world where conservation efforts are too often compromised by civil conflict and war. Since 1990, conflicts have occurred in wildlife habitat in a number of African countries, including Angola, the Central African Republic, the DRC, Liberia, Rwanda, Sierra Leone, and Sudan. More than 90 percent of major conflicts between 1950 and 2000 occurred in countries of exceptional biodiversity, and more than 80 percent took place in areas considered to be sensitive habitat.[1] Even small conflicts can unravel years of concerted conservation efforts.

Knowing how war-torn parts of the DRC are—and how critical that immense country and its Congo Basin forests are to the future of chimps, it seemed important to learn whether there is any hope for putting an end to the conflicts there. The more I read of rapes, killings, and corruption, the easier it was to forget the conservation consequences and to get lost in the horrible realities of the toll on humans. (Millions were killed during the 1998–2003 civil war, and each year since, thousands more have died.)

So much had been tried and failed—the involvement of UN peacekeeper troops, negotiations and a peace treaty, and interventions by world leaders at the national and regional levels. Of all the thorny issues in saving chimps, this seemed to be among the most hopeless.

One of the greatest good fortunes of my life has been to have Dr. David Hamburg as my mentor for forty years. I can't claim to have earned this mentor; his life and mine, and the lives of all of us who worked at Gombe in the 1970s, simply collided.

It was on May 20, 1975, when Dr. Hamburg found a pad's worth of urgent sticky notes fastened onto his office door that would profoundly alter his day—and, for that matter, his life. Forty guerrillas from the DRC, then known as Zaire, had boated across Lake Tanganyika to Jane's camp in Tanzania, kidnapping three Stanford University students and the Dutch camp manager. The United States Department of State, Stanford's president, the students' parents, the media, and others were urgently calling.

Dr. Hamburg was on sabbatical at Caltech at the time, taking time off from his duties as chair of Stanford's Program in Human Biology and the Department of Psychiatry. He was also in charge of Stanford's Gombe programs, and people were clamoring for more information and a plan. Little did he know that the unfolding events would not only send him to Tanzania to negotiate with rebel leaders and the governments of three countries but also ultimately lead him to become one of the world's foremost experts on prevention of human conflict and genocide.

Upon learning the shocking news, he immediately left for Tanzania, leaving behind his savvy wife, Dr. Betty Hamburg, to research any avenue that might reveal who had kidnapped the students and what it would take to get them back. That same evening, I received a phone call from Dr. Betty informing me of the kidnapping. The unfortunate foursome included three friends of mine from Stanford: Carrie Hunter, Steve Smith, and Barbara Smuts, as well as Emilie Bergman, a friend I had made at Gombe.

"I know we'll get them back safely," Dr. Betty said reassuringly, but I wasn't convinced. I knew that life across the lake in Zaire was volatile and dangerous beyond what we could imagine.

❖ ❖ ❖

It was David Hamburg who had initially forged Stanford's relationship with Jane Goodall. Interested in understanding the biological underpinnings of human aggression, he had been instrumental in creating the program in 1971 through which I, and others, had worked at the Gombe Stream Research Center. He had also created Gombe West—the Stanford Outdoor Primate Facility.

Arriving in Tanzania, Hamburg was thrown into the heated mix of release efforts by the governments of the United States, the Netherlands, and Tanzania, by the students' parents, and by Jane Goodall and her husband, Derek Bryceson, director of national parks in Tanzania. The four young people, he would learn, had been kidnapped by members of the Parti de la Revolution Populaire, a group whose mission was to remove President Mobutu Sese Seko from power and establish a Marxist society. The group's leader was Laurent-Désiré Kabila, the man who, twenty-two years later, would finally succeed in overthrowing Mobutu. (Kabila was murdered in 2003 by a bodyguard as part of a plot devised by his military officers. His son is now president of the Democratic Republic of the Congo.)

Back at Stanford, Dr. Betty was uncovering crucial information and devising some brilliant strategies, but communicating the information was proving difficult. The Tanzanian government, which had bugged Hamburg's room, monitored all his phone conversations. It was going to take inspiration to find a solution—but they succeeded. The pair knew one another so well that they improvised a code by making uncharacteristic comments and using odd words to make their true meanings understood. Hamburg would prove to be central to the efforts and negotiations to get the students' release.

After four days, the rebels released Barbara Smuts, who carried letters with the terms of release the Parti de la Revolution Populaire was demanding for the three remaining hostages. Meanwhile, the others remained with the rebels, their lives on the line not only from threats by their captors but also from Mobutu's gunboats firing on the rebels. The next five weeks proved contentious as disagreements broke out among all parties involved in negotiations. Ultimately, however, an agreement was reached in which the three remaining hostages were to be released forty days after their kidnapping.

Rescuers went to retrieve the three but returned only with Carrie and Emilie. Betraying the agreement, the rebels failed to release Steve. Instead, they presented new demands and greatly escalated concerns for Steve's life. Betty Hamburg's spousal telepathy told her to get on a plane to Tanzania immediately, and with good reason: instinct told her that her husband was considering offering himself in Steve's place, and she feared that such an action could result in the deaths of both. Thankfully, she arrived in time and quashed any such offers.

Steve's release finally came a month later, after three of the rebels' demands were satisfied—ransom, publicity for their cause, and release of political prisoners. Heroic efforts to save all four of the captives had finally succeeded, but there would be consequences: American ambassador Beverly Carter had gone against State Department directives in his effort to do everything possible to secure the students' release—and, as a result, his new appointment as ambassador to Denmark was canceled. Furthermore, Gombe was changed, and for now, it was no longer a place for international students. Africans would continue the work until conditions were deemed safer.

❧ ❧ ❧

Dr. Hamburg, greatly affected by the kidnapping, was also deeply distressed by the Tutsi-Hutu ethnic violence of the African Great Lakes region that he had witnessed during this and earlier visits to the region. His experiences provided real-world experience with human aggression, the subject he had dedicated his life to studying.

"These several months," he would write, "exposed me vividly to some of the sources of violent conflict: social breakdown, abject poverty, rampant disease, oppressive dictatorships, fear and hatred, and egregious violations of basic human rights. I was never the same again."[2]

The American ambassador noted Hamburg's masterful abilities at negotiation, and when he suggested it was time to consider a career shift, Hamburg knew he was right. Accepting the Institute of Medicine's offer to serve as president, he spent five years refocusing the nonprofit organization (part of the National Academy of Science) and adding an international health division, which profoundly influenced policymakers in the United States. He also became involved with the World Health Organization's work in developing countries and moved to Harvard University to develop a prestigious new health-policy program there.[3]

With Dr. Hamburg's next assignment, he attained perhaps even greater distinction. As president of the renowned Carnegie Corporation of New York (1983–1997), he created a new focus on avoiding nuclear war. When he began, it was the time of the Cold War and the Reagan presidency, and he risked taking heat from the State Department for involving the foundation where it potentially wasn't welcome. Nevertheless, he persevered, convening working groups of world experts and asking them to address arms control and crisis prevention. The panels responded, identifying feasible, often simple steps such as strengthening the hotline between Moscow and Washington. He next brought leading experts and the nation's most influential legislators together to discuss how to prevent inadvertent nuclear launch and accidental war. Their proposals led to the establishment of nuclear risk-reduction centers with dedicated personnel available twenty-four hours a day and the initiation of regional consultations to build confidence among international neighbors.

As the Cold War ended, it was time to address other kinds of conflict, including religious tensions, regional disputes, and genocide. The Carnegie Commission on Preventing Deadly Conflict was created, and Hamburg joined forces with the distinguished statesman Cyrus Vance, a man who had devoted his career to federal service, including serving as secretary of state under President Jimmy Carter from 1977 to 1980. Together, Hamburg and Vance cochaired an international commission composed of sixteen international leaders and scholars to develop tools and strategies for the future.

Working groups employed the wisdom of scholars to study issues such as effective community interventions for averting violence, as well as international mediation in ethnic conflicts. They reviewed case studies, identifying critical steps that might have averted tragedy. One such report concluded that deployment of a force of five thousand troops during the first two weeks of Rwandan violence in 1994 might have averted much of the genocide that ultimately killed more than one million people.

The commission developed a three-pronged strategy for preventing deadly conflict that focused on detecting looming crisis and defusing it, alleviating international and internal strife so as to avoid conflict, and instituting longer-term strategies to address root causes of war, including economic, social, and humanitarian need. In each case, expert panels identified critical actions and a protocol for preventing conflict. The recommendations were shared within the United Nations and multination groups like the European Union, ultimately leading to implementation of many of them and providing a tool kit that would be used to avert crisis in Africa and elsewhere.

Hamburg guided the Carnegie Corporation of New York's other programs with an equally clear vision, addressing the education and healthy development of children; fostering human resources in developing countries, especially in sub-Saharan Africa; and strengthening democracy in the United States, Africa, and the formerly Communist countries of Europe.

✦ ✦ ✦

My children had asked to someday meet Dr. Hamburg, much to my delight, and I was only too happy to make the connection during our trip to the East Coast to visit colleges. At eighty-three years of age, there he was, strolling down the streets of Manhattan looking as smart and casual as if he were thirty-three, and right beside him strode Betty, bright and smiling. The two were still reeling with delight at the recent appointment by President Barack Obama of their daughter, Peggy Hamburg, as the new chief of the Food and Drug Administration.

No sooner had we sat down for lunch at a downtown restaurant than Dr. Hamburg launched in, telling my children everything they needed to know to create world peace. They were hearing it from the Source, the man who had made conflict prevention a science. This was the man who, in the last segment of his career, had worked closely with Kofi Annan, then secretary-general of the UN, and others to establish a number of programs within the UN and the European Union that could provide the brain trust and resources needed whenever conflict threatened. In a manila folder, he carried a new chapter for the new edition of his book *Preventing Genocide: Practical Steps Toward Early Detection and Effective Action*.[4] This particular afternoon, he planned to send a memo to Secretary of State Hillary Clinton, hoping to see similar resources created within the State Department.

So, how does one prevent genocide? Robert L. Strauss, former director of the Peace Corps in Cameroon, writes about Africa being a house of cards, its countries being, one day, one catastrophe away from collapse into instability, internal strife, and the use of rape and murder as a political weapon. But both Strauss and Hamburg believe it is possible to predict impending conflict—and to act. Strauss writes,

> What is particularly infuriating is that time and again, as ethnic and political tensions begin to simmer—with tragic consequences looming ahead as predictably as the iceberg in front of the Titanic— the international community . . . invariably says that only the local

community can resolve its problems. When locals beg them to intervene, their response is invariable. "We are not the police," they say. "The local community must come together to find lasting solutions to their problems."[5]

Thanks to the concerted efforts of Hamburg and others, the United Nations and the European Union now have a host of advisers, handbooks, and other resources to monitor emerging situations and to provide meaningful actions—both preventively and at the time of crisis—to defuse them. The methods have proven effective, one of the best examples being an intervention by Kofi Annan in 2008 following disputed elections in Kenya that were threatening to unleash civil war. Annan and the tactical team of conflict-prevention experts mediated and defused the polarity between rival leaders Raila Odinga and Mwai Kibaki and their respective parties. Their actions, contributing to a peaceful settlement, averted not only mass violence but political and economic collapse as well.

Always the gentleman, Hamburg gives the credit to his peers—people such as Annan and Vance, as well as UN secretary-general Ban Ki-moon, South African activist Desmond Tutu, Jeffrey Sachs (director of Columbia University's Earth Institute), and others. Hamburg and his son Eric created a film collection of interviews with these and twenty-three other world experts entitled *Preventing Genocide: Pioneers in the Prevention of Mass Violence*.[6] The interviews, constituting a treatise on the practice of world peace, provide a refreshing antidote to insular policy notions that the best defense is always a good offense.

✳ ✳ ✳

After our lunch, I think about all Dr. Hamburg has accomplished and about the courage it must have taken to address such monumental problems. Imagine the number of naysayers who undoubtedly called his work misguided. Yet a community of committed world leaders joined in, daring to propose pragmatic methods of diplomatic and emergency response to threatening human violence—and even delving into questions of how to ameliorate the poverty that too often is the root cause of human conflict. It is hardly chance that, over the past fifteen years, 80 percent of the world's poorest countries have suffered a major war. Hamburg and Vance have written, "When poverty runs in parallel with ethnic or cultural divisions, it often creates a flash point."[7] Clearly, we have seen this time and again in East Africa, particularly in the struggles between Hutu and Tutsi tribesmen.

Although most of us would consider solving extreme poverty an impossibility, experts like Jeffrey Sachs offered knowledge and real-world possibilities worthy of action. Sachs, well known for his work with the United Nations and the World Bank, has elegantly outlined how global cooperation could alleviate extreme poverty by heading off global warming and environmental destruction, stabilizing the world's population, and providing key economic assistance. If the "rich world" contributed even one-tenth of 1 percent of its income to global stabilization, he claims, goals of reducing poverty, hunger, and disease could be realized and more than eight million lives could be saved per year.[8]

Sachs's frustration is obvious as he points out that in the late 1990s, the developed world was contributing less than $100 million annually—a dollar amount he says is a "rounding error" for programs like the United States Department of Defense—to sub-Saharan Africa to deal with the AIDS epidemic, which had infected twenty-five million people. His theory that a little money goes a very long way in the less developed world would be borne out, however, as President George W. Bush committed $15 billion to AIDS treatment in the most stricken countries of Africa from 2003 to 2007. The program reduced AIDS deaths by 1.2 million and provided lifesaving treatment to 2.1 million people.[9] Effective AIDS treatment provided affected families with the economic and social stability they had formerly lacked to raise themselves out of abject poverty. The program was reauthorized and expanded in 2008, with a budget of $48 billion for a five-year period.

❧ ❧ ❧

It can be easy to forget that human violence has impacts far beyond human suffering and can exact an appalling toll on the natural world. Forests are frequently destroyed or are claimed by rebels and refugees, and animals die from slaughter. During Idi Amin's ruthless dictatorship in Uganda, millions of animals were killed, even in the national parks, a tragedy that required more than twenty years of concerted recovery efforts.

Similar scenarios have played out during ethnic warfare in Rwanda and Burundi. In years of genocide, the multimillion-dollar tourist industries in those countries collapsed, international funding was lost, and refugees flooded into parks, desperate for food and fuel, posing an immediate threat to the forest and animals. In 1994, some 850,000 Rwandan refugees fled to the forests of Virunga National Park and not only deforested more than a hundred square miles of forest but also depleted the elephant and hippo populations while greatly increasing the risks to the last remaining mountain gorillas from disease and poaching.[10]

Most important, millions of lives were lost during these and other outbreaks due to unspeakable brutality. The world watched and did very little to intervene, despite knowledge of the dimensions of the slaughter. Given that experience, and a collective vow of "Never again" when we talk of the Holocaust, programs like those Dr. Hamburg and others have crafted offer a road map to the world about what it can meaningfully do to try to dissuade violence.

Now, the Rwandan and Burundian genocides are in the past, Idi Amin is only a horrific memory in Uganda, and economic and political stability seems to have returned along with programs to help the people, the wildlife, and the forests in these countries. Kenya survived its 2013 elections and, thankfully, Tanzania remains stable.

But nearby lies an unruly giant, the Democratic Republic of the Congo. This country, one-fourth the size of the United States, has suffered the loss of millions of lives over the past twenty years of political instability, and there appears to be no end in sight.[11] Violent uprisings have been particularly problematic in the east, where rebel groups that fled Rwanda years ago are perpetrating murders and brutal rapes that have numbered in the tens of thousands over the past ten years. More than 130 rangers have been killed since 1996 by armed rebels in Virunga National Park alone. And it is here that we are now playing the waiting game, as meaningful conservation programs are often stalled until stability and enforcement can be achieved. Meanwhile, we must hope that the DRC's heretofore-untouched forests, home to the last sizable populations of African great apes, survive until peacemakers like Dr. Hamburg and his colleagues are heard.

CHAPTER 18

CAROLE NOON AND
THE POWER OF ONE

Although my focus was on African chimps, I also wanted to know about chimps in the United States. About 1,900 chimps, a population that rivals that of chimps living in the wilds of Tanzania, are in captivity in the country, and I wondered whether their conditions had improved from the past and what their future held.

I set about trying to reconnect with my friend Carole Noon, who had dedicated her life to helping captive chimps. Unbeknownst to me at the time, Carole, fifty-nine years old, was rapidly succumbing to pancreatic cancer just at the prime of her career. A David who overcame a Goliath called the Coulston Foundation, Carole left behind an amazing legacy and a wonderful story about the power of one.

✦ ✦ ✦ ✦ ✦ ✦

The door of his cell opens, and Carlos surges out into the sunshine, completely out of a cage for the first time in forty years. The excitement on his face is obvious as he glimpses sunshine and the horizon.

Carlos was kidnapped from his home in Africa decades ago, after scientists killed his mother and pried him off her. He was sent to the United States with others who shared his story, one of sixty-five young chimps captured in the 1950s and used to gauge the effects of space travel on humans. Humanity's closest relatives, sharing more than 98 percent of our DNA, they were the next best thing to experimenting on humans.

Carlos lies down on his back, dabbing the grass with one hand and whiffing its scent. A vast expanse of the green stuff carpets the three-acre enclosure his new family and he will share for the rest of their lives. Carlos's chimp companion, Mimi, ventures out to join him.

It is eerie to look back at the photo of Carlos's release. A picture I once found dazzling, it is now bittersweet to see the image of a blonde and sun-weathered Carole Noon standing by, encouraging Carlos as though she were a soccer mom at her son's big game. The video shows the now-deceased heroine wearing her characteristic baseball cap, pleased at the reunion between Carlos and grass. Moments like these were the passion and purpose of the founder and director of Save the Chimps, who dedicated her life to rescuing laboratory and entertainment chimps—and what a fantastic ride it was.

Starting as a graduate student in the mid-1980s, Carole rescued chimps from the abysmal conditions of Florida's roadside zoos and railed against biomedical laboratories that frequently held even baby chimps in isolation for medical testing. During the next ten years, she expanded her advocacy work and volunteered in Africa, where she learned the ins and outs of running a chimp sanctuary.

But it was in 1997 when her success in rescuing abused chimps surged radically. Hearing that chimps who had been used in NASA's space program were being transferred to a biomedical laboratory notorious for its violations of the federal Animal Welfare Act, Carole launched a campaign, and, ultimately, a lawsuit, on behalf of the chimps. It was a contentious fight that dragged on for some time, but she prevailed and was awarded the custody of twenty-one chimps, survivors and descendants of the space-program chimps.

Carole now faced the challenge of providing a proper home to a group of chimps damaged by social isolation and experimentation—and of constructing a sanctuary to house them. Carole obtained huge grants and awards, enough to purchase two hundred acres of land in Fort Pierce, Florida, and built an island and support buildings on several acres. Her singular purpose was that the chimps would live the rest of their lives in a clean and decent environment with fresh air, climbing structures, hearty fresh food instead of prepackaged dried fare, and respect.

A good story would end here, but Carole's became considerably richer six months later when she received a phone call from Frederick Coulston himself—the man from whom she had wrested away the twenty-one chimps. His laboratories were on the brink of bankruptcy, a result of Animal Welfare Act violations and lost grant money. He would be willing to sell her the facilities and donate the remaining chimps to her—all 266 of them.

Few of us would take on the care of a single rambunctious chimpanzee, let alone 266 of them in need of nurturing back to mental health, but Carole reportedly never hesitated. She secured $3.7 million in support from the Arcus Foundation and other backers, purchased the facilities, and launched a plan to immediately improve the conditions of the chimps at the Alamogordo, New Mexico, laboratory facility. Walls were knocked down and adjacent cages linked. Chimps who had not seen the sun for years were now able to walk into the daylight. Others who had lived in isolation cages were rejoined with their fellows, finding comfort, friendship, and a reason to live.

These improvements were important but only a temporary measure. Carole's ultimate plan was to move the chimps—ten at a time—from New Mexico to far bigger surroundings at her Florida sanctuary. She fitted a tractor-trailer for the job so that the Coulston chimps could, over time, be driven to their new home. It took six years, but the last chimps left the dismal facility and arrived at their island home in December 2011.

The Save the Chimps newsletter chronicled each new arrival. One of my favorite stories was of Jaybee, whose big day came in July 2008. It was his turn to start the thirty-seven-hour trip from Alamogordo to Fort Pierce as part of what had become dubbed the Great Migration. The chimp had spent all but a few years of his life in biomedical laboratories. He had been anesthetized more than 150 times, had undergone nineteen liver biopsies for hepatitis research, and had been castrated. The fact that he knew how to eat using utensils suggested that his early years were in the entertainment industry. No doubt, as he grew stronger—and harder for his trainer to manage—he had been turned over to medical research, and the trainer had likely acquired a younger and more Hollywood-friendly chimp in his place.

Jaybee's life had improved considerably once Carole arrived in 2002. At that time, she found him alone in his small cell, lying on a nest he had fashioned from extra bits of monkey chow. She told of how appreciative he was when she gave him a blanket, which he treasured and kept fastidiously clean for three days. She fed him, gave him toys, and did all she could to make his isolation bearable. Eventually, he was introduced into a group of twenty chimps who included his special friend, nine-year-old Kiley. Because the tractor-trailer that transported chimps to Florida could hold just ten chimps, the group was temporarily divided in two until it could be reestablished in a few months in its new island home.

Jaybee was loaded into the truck in his metal cage and positioned next to a window, *his* window. The other nine chimps had already been loaded into the climate-controlled van, and it was time for departure. There were a few pant-hoots as the truck started up its engine, but then silence again.

The chimps looked intently out their window at scenery they likely had never imagined. A quiet "Hoo" occasionally sounded when the truck passed a cow or a dog or an especially picturesque field.

The truck pulled over about once an hour to allow someone to check on or feed the chimps. People present at the stops were fascinated, and a truck driver offered up a bag of oranges. At a gas station, a storekeeper donated all the bananas he could find on his shelves. A heretofore shy female chimp made eyes at the onlookers and tried to get their attention. As the truck departed, the chimps sat eating their oranges while watching out the window, like children on vacation.

After one and a half days on the road, the truck pulled into the Fort Pierce sanctuary. The resident chimps pant-hooted out on their islands, excited by the arrival of the truck. The ten newcomers vocalized in reply, still studying the scenery and the circumstances, and Carole was there as they arrived. She walked along each of the cages in the back of the trailer, checking the chimps and assuring them that their long ordeal was now over. (No doubt she had given this same welcome to the one hundred chimps who had preceded Jaybee and his group.) One by one, the chimps were then moved into the holding area in the group's new building, where all would be reintroduced and held until time for their release onto their three-acre island. As they moved into their facility, the chimps touched and studied every corner of it. What a relief it must have been to be there, in an environment that spoke of hope and comfort.

✤ ✤ ✤

Although the sanctuary vet had performed vasectomies on all the male chimps, one procedure apparently failed, as proven by the birth in 2007 of a baby chimp nicknamed Mel, short for Melody. Mel, now one year old, was conceived by an eight-year-old chimp, equivalent to a human mother of eleven or twelve. When the mother proved uninterested in parenting, Mel was removed in search of a better environment and ultimately placed with adult chimp April and her friend Ron.

YouTube videos capture Mel as she frolics after her adoptive mother.[1] Mel takes a great leap and lands spread-eagled on top of the blanket April is dragging along behind her. Mel's white tail tuft sticks up as she rides along on the blanket, looking as though she is wakeboarding behind April. Her tiny play face matches the larger one April is wearing, and every now and again some breathy laughter can be heard.

Adult male Ron comes up to join the two, as though afraid he'll be left out. He is gentle as he reaches over to tickle Mel. The affection among these three is obvious. "If he's given two bananas, he'll usually share one with Mel," Carole says. "And when Ron is given Gatorade, he finishes only a portion and saves the rest for Mel."

Mel is lucky to be one of the only sanctuary chimps not to have suffered medical experimentation. The space chimps, we know, were used as crash-test dummies and spun in centrifuges as babies until they passed out. The others have undergone experimental surgeries and have been inoculated with hepatitis, exposed to pesticides, and isolated so severely that many developed disturbed behaviors characteristic of posttraumatic stress disorder.

The keepers smile as they watch Mel bouncing along on the blanket behind April, tail tuft disappearing into the distance, Ron loping alongside.

❋ ❋ ❋

In truth, starting when I met Carole in 1987, I was always a little intimidated by her. We met as junior participants in a conference featuring animal-welfare greats. The group was to propose standards to the United States Department of Agriculture's Animal and Plant Health Inspection Service to ensure the psychological well-being of captive primates, and we were giddy at the opportunity to work with Jane, as well as primate researcher Dr. Roger Fouts, Shirley McGreal of the International Primate Protection League, Christine Stevens of the Animal Welfare Institute, and others whose work we so admired.

"So, how do you fit into all of this?" I asked.

"I'm working on my doctorate and doing what I can to help chimps in Florida," she said. "You can't believe the roadside zoos they have there. There's no regulation whatsoever. People just keep chimps in cages by themselves in really miserable situations. I'm doing what I can to get them out of these places and trying to figure out how to help them recover."

I was already starting to feel like the shrinking woman, dwarfed by this phenomenon, when I heard her add, "How about you? I hear you worked with Jane."

"Uh, yes, I did," I answered. "Yes, I worked for seven months at Gombe and then for a couple of years with captive chimps at Stanford's primate facility."

"You worked with captive chimps? What was the facility like?" Carole's intense blue eyes were sending signals that she wanted a detailed description. Thankfully, the Stanford Outdoor Primate Facility was a well-designed and spacious facility with outdoor enclosures that minimized stress and were well suited to the chimpanzee groups that lived within them. I described it to her as the respectful setting it had been, and all seemed to go well—until the moment when she asked, "Where are the chimps now?"

"They're at a government facility. I don't know which one," I whispered awkwardly.

"Wait, what? What do you mean, you don't know? Aren't you worried about them and trying to do something about it?"

It suddenly felt like a hot beam of intense light was shining on me, revealing my every defect. Hearing her words was my first full recognition of the truth—that I had not done nearly enough and had been far too sanguine that they were all right. I was in my second year of medical school, miles away in Cleveland, when the chimpanzee research ended. A majority of the chimps were going to a breeding program and would not be used in experiments. I empathized with the directors who had been unable to keep the facility running and had little or no understanding of the life of laboratory chimps. I knew that Pal Midgett was still working with them, and I contented myself with his brief Christmas-card updates about them and reassurances during phone calls that they were all right. But now, Carole's penetrating questions were making me feel unworthy.

From then on, I tried to learn from Carole and to live up to her very high standards, but it was impossible. Carole was simply far more outspoken and far more willing to do whatever it would take. What the rest of us saw as impossible or outrageous, Carole saw as necessary and achievable.

"How can I help?" I asked Carole one day in 1999 after I learned she had won her lawsuit and successfully secured the original twenty-one space-program chimps. Without a moment's hesitation, she threw down her request.

"I need you to get ahold of the director of the California Science Center and ask him to let us put Ham's space capsule on display here at our education center." Ham was a three-year-old chimp when he was sent into space in 1961. His space flight, which provided the necessary evidence that it was safe to send a human next, was the subject of newsreel reports and television news programs, making him a celebrity at the time.

"What makes you think they'd be willing to do that? Isn't that a really important part of their collection?"

"They don't even have it on display. You just need to let them know how important it is for us to have and how much good it will do here."

After discussing Carole's plan with my sister, director of exhibits for a natural history museum, I knew that Carole might just as well have charged me with finding and bringing back the Golden Fleece. But that was the difference between Carole and me. She didn't know the meaning of *impossible*, and three hundred rescued chimps are testimony to her superpower.

❋ ❋ ❋

It had been awful, Jane told us on that first day of the conference. She had visited a laboratory several months before, where she saw firsthand the appalling circumstances in which chimps were being experimented on.[2] She had seen babies living in isolation, devoid of contact or stimuli—so disturbed by their deplorable living conditions that they rocked, pulled their hair out, or were completely withdrawn and sullen. It had been an awakening for her, and hearing the dreadful tales of it was shocking to me as well. Jane had been an advocate for zoo chimpanzees for decades, and now the plight of chimpanzees in biomedical research was also high on her list, a passion that persists to this day.

These events also prompted me to begin to investigate the medical use of chimpanzees, a journey involving some extremely difficult ethical questions but one that I felt a strong obligation to explore, especially because I am a doctor. I needed to know whether their use truly was essential to solving serious human medical problems. Some investigators claim to this day that they are essential for cancer, hepatitis, addiction, dementia, and AIDS research. Because they are humanity's closest relative, they are sometimes used to test immunologic responses and toxicity of new treatments. Chimps in hepatitis research, for example, are initially infected with the virus so as to become living test tubes. Over subsequent years, they are then injected with various substances scientists hope will prove therapeutic, and then blood tests are drawn to see whether the substance invoked an antibody response, suggesting that it might be effective in treatment. Other, more invasive studies require repeated liver biopsies under anesthesia and worse. Some chimps have had organs removed, have received implants in their skulls to deliver drugs directly into their nervous system, and have given birth numerous times, only to be anesthetized and to have the baby taken away.

Over the years, medical professionals proposed other uses that would subsequently go down in flames. One example, proposed in the 1970s, was xenotransplantation, the idea of using chimps and other primates as organ donors. Not only did scientists quickly find that human donation was far more successful and less risky, but they were also faced with the grim reality that killing higher primates is costly, cruel, and impractical.[3]

One of the most poignant reflections on xenotransplantation comes from famed transplant surgeon Dr. Christiaan Barnard, an early advocate who quickly changed camps.

> I had bought two male chimps from a primate colony in Holland. They lived next to each other in separate cages for several months before I used one as a [heart] donor. When we put him to sleep in his cage in preparation for the operation, he chattered and cried incessantly. We attached no significance to this, but it must have made a great impression on his companion, for when we removed the body to the operating room, the other chimp wept bitterly and was inconsolable for days. The incident made a deep impression on me. I vowed never again to experiment with such sensitive creatures.[4]

Chimps have given their lives and their well-being to quite a number of experiments on marginal issues. Was infecting chimps with the deadly but little-seen kuru virus really warranted?[5] Is there any possible way to justify the failed experiment in which a chimpanzee was anesthetized and his circulatory system connected to that of a three-year-old girl with liver failure in hopes that the chimp's liver could remove the toxins in her bloodstream and allow her liver to heal?[6]

When the AIDS epidemic developed, scientists once again became excited about using chimps to find a vaccine and identify effective treatments. Their enthusiasm dampened, however, as they recognized the tremendous costs of experimentation (about $50,000 annually per chimp), the fact that chimps do not develop an AIDS illness comparable to that of humans, and that there are other, better animal models. And by the way, it is now twenty-five years later, and we still lack an effective AIDS vaccine. Over a hundred vaccines have been tested, many showing great promise in chimpanzees, only to result in far more limited effectiveness in humans. But all this can be of little consequence to a chimp named Tom, who was finally retired from research after more than 360 knock-downs (general anesthesia) and inoculation with the AIDS virus.

Hundreds of chimps have been used over the years for cancer research, but here again, other animals—often mice—have proven to be superior experimental subjects, not only because the types of tumors they develop more closely resemble those of humans but also because they are far more plentiful and far less costly to conduct research on. Still, a number of entrenched research scientists claim that chimpanzees are absolutely key to future gains.[7]

So, what happens when other scientists examine the literature to see whether experimentation on chimps is really essential, especially to emerging new medical therapies? Research scientist Dr. Jarrod Bailey has published a wealth of papers on this topic, casting doubt on claims of many lab scientists. In one study, while examining more than 65,000 articles on development of monoclonal-antibody cancer treatments, he found that cell cultures, other species, and even human trials often provide alternatives.[8] Of the articles, fewer than 30 concerned chimpanzee research, and only one of 700 antibodies tested on them proved effective in humans.

Laboratory scientists frequently tout the critical role chimps have played in development of vaccines to prevent hepatitis B—and of their potential to do the same for hepatitis C. Yet scientists are beginning to forgo such testing on chimps, instead using safety information from mice and other models, then proceeding directly to human trials in high-risk populations.[9] Thankfully, new laboratory alternatives are increasingly available today. Development of swine flu vaccine, for example, depended not on chimps but on humans for testing of effectiveness and safety and relied on cell cultures for vaccine production.

The United States and Gabon are the last countries where invasive research on chimps continues. By 2008, restrictions on great ape experimentation had been enacted by seven European countries, Japan, Australia, and New Zealand—countries where scientists agreed that chimps are no longer vital to such research. Recently, however, there has been some significant movement in the United States to limit research on chimps. The National Institutes of Health implemented a permanent funding moratorium on chimp breeding in 1995 and in June 2013 announced that it plans to retire to sanctuary all but 50 of its 360 chimpanzees available for research.[10]

The decision was based on the recommendations of a panel of experts convened by the Institute of Medicine, which concluded that invasive research on chimps is essentially not currently warranted—with one possible exception, and even here, there was considerable difference of opinion.[11] Although the discussion was contentious, some panelists felt that a group of about fifty chimps should be retained for early hepatitis C vaccine testing to rule out ineffective candidate vaccines, and in case a new emergent need should arise. In addition, several hundred privately owned chimpanzees will remain in biomedical laboratories, subject to invasive testing.

After all these years, it is clear to me that experimenting on chimps is just plainly unethical. Scientists would never consider performing experiments on children, yet chimps share many intellectual abilities and the emotional potential for suffering a young child does. If it is morally wrong to perform experimentation on humans, it is equally wrong to perform on chimpanzees.

❦ ❦ ❦

Carole was a do-it-right person, and it showed in every decision she made. One of her best such decisions was to build the Florida sanctuary so that it could withstand hurricane season. She knew evacuation was never going to be an option, so she built sanctuary facilities strong enough to serve as hurricane bunkers when needed. Her strategy worked. Now, whenever there is a serious threat of hurricane, the chimps are simply brought inside, and a keeper stays with them. Sometimes, the chimps sleep right through the storm.

I like to picture Carole walking the grounds of one group's enclosure, dropping toys, branches, and a blanket for the chimps to play with once they are rereleased into the area for the afternoon. The chimps are inside the building, where they are receiving a lunch of warm oatmeal and fruit, not the tasteless monkey-chow biscuits they survived on for so many years.

The islands are all full now, most residents brought from the Alamogordo facility but others rescued from equally awful circumstances. It is amazing to see these former prisoners, now healthy and active, walking and grooming with friends. They are resilient beyond reason and proof of the healing that can result from humane and loving care. These formerly hollow-eyed, hopeless beings have now been restored to life.

I wish all captive chimps could be here to live on these islands—and I wonder what is to become of the 850 imprisoned in laboratories and 300 others kept by owners, trainers, and unaccredited facilities throughout the United States. Will they ever be excused from liver biopsies and blood draws, or unnatural lives as entertainers or pets, and retired to a life of dignity and kindness? I hope so.

I had planned to interview Carole about her view of the future, but time and again, the interview was postponed. Then, after several weeks, I received an e-mail informing me of her sudden death from pancreatic cancer. She had succumbed in a matter of months, having finally encountered a force she was unable to overcome. I had not known about it—perhaps she did not want the world to know of the battle she was fighting—and I was stunned by the loss of her great spirit, as were so many others. We needed Carole—her inspiration, her fortitude. How could anything have touched this incredibly strong-willed woman?

Knowing that the interview would never happen, I visited the sanctuary, where it was clear to me that those carrying on Carole's work share her absolute commitment to the chimps and to her legacy. With the Great Migration now over, the sanctuary will receive new chimps as they are rescued from individual owners and laboratories, educational efforts will continue to promote better public understanding of the social injustices that chimps experience, and campaigns to eliminate invasive research will be fought with even greater immediacy.

✦ ✦ ✦

When I think of Carole, I also envision an image of Carlos, dabbing the grass with his toe for the first time in forty years, and it haunts me. His hair and his snout are gray with age, and as he moves, the arthritis he has developed over the years is obvious. He pauses briefly, looking up at the blue sky with the same look my children have when they see the night sky. I smile inwardly, registering what a gift this woman gave him. And then I hear her familiar refrain: "Chimpanzees—they are amazing people."

CHAPTER 19

ZOOS

Captivity is rarely a good place for chimps, but zoos and sanctuaries are working to create settings that allow chimps to be chimps. Prior to the 1970s, many zoo chimps suffered serious psychological problems as a result of social deprivation and boredom. But good zoos now provide plenty of activity and keep chimpanzees in social groups so they have more normal lives and relationships. Zoos today also play a key role in educating the public about critical conservation issues, and several are even involved in supporting chimps in the wild.

☀ ☀ ☀ ☀ ☀ ☀

An editor once suggested that the opening chapter of this book must explain why chimps matter so much to me. She was hardly the first reader of my manuscript to mention it, but just as I had every time before, I felt clueless. There was no life-altering incident with one or more chimps, no toy chimp I had whispered secrets to as a child. The simple truth is that I have loved chimps ever since the moment I first saw them—and even after all these years, I still don't know why.

I remembered the editor's challenge as I walked into the inner sanctum of the chimpanzee exhibit at the Los Angeles Zoo with Candace Sclimenti, senior animal keeper for the zoo's ape section.[1] The woman giving a special behind-the-scenes tour of the exhibit was someone I knew had created an environment for the chimps in her care that was exceptionally humane—and a model for other zoos. As we toured the facility and were introduced to its fourteen chimp occupants, I felt just as excited as I had the first time I saw a wild chimp. Realizing this, it hit me—this visit might provide the chance to finally tease out what it is about these musky-smelling, excitable animals that so completely enchants me.

Candace talked about each of the chimps as we toured, speaking of them almost as though they were her children. Gracie, the beauty queen of the group, was also a talented escape artist. Years ago, she had managed to escape the exhibit four times despite the zoo's best efforts to thwart her. Gracie would somehow muster the strength to jump sixteen feet into the air from a standstill, landing on the top of the wall, where she could pull herself up and over. Gracie's mother, Pandora, was one of Candace's favorite chimps of all time—even tempered and a wonderful, caring mother. Gerard, Pandora's son, was another favorite, always wanting to play. Joanna had been stubborn and difficult, but she had a special fondness for Candace and her own unique charm. And so it went, Candace regaling us with tidbits about each of her remarkable chimps and their special qualities.

Candace led us to a room next to the outdoor enclosure where only metal bars separated us from the chimps. A fine-looking adolescent chimp named Ben instantly ran up to the grate, excited to see Candace. His head nodded mischievously as he picked up a stick and poked at Candace's feet, causing her to laugh and almost to dance while addressing us. Two other males played nearby, laughing as they tickled one another. Candace's amused smile conveyed just how much she adores chimps, and I think she could tell I understood, for fairly soon, she was frequently looking at me as she spoke.

❧ ❧ ❧

Perhaps it is not surprising that Candace admires Gracie's energy and spunk, for these are traits they share. Candace's own star quality led her to become an actress as a young person, working regularly through an agency. But in 1995, she left the Los Angeles area and moved to New Orleans, where her husband pursued graduate studies at Tulane University. Candace became a volunteer at the Audubon Zoo, where she was soon thoroughly enamored of primates. By 1997, she was back in Los Angeles, volunteering at the zoo while getting a master's degree at California State University, Fullerton, and in 1999, she became a zoo employee.

Today, she presides over the zoo's phenomenal groups of gorillas, orangutans, chimps, and gibbons. The gorillas and orangutans are in dazzling exhibits that are models for zoos throughout the world. But even more world class, if it is possible, is the Los Angeles Zoo chimp exhibit and its residents—to whom, I'd wager, Candace's heart truly belongs. Such a large group of zoo chimps who are so healthy and exemplary is a tribute to Candace and others at the zoo, and it provides visitors with a rare opportunity to see chimps living as the active and interesting primates they were meant to be.

As in the wild, these chimps generally share alliances often based on their maternal family groupings. Pandora is mother to four of the group's chimps and the grandmother of three. Many visitors swear you can tell her family members instantly, as they share a tendency to be bald from the forehead down. Nan, matriarch of the other familial group, is the mother of two strapping males, Shaun and Glenn, and grandmother of Jean and Jake. Just two of the fourteen chimps were born elsewhere: Zoe, who arrived as an infant from Lion Country Safari, in Florida, where her laboratory-raised mother abandoned her, and young Ben, who was purposefully transferred to the Los Angeles Zoo from Zoo Miami as a potential mate for a number of the younger females.

Candace moved us up to the penthouse area of the enclosure, pointing out the features of this state-of-the-art exhibit along the way. The exhibit, *Chimpanzees of the Mahale Mountains*, which opened in 1998, is named for a well-known chimp study site that, like Gombe, lies on Lake Tanganyika, in Tanzania. The exhibit was built with extensive holding areas behind the outdoor enclosure, allowing keepers maximum ability to divide the larger group into subgroups and to simulate the fission-fusion community groupings chimps enjoy in the wild.

The day's penthouse occupants were Pandora, her daughters Gracie and Regina, and granddaughter Yoshiko. The ladies were enjoying the relative tranquility of their all-female group, and Pandora reigned over it all with her calm, commanding presence. In truth, Pandora looked a bit odd, lacking even a single hair on her well-groomed head and her Shrek-like ears protruding at right angles from her skull. Yet she seemed somehow regal as she sat listening in on Candace's talk.

Next, we walked into an adjoining area occupied by two elderly and two younger females. The older females had serious health problems, and being separated from the larger group was not only helping them enjoy a slower pace of life but also facilitating medical care and monitoring. They had been trained to present their bellies for insulin injections on cue and to press their chests to the cage bars for occasional ultrasounds of their hearts.

The zoo has lost a number of chimps over the years, usually to age, heart problems, or other natural causes. In the process, they have witnessed the emotional impact these deaths have on the other chimps, causing mourning and disbelief not unlike that people experience.[2] In response, zoos and sanctuaries have adopted policies that ensure that the chimps are given the opportunity to come to terms with and mourn the death of one of their members. The protocol calls for presenting the body just outside the caged area for the living chimps to see and be with.

"It can be heartbreaking to witness," Candace tells me. "Some scream. We've seen a couple fill their mouths with water and spit it at the body. Others poked at it and then just sat nearby, sometimes for more than an hour. They don't tear up and cry like people, but they do 'cry' in a way." When I ask her what it sounds like, she describes the sound of a high "hoo" that is sad and quiet.

Candace tells us that it is especially challenging to protect the chimps' mental health. I've seen it myself, a throwback to the early 1970s, when many zoo enclosures were austere. Chimps were often kept singly or paired with just one or two others and given little diversion beyond watching the daily zoo visitors and dreaming up ways to taunt them. With food provided for the zoo chimps, the hours normally spent foraging for food were now devoid of activity. Even the Los Angeles Zoo enclosure, at the time, was a concrete structure with the quintessential dry moat and some logs placed on the central platform slab.

In his 1967 best seller *The Naked Ape*, Desmond Morris was one of the first people to discuss the mental health issues of captive chimps. Hours of boredom, meager social activity, and the zoo practice of removing the chimps from their mothers at birth were taking a huge toll on chimp well-being. The result was that a majority of zoo chimps rocked and swayed, plucked much of their hair, and showed signs of mental illness readily recognizable from similar behavior in humans.

A new revolution was beginning, however, that would lead to today's improved conditions for many zoo chimps. Zookeepers at leading zoos turned up their efforts to provide activities for chimpanzees in order to keep their minds active. Behavioral enrichment was offered by giving chimps branches and by making them work to obtain their food. The Los Angeles Zoo, for example, improvised an artificial termite mound from which chimps could use sticks to fish for honey. Most zoos stopped housing chimps singly or in stultifying small cages, and efforts began in earnest to keep babies with their mothers whenever possible.

Ask Candace what the most important function of today's zoo is, and she'll tell you it is to take the best possible care of the animals entrusted to it. Zoos also need to allow animals to be what they are—to live their lives as closely as possible to how they would have lived in the wild, she adds, "so people can experience them for who they are." She bristles at the thought that bad zoos might leave people thinking that chimpanzees are feces-throwing monsters that sit in boredom. A good zoo must provide what the animals need to be normal and healthy—and in the case of chimps, that means plenty of activity and a social group.

Today's zoos may be increasingly taking on other responsibilities that go far beyond education and animal care. As wild populations are increasingly pushed to the brink, zoos could one day be a critical link in ensuring the survival of the species. If zoos are among the last places where chimps survive, they could provide a critical reservoir of breeding chimps, essential to any efforts to restore chimpanzees to the wild.

To ensure a healthy assurance population of zoo chimps, the Species Survival Plan of the Association of Zoos and Aquariums brings the nation's zoos together to work cooperatively to breed their chimps in a controlled, planned way. The Los Angeles Zoo chimp group, in which there has already been a good deal of inbreeding, exemplifies why this is important, since continued inbreeding could lead to genetically inferior and vulnerable chimps. To prevent this, however, the SSP called for moving Ben from his home in Miami to become a mate to several of the younger Los Angeles Zoo females, thus enriching the genetic pool. Further transfer of chimps between zoos will continue according to the regularly updated plan.

Zoos are also playing a critical role in supporting field research and wildlife conservation. The Lincoln Park Zoo, in Chicago, for example, is a leader in chimp-conservation efforts, promoting field research at Gombe and in the Republic of the Congo's Goualougo Triangle and developing models to help wildlife sanctuaries in Africa predict the number of chimps they will be called on to care for in the future. The zoo's Project Chimp-CARE assesses the status of the more than two thousand captive chimps in the United States to envision a plan for appropriate care of all of them in the future.

❦ ❦ ❦

I asked Candace what the best part of her job is, and once again, she answered readily: "It's the interaction with the chimps. I just feel so blessed and honored to be around these incredible beings. They're constantly teaching me and amazing me."

A little puzzled by her comment, I asked what, exactly, they had taught her, and for once she took a moment to think before responding. Finally, she offered a story as illustration: Gracie, due to give birth at any time, was being kept with the comfortable subgroup of her mother, sister, and niece in anticipation of her impending delivery. Candace and the other keepers were staying close, watchful for any sign that Gracie's labor was starting. It was a momentous occasion, and they had hopes of not only being one of the few humans ever to witness a chimp birth but also sharing the moment with this favorite chimp. As they monitored the group, they were struck by how attentive the other females were, appearing as though they were aware of what was soon to transpire and even seeming emotionally supportive of Gracie. Candace felt excited and honored to be part of this most intimate moment. But when Gracie's bag of waters broke, signaling that labor was in progress, the females began barking at the keepers.

"It was as if they were telling us, 'This doesn't concern you—leave us alone,'" said Candace, admitting to having felt a bit wounded. "In all the years I've worked with them, I have always felt accepted and as though there was a trust. But this was the only time in all my years I didn't feel connected. They were telling me to take a step back and to respect the sanctity of this moment—and their right to it. I'll never forget it. They were teaching us."

Perhaps it was the epiphany I had been looking for. Candace had just described a moment that summed up so many of mine—that sense that whatever it is that lies at the core of being human also lies within chimpanzees, something spiritual and urgent, something that absolutely demands our utmost respect.

❧ ❧ ❧

I left the zoo thinking about yet one more story Candace had shared, this one about the gregarious and playful Gerard and his gruff father, Judeo. Gerard was always playing with the keepers, charging toward them, prompting the keepers to pretend to be totally surprised and amazed. It was Gerard's favorite game, but whenever possible, Judeo would break it up, usually chasing and sometimes attacking Gerard.

One day, as Candace sat crying quietly over a video of her grandfather, who had recently passed away, Gerard came and sat near her, seemingly offering comfort and registering her sadness. Seeing the two together, Judeo approached. Candace braced for him to chase Gerard away, but to her surprise, Judeo simply joined them, sitting quietly and sharing the sad moment in a most uncharacteristic and poignant way.

"Judeo was like that," she told me. "One of the best alphas I've seen. Tough on the outside but soft and squishy on the inside," words so descriptive of the chimp—and human—males I have loved.

And with that I wondered, what need could I possibly have to explain why I love chimps? They are us, but softer and simpler. And though circumstance can on occasion push some to ferocious acts, in the end, they are children—extraordinary children who teach us what lies at our own core.

CHAPTER 20

FOR YOUR ENTERTAINMENT

Hollywood loves a baby chimp, and chimp advocates have had little success in keeping the industry from featuring them in commercials, movies,
and television. But few people realize the price those chimps pay and how
handlers usually dump them as soon as they are no longer easy to handle.
Pet owners, too, often rob chimps of more normal lives for their own self-
gratification, paying upwards of fifty thousand dollars per chimp for the
privilege.

✢ ✢ ✢ ✤ ✤ ✤

It is a long fall, going from life as a Hollywood star to the squalor of a
small, remote zoo in Nebraska—but such is the life of Ripley, the entertainment chimp whose life has had no end of twists and turns. Purposely
taken away from his mother at birth, Ripley was sold to a Hollywood
trainer to begin his career, which would include appearances in movies
like *Ace Ventura* and *Junior* and even have him spitting at Kramer in one
episode of the television series *Seinfeld*. But chimps don't last long in Hollywood, no matter how faithfully they have performed. Once they reach
six to eight years of age, they are all washed up because they are often
unmanageable, stronger than their trainers, and no longer the cute youngsters directors want to hire. It wasn't long before Ripley found himself
living in a small, unaccredited zoo, living with three other retired entertainment and pet chimps.

The four shared a cage until one memorable day in September 2005,
when keepers failed to firmly latch and lock the door. One of the chimps
spotted their mistake and jimmied the door open. Soon, the four were out
exploring the grounds. As employees discovered the escape, they quickly
herded zoo visitors to the administration building, holding them there
until the chimps could be recaptured. One chimp even wandered into the
nearby town, trying to enter a small store, but returned to Zoo Nebraska
when he found the store's front door locked.

During all the commotion, Ripley chose to close himself back into his
cage, apparently feeling safer there. Perhaps he knew what awaited the

others—being tranquilized with medicine shot from a dart gun. Unfortunately, the zoo staff was poorly trained in recovering escaped animals, and although they managed to dart two of the escapees, they used the wrong tranquilizer, one that had little effect on the chimps. Finally, the zoo director decided to shoot and kill the three chimps, doing so from a golf cart. The incident, tragic all around, should not have played out as it did.

Ripley, just fifteen years old, had endured far more than his share of tragedy. Not only had he been separated from his mother at birth and abused as an entertainment chimp, but now he had also witnessed the killing of his two friends and his younger brother. Three days later, he found himself being shipped to Missouri as breeding stock to procreate more baby chimps for Hollywood. There, over the course of three years, he failed to breed with any of the females, so he was shipped back to California to see whether he would successfully breed with a different group of females. This attempt, too, proved a failure.

Ripley's life finally took a turn for the better. The trainer released him to the Center for Great Apes, a sanctuary in Florida where many of his original companions and siblings from Hollywood were retired. Ripley arrived at the center in December 2009, where he was reunited with his sisters, Maggie and Bella, his brother, Mowgli, and several old friends. In 2007, he was joined by his only offspring, Kodua, whom he had sired at age twelve before being sent to Nebraska. Today, he lives at the center in a group that includes Kodua, Kodua's mother, and Michael Jackson's former pet, Bubbles. Patti Ragan, founding director of the center, says Ripley had "an immediate connection with them—hugs, pant-hoots, and grooming."[1]

Ripley's story is fairly characteristic of entertainment and pet chimps—except that his has a happier ending than most. The simple facts are that most chimp performers have been taken from their mothers at birth, have been hit or psychologically abused in order to get them to perform, and will spend only a few years in entertainment before being turned over to a squalid roadside zoo, a lab, or a breeding operation to spend the next thirty to forty years in a miserably small cage with little to do. No wonder that so many animal rights groups have declared war on businesses that use chimps for advertising, television, and movies.

Even the disclaimer at the end of a movie that reassures viewers that "no animals were harmed in the making of this movie" is somewhat misleading. The American Humane Association has been monitoring Hollywood's use of animals on set since the 1940s, certifying that the animals were not abused during the actual filming. Unfortunately, however, its protections pertain to the set only, and it is what the organization doesn't monitor that is cause for greater concern. Its assessment might be different if monitors could see the chimp's living conditions, the abusive training that went on during preproduction, and what will happen to the chimp as it approaches adulthood.

Plenty is known about how chimps and orangutans are abused by their trainers, quite a number of whom have been run out of the business as a result. One eyewitness to abuse of chimp actors is Sarah Baeckler, who went undercover for fourteen months in 2002 in order to document their daily lives. Baeckler, a primatologist, worked at the Amazing Animal Productions training facility, in Malibu, headed by the now-infamous animal trainer Sid Yost. At the facility, Baeckler witnessed countless displays of abuse. "The trainers physically abuse the chimpanzees for various reasons, but often for no reason at all," she testified at a briefing. "If the chimpanzees try to run away from a trainer, they are beaten. If they bite someone, they are beaten. If they don't pay attention, they are beaten. Sometimes, they are beaten without any provocation or for things that are completely out of their control."[2] She also writes, "I saw volunteers and trainers hit Cody on the head with a lock, take a full windup and punch him in the back, kick him in the head, and hit him with a blunt instrument known as the ugly stick." And finally, she writes, "The plain truth is this: the only thing that will make them stop behaving like curious, rambunctious chimpanzees and, instead, routinely perform mundane tasks over and over again on cue is abject fear of physical pain." Thanks to her investigation, Yost was ordered to retire all five of his chimps and release them to sanctuaries.

✳ ✳ ✳

Hollywood's use of chimps causes other problems as well. Studies show that because people see chimps in movies and advertisements on a fairly regular basis, they assume that chimps are small, cute, and cuddly and would make great pets. They also wrongly assume that chimpanzees are thriving as a species. One can understand why many Africans resent pressure from the Western world to protect wild chimps when they learn that Westerners are using chimps as pets, actors, and lab subjects.[3]

The pet trade is also infamous for its abuse of chimpanzees and other exotic animals. One notorious business, for example, calls itself a sanctuary but is actually in the business of selling chimps for upwards of fifty thousand dollars each. Female chimps giving birth to new infants are tranquilized and their babies snatched away and sold. Few of the people purchasing the infants, however, are adequately prepared to care for them and often give them up as they reach adolescence at around eight to ten years of age. Meanwhile, the pet trade continues breeding as many as it can sell.

Too often, we hear horrific accounts of pet chimps harming their owners. One of the most infamous cases involved a chimp named Travis. In 2009, the fourteen-year-old adult chimp used owner Sandra Herold's keys to escape from the home in which he was living as her companion. All his life, Travis had been treated like a human, eating at the table and sleeping in bed with Herold. She kept the chimp in diapers and gave him Xanax to control him when he became difficult. The chimp grew to weigh two hundred pounds, twice the weight of a wild chimp, and had no chimp companions to socialize or mate with.

One day, Travis viciously attacked Herold's friend Charla Nash when she attempted to herd the escaping chimp back into the house. When the owner's efforts to get the chimp to stop attacking Nash were unsuccessful, she resorted to stabbing Travis with a knife. Finally, he was shot to death by police. Charla Nash spent months in the hospital, lost both hands, and required a face transplant as a result of her terrible injuries. She will live out the duration of her life blind and without the use of her hands. A lawsuit against the estate of Sandra Herold (now dead of an aneurysm) has resulted in a $4 million award, and Nash is suing the State of Connecticut for $150 million for failing to enforce existing laws and prevent the attack.

Was Travis a bad chimp? Presumably not. By age eight, chimps are already far stronger than humans and nearing sexual maturity. They become unmanageable, and most owners and trainers turn them over to a sanctuary or a medical laboratory at this age, having thoroughly exploited them. Other owners build large cages to keep them in, such as was the case with one chimp owner whose "pet" severely mauled him when he failed to securely fasten the door. Some owners, nevertheless, insist on keeping pet chimps in their homes, putting themselves, their neighbors, and the chimp at risk. There is nothing remotely normal about pet owners who give Xanax to grown chimps to keep them "manageable," serve them wine and food at a dinner table, make them wear diapers, and share their bed with them.

Another well-known and horrific incident also reminds us of the folly of owning wild animals. In 2011, in Ohio, exotic-animal handler Terry Thompson released his menagerie of animals from their cages shortly before killing himself. The animals posed a serious threat as they wandered near highways and onto private property, and ultimately, almost all were shot and killed by local sheriff's deputies. When the carnage was over, forty-nine animals had died, including eighteen tigers, seventeen lions, six black bears, a pair of grizzlies, three mountain lions, two wolves, and a baboon. The owner had spent one year in jail on federal weapons charges and had received thirty-six citations for animal cruelty, allowing animals to roam, and other infractions. Animal expert Jack Hanna remarked, "It sometimes takes things like this to make things better," and although the State of Ohio did, in fact, create new laws prohibiting ownership of large exotic animals, there remains substantial room nationwide to prevent such abuses.

❧ ❧ ❧

Thankfully, pet chimps have good people fighting on their behalf, and one of the best is Dr. Steve Ross, director of the Lester E. Fisher Center for the Study and Conservation of Apes, at the Lincoln Park Zoo, and founder of Project ChimpCARE. His innovative program seeks to catalog the housing and management of every chimp living as a pet or performer in the United States and to improve the lot of this often-unseen population. Project ChimpCARE estimates that 58 chimps in the United States remain as pets or breeding stock. Another 23 are in entertainment, and 210 are living in unaccredited facilities, some in unforgivably bad conditions.[4]

Early on, Ross and Vivian Vreeman, the project's coordinator, went on the road to find each of them. In the process, they reached out to the chimp owners, building lasting bonds whenever possible that eventually led to several chimps being turned over to sanctuaries. For example, one Montana owner of two seven-year-old chimps had vowed that "her boys" would be taken away only "over my dead body." The woman, who had appeared on shows such as *Good Morning America* and *Today*, was proud of the in-home cages she had invested thousands of dollars in. However, Ross's even-handed influence, along with a misdemeanor public-nuisance charge she received when one of her chimps bit a woman, finally led her to turn the chimps over to the Save the Chimps sanctuary.

Ross has a knack for pointing out the irony of how we treat chimps in the United States. He has led a successful campaign to correct inconsistencies in how the United States Fish and Wildlife Service classifies the conservation status of chimps. Despite the fact that worldwide, chimps are known to be endangered, captive chimps in the United States have been designated as merely threatened, a status lower on the scale of risk of extinction. Ross, representing the Association of Zoos and Aquariums and joining with seven cosponsors, has campaigned for an upgrade in status that would require permits for any invasive medical use of chimps or sales across state lines and would prohibit the killing or harming of a chimpanzee. Pet owners would still be allowed to own chimps but would need permits regarding their care. If this proposed rule is implemented as expected, the Fish and Wildlife Service will likely finalize it in early 2014.

Thankfully, chimps are no longer brought into the United States from Africa. That practice has been banned for many years; the last African chimp arrived at a zoo in the United States in 1976. However, the pet trade is alive and well in Africa, often operating under the radar due to laws against trade in great apes. For example, chimp researcher Cleve Hicks encountered forty live chimp orphans between September 2007 and February 2009 in Aketi, Bambesa, and Buta, three regions of the northern region of the DRC where bushmeat hunters were savaging the local forests. The infants and juveniles had been orphaned when their families were shot, and they now found themselves tethered in the backyards of owners ranging from peasant farmers to Catholic bishops and government officials; some of the youngsters had had their front teeth knocked out to prevent biting. Hicks was unable to get local law-enforcement officers to assist, but he eventually talked five owners into surrendering the chimps to sanctuaries.[5]

In another case, a chimp sanctuary in Sierra Leone investigating the local pet trade discovered that two wildlife dealers had actively captured and exported live young chimps for years, and there were reports of sixty chimps kept as pets in the capital of Freetown alone in 1989. Studying records from 2001 to 2006, the sanctuary found it had received thirty-three chimps who had been owned or bought by expatriates, most of whom were do-gooders who rescued the chimps from bad situations in marketplaces or with abusive owners. Thirty-nine other chimps, nineteen of which had been intended for sale, had been turned over by locals.[6]

The trade in great apes is becoming increasingly widespread and sophisticated, as transnational criminal networks supply great apes to the tourist-entertainment industry, disreputable zoos, and wealthy individuals who want them for pets. It is estimated that some 22,000 great apes were taken from the wild between 2005 and 2011, and nearly two-thirds of them chimpanzees.[7] Almost unbelievably, however, only twenty-seven arrests were made for great ape trade, and one-fourth of the arrests were never prosecuted.

The stories are powerful: picture a mysteriously moving cardboard tube in a Qatar airport baggage area that, when opened, was found to contain two baby chimps, one stacked atop the other, both barely alive. Fortunately, they survived and were sent to a sanctuary in Zambia, but many stories have far more tragic endings. In 2001, a baby chimp and a baby gorilla were intercepted in Cairo in an illegal shipment from Nigeria, and although several NGOs attempted to intervene, they were euthanized by drowning in a vat of chemicals due to officials' concerns that they might harbor disease.

Chimps and other wildlife are smuggled out of their countries of origin using every mode of transportation. Some are transported via ships or in the back of trucks, both riskier methods in which the cargo is more likely to be inspected and intercepted. But sophisticated international traffickers are increasingly turning to flying them out of small airstrips so as to avoid inspections. The planes fly directly to places like the Middle East and Southeast Asia, arriving at small airports, where it is relatively easy to bribe local inspectors and police. Other destinations include Eastern Europe, and 10 gorillas and more than 130 chimps are known to have been exported to East Asia from Guinea alone since 2007. The pet trade, thriving relatively unchecked, is becoming an increasingly serious threat to the last intact populations of chimps and great apes.

What will it take to stop these international crime rings? So much can be done. Effective efforts start with surveillance of local trappers, who generally leave telltale signs of their activity and thus can be a conduit to tracking down the buyers and traffickers. African countries need to create antismuggling units to work with their criminal-intelligence units in order to routinely inspect the cargo of noncommercial flights from small airstrips and to monitor road and river traffic.

New international consortiums hold promise for better identifying and combating sophisticated international crime rings and for sharing information with Interpol, customs officials, and local police. Organizations such as Ofir Drori's Last Great Ape Organization are also proving critical in pushing African countries to fight corruption, enforce existing wildlife-protection laws, and prosecute criminals to the fullest extent of the law, and we need to support them so they can grow their mission. So, too, must we use our voices to discourage the use of great apes in entertainment and advertising.

Imagine! Twenty-seven prosecutions in the face of thousands and thousands of smuggled baby great apes. Citizens tired of the status quo can become part of a connected activist community through organizations such as the Last Great Ape Organization, as well as ChimpSaver.org, Conservation Justice, and the International Primate Protection League, and can visit these groups' websites to stay abreast of new reports. This is a problem with a solution, but only if we make it so.

PART IV

MAKING IT HAPPEN

CHAPTER 21

THE FUTURE OF THE GOMBE CHIMPS

Inspirational leaders and cutting-edge programs are doing all they can to bring chimps, other great apes, and so many other species back from the brink, but so far their efforts are not nearly enough. Chimp lives and forests are being lost at a rate we can barely imagine. It is time to jump in with everything we've got.

✤ ✤ ✤ ✦ ✦ ✦

Scientists say we humans are a species easily overwhelmed by problems, able to manage only a finite pool of worry that can easily reach capacity just dealing with family issues and the nightly news reports. So, perhaps my worry pool was full that July day in 2008 when we arrived at Gombe and saw the problems the park was facing. All the evidence was there, but it only partly registered at the time.

Back at home, it was a screensaver photo of Fifi's daughter Fanni and her granddaughter Fadhila that floated chimpanzees back to the top of my worry pool. In the photo, one-year-old Fadhila is innocently peering up at the camera as though nothing could possibly go wrong there in her mother's arms. It made me feel a little dishonest, given that I was not at all certain she was truly safe, and it began tugging at me every time I sat at my computer. I wanted to believe that she really would one day grow old, just as her grandmother had, at Gombe.

The photo spoke to me for other reasons as well. I couldn't look at Fanni without seeing her mother, Fifi. The resemblance was haunting and wonderful. Fifi had always been my favorite of the Gombe chimpanzees. I found myself feeling an odd obligation to her, as though I needed to look after her family now that she had passed. It didn't make sense—emotions don't—but over time, the image of Fanni and Fadhila became a daily reminder of the remarkable souls I needed to not forget. These were the next generations of the chimps I had known and been forever changed by at age nineteen. They were innocents, without an inkling that their destiny was in the balance.

My initial web searches were fairly half-hearted, but the results were as glaring as Las Vegas neon. The chimpanzees of Gombe National Park are endangered by a disturbingly long list of factors, the biggest blow having been dealt more than fifty years ago, when a survey error gravely misjudged the perimeter of what was then the Gombe Stream Game Reserve. The mistake meant that the protected area that would eventually become Gombe National Park was now just a fragment of what had been intended, barely large enough to fit three healthy chimp communities. The blunder would have critical consequences years later as villages developed along the park's perimeter. This, and the fact that Gombe had become a tourist destination, meant that the Gombe chimps were at risk from human disease, deforestation, and isolation from chimp populations outside the park.

Thankfully, Jane and others began coming to terms with the issues decades before I did. She tells of attending a conference in 1986 at which chimp researchers from throughout Africa described how habitat loss was threatening the chimp communities they were studying. One after another, each shared the same message that a new demon was afoot in Africa's natural world. This was a call to action for Jane that took on even greater urgency in 1992, when she flew over Gombe and saw how denuded the surrounding hillsides had become as people had cleared the land for farms and harvested fuelwood for cooking. Recognizing the stakes of the game, she became a warrior for chimpanzees, traveling three hundred days a year to get the word out.

❦ ❦ ❦

Jane had recognized the need to win the support of locals even at the time she first arrived in 1960. She had innocently stepped into the midst of ill feeling that dated to the 1940s, when the Gombe Stream Game Reserve was first created. Establishing the reserve had required forcible evictions that, in turn, produced enormous resentment among the local people. Others felt contempt that arable land was being reserved for chimpanzees when there was so much human need. So, in 1994, the Jane Goodall Institute created a multifaceted community-based program, the Lake Tanganyika Catchment Reforestation and Education Project (TACARE), which created tree nurseries, women's cooperatives, health-education centers, family-planning and AIDS clinics, and microcredit and other programs while also promoting sustainable technologies to reduce pressure on the remaining indigenous forests.

The programs, which had an important impact on the health and economy of the local human community, resulted in more sustainable lifestyles and conservation. But even this array of programs was unable to fully compensate for the tremendous growth in population in the region. The population was increasing 4.8 percent per year, and more and more people were living near Gombe National Park. Time was of the essence. If the chimps were to be protected, it was increasingly clear that forests adjacent to the park needed to be protected. And if possible, wildlife corridors had to be established to ensure that chimp communities would not become further cut off from one another. Isolation could put the chimps at risk of being completely wiped out by an epidemic or a forest fire and could result in inbreeding and less resilient populations of chimps. But how to shield these key unprotected areas, especially given the fact that some of the critical acreage is managed by individual villages and even, in one case, a local jail system?

✦ ✦ ✦

My family and I had the opportunity to meet some of the people key to this effort as we visited the headquarters of the Jane Goodall Institute, in Arlington, Virginia, in summer 2009. Standing at the elevator was Dr. Lilian Pintea, a man who has been key in understanding the dimensions of the problem and determining which areas are most important to maintain and restore. As a Fulbright scholar, Lilian, a native of the Republic of Moldova, had studied the use of remote sensing and satellite imaging, and later worked as an environmental consultant at the World Bank. Eventually, his studies took him to the University of Minnesota, where he studied under Dr. Anne Pusey.

We had barely finished shaking hands when Lilian eagerly turned his attention to our friend Megan, his coworker. He had a surprise in store for Jane. He had arranged for a giant peace dove to be placed in front of Pan Palace at Gombe and to produce a satellite image of it. Similar doves had been made from sheets and poles by Roots & Shoots groups all over the world in celebration of United Nations International Day of Peace, and Lilian knew Jane would be delighted to see that Gombe was a part of it. He would personally present the image to Jane the following week at an international conference they both would be attending.

Satellite imaging was to Lilian what the cell phone camera is to the rest of us—something used often and matter-of-factly. He had worked with it for years and accomplished important breakthroughs in linking high-resolution satellite-imagery data on forest resources with land-use maps. This allowed him to monitor human encroachment on Gombe's forests and even to contemplate how to achieve a successful chimp corridor. The photos had made clear that Gombe is a virtual island of forest, with low-lying village lands on one side and the steep slopes of the Great Rift Valley's escarpment to the east. Until now, the slopes had proven too steep for villagers to cultivate, and the chimps were still able to use the forest, but increasingly, trees were being harvested or being destroyed by fires. Forests had disappeared from half of the slopes, damaging the watersheds that both villages and chimps depended on, and farmers were now driven to cultivate even these impossibly steep areas.

The satellites also showed the impact of the region's population explosion. The number of local settlements had increased from thirteen to twenty-four in the space of about ten years, and the populations of the initial ones had grown substantially. This explosive growth reflected that of the general region, which had swelled to 1.7 million people. The rapid growth rate was double that of regions elsewhere, owing not only to a high local fertility rate but also to arrival of refugees from Burundi and the DRC. Topping all this was the region's poverty, with a gross domestic product just half that of the rest of Tanzania, meaning that chimps were vying for land and forest with the poorest people in the country.

Thirty years of research at Gombe had documented the drop in its chimp population from approximately 140 individuals to fewer than 90. The Kasekela chimp community, which I had studied years ago, had grown and expanded its territory, squeezing the chimp communities on either side and forcing them into less suitable habitats, some of which overlapped local village land. Population analyses modeling the future of the Gombe chimps found that if nothing were done, their population would decline to half of its current size within fifty years. But if forest could be preserved and the escarpment replanted, the chimp communities could likely survive and even expand by accessing forest outside the park boundaries. The difference between dwindling toward extinction and rebounding to a more sustainable population of perhaps as many as 230 chimps depended on working with those thirteen local villages.

Enter Grace Gobbo, a Tanzanian ethnobotanist who happened to be at the Jane Goodall Institute's offices during our visit. She was being honored as one of the National Geographic Society's Emerging Explorers, a prize that carries a ten-thousand-dollar award as well as considerable prestige.

Gobbo and her predecessors had helped win the cooperation of the lo-cal villages, developing trusted relationships with them and helping them understand the environmental, agricultural, and even medicinal benefits of preserving their woodlands. The Tanzanian government requires vil-lages to have land-use plans, so Dr. Pintea's team had strategized how to coordinate the thirteen plans to ensure a contiguous corridor of forest next to the park. If successful, these plans would secure the forests of the Rift escarpment the Gombe chimpanzees so badly needed access to, and replanting the areas would protect and improve the watershed on which people and chimps depended.

✦ ✦ ✦

Gombe is relatively small, about 8 miles long and 1 to 2 miles wide. Its total area of 13.5 square miles is a fraction of most national parks. Yosemite National Park, for example, consists of 1,190 square miles, and Yellowstone National Park covers 3,468 square miles. Imagine yourself in charge of protecting the Gombe woodlands from Tanzania's poorest people, who are eyeing the land for fuel and farms and unaware of its importance to their watersheds and future. Protecting it would be no easy task.

Jane and her institute have long been engaged in trying to find what works. By 2006, they were initiating land-use planning in earnest with the local villages and had become seasoned experts in developing and running social programs through TACARE to improve the well-being of locals—all this in addition to years of work developing a management plan to pro-tect Gombe and the chimpanzees. But even these efforts were not enough to ensure the future of the chimps. Problems posed by those living nearby were spilling into the park. Fires set for clearing land for agriculture too often burned into Gombe, threatening vital food resources for the chimps. People living near the park posed infection risks, and without the con-tinued support of the entire region and the national government, Gombe would remain in jeopardy. The only way to fully address these issues would be to create a comprehensive Conservation Action Plan.

The Jane Goodall Institute team, which brought local people, councils, and government officials together to spell out a detailed plan of action for the future (2009 to 2039), finalized and officially presented their re-port in March 2009.[1] The CAP called for bans on creation of new vil-lages and roads in critically sensitive areas, replacement of slash-and-burn agriculture with higher-yield and more sustainable methods, and use of fuel alternatives to charcoal and wood burning. The plan also called for new protections against human disease that had killed twenty-four chimps over the years by further limiting the number of daily tourist visits and ensuring that tourists and locals have been adequately immunized. A timeline and a task list are now in place, and collaboration is under way that, if fully implemented, could greatly improve the outlook for Gombe's chimpanzees. Getting all stakeholders to do their part will undoubtedly require tremendous finesse and energy on the part of the core team, but the CAP is a vital first step.

❖ ❖ ❖

If the world's most famous chimpanzees are in trouble despite their fame, what must be the circumstances of the other two-thousand-plus Tanzanian chimps? This was the question scientists and government officials asked as they crafted a nationwide conservation plan in 2010.[2] Their populations, found exclusively in western Tanzania, face a very high threat level because the great majority live in unprotected regions with unchecked human population growth. Chimps in southern Tanzania are at such severe risk that they could disappear entirely within fifteen to twenty-five years.

The group focused on the difficult question of how to conserve current chimpanzee populations and maintain wildlife corridors, quickly encountering the reality of just how complicated controlling land use is in much of Africa. Accomplishing this would require concerted coordinated effort by villages, local governments, government agencies, and NGOs—no small task. Not only would the effort require getting the cooperation of an extensive number of villages, but restrictions would also need to be enforced in sensitive areas against road building and charcoal production, with sanctions imposed if villages failed to comply. Where critical corridors fell on general land, new protected areas would need to be established and management plans created. And even where corridor habitat fell within the boundaries of reserves and national parks, comprehensive management plans would be needed. It would require a huge effort—just ask any city council in the United States that has tried to enforce building codes or any landholder asked to give up property under eminent domain for the building of a highway. Whether the CAP will succeed remains to be seen, and more than two thousand chimp lives are hanging in the balance.

The story is much the same in other countries of Equatorial Africa. In West Africa, hunting and disease have resulted in more than half of its ape populations disappearing between 1983 and 2000. Here, commercial hunting, deforestation, and exposure to disease, particularly the Ebola virus, have been devastating. A consortium of great ape researchers sounded the alarm in 2003, calling for the immediate elevation of gorillas and common chimps to critically endangered status. "Without aggressive investments in law enforcement, protected area management, and Ebola prevention," they told the world, "the next decade will see our closest relatives pushed to the brink of extinction."[3]

Simply put, great apes need great spans of forest and woodlands, areas big enough to support large populations, to survive. In the case of chimps, scientists believe that populations of at least 500–600 individuals stand a good chance of long-term survival if sufficiently protected and that even groups of as few as 250 might be viable. Large groups are able to breed healthy future generations because there is sufficient breeding and cross-group genetic exchange to provide a healthy gene pool. But it takes huge tracts of protected forest to support groups of this size, and this is precisely why great apes in Equatorial Africa are faring poorly. Wherever there is high human density, such forest swaths no longer exist, with the exception of scattered large national parks. In effect, expanding human populations have devastated the forests of Equatorial Africa, leaving mere forest remnants, much as we had seen in western Uganda. And even forested national parks are now surrounded by human populations. Big stands of forest remain almost exclusively in the Congo Basin.

✦ ✦ ✦

Scientists have little difficulty identifying critical areas and landscapes that can and must be protected in order to safeguard the planet's chimpanzees, but they formulate these plans while recognizing that their all-too-reasonable recommendations may well go unrealized. They tell us that governments have to get more involved in patrolling the protected areas and must stop looking the other way while rampant corruption persists in their ranks. Land-use planning, a task that governments are generally slow to tackle for fear of repercussions from locals, needs to be pursued. Degraded habitat must be restored, necessary infrastructure put in place for coming REDD+ programs, and land redesignated or even purchased in areas constituting critical wildlife corridors. Safeguards against disease must be instituted, with ample veterinary care and monitoring as well as the capacity to respond rapidly to potentially catastrophic disease outbreaks.[4]

These are big steps, but a dollar goes a long way in Africa. The conservation plan for the chimpanzees of East Africa, if enacted, could protect more than 90 percent of the population known to be alive today, and this could be achieved at a cost of several million dollars per year, simultaneously benefiting other endangered animals as well. The cost of enacting the recommendations for Uganda, for example, carries a ten-year price tag of $3.85 million, a tiny fraction of the much-needed billions the United States has contributed to Uganda for AIDS treatment.[5] Estimated costs for the CAP for West African chimps are similar and achievable.[6] In fact, the costs of most programs to benefit great apes are reasonably affordable. However, it is the cost of protecting forests and providing livelihoods for local people that will require substantially greater funding, estimated worldwide to be in the billions.[7]

❧ ❧ ❧

So, what is the situation for the Gombe chimpanzees we have known since Jane's first astounding description of them in the 1960s? In short, they are at risk of dying out. The more the population dwindles toward a size of fifty or less, the more vulnerable they are to being wiped out by a catastrophe. But the Tanzanian government and the Jane Goodall Institute are working to increase the available area outside the park and to connect a small remnant group to the other three communities.[8] If they succeed in more than doubling the current population, doing so will mean a hopeful future for long-term survival and a giant win for conservation. But should their efforts fail, we will have lost a community of sentient, intelligent beings and their culture. The difference between success and failure is the difference between little Fadhila having a normal life and fostering healthy future generations of chimps and Fadhila witnessing the collapse of her Gombe "tribe" in her lifetime. And though it is possible that a group of ninety might possibly persist over a one-hundred-year period if sufficiently protected, that scenario seems unlikely, given regional conflicts, global warming, disease threats like Ebola, and the general unpredictability of life in Africa.

Thousands of other chimp lives are in even more immediate danger— today and every day. Take the example of Gabon, for instance, one of two countries with the highest number of chimps, and one with a relatively low human population density. Yet even in a forested country like this, the toll has been heavy. One Gabonese park, Minkébé National Park, lost 98 percent of its gorillas and 99 percent of its chimpanzees at the time of an Ebola outbreak in the 1990s.[9] As timber sales became more profitable, Gabon's logging production doubled between 1987 and 1996, bringing with it new roads as well as hunters and poachers. Meanwhile, the great ape population declined 56 percent between 1980 and 1983 and between 1998 and 2002.[10]

A majority of wild chimpanzees live in unprotected areas—both in the Congo Basin and in more populated regions—and all of them are in trouble. Imagine being a chimp in Equatorial Africa in danger of being hunted and killed for bushmeat, or a baby at risk of seeing its mother killed and then being sold into the pet trade. One in five Ugandan chimps have been caught in snares and mantraps, many of them losing a limb or even their lives. Even chimps in protected national parks are prey to snares.[11] And then there are the chimps living in populated areas, trying to survive in small bands and in remnant forests and having to steal crops or leave the forest even for basics like water.

If we fail to get involved, chimps will soon survive only in national parks and other extremely well-protected areas, and their habitats will appear as small dots on the map of Africa. And although chimpanzees may not be extinct by 2030, thousands and thousands of them will have died as their communities first become cut off from one another and then are cut out from beneath them, just as we saw at Hoima.

We can and must get involved.

And we must protect the planet's one last great reservoir of chimpanzees.

CHAPTER 22

THE CONGO BASIN

A magical book, *The Last Place on Earth*, sits on my coffee table for times when I need to believe there still is unspoiled wilderness on the planet.[1] It is the journal of Mike Fay's expedition through Africa's last untouched forest, featuring the extraordinary photos of Michael Nichols. Like photos of the Moon, these images of Fay's Megatransect (the term refers to a massive ecological survey) reveal a world that few have seen—one at risk of being lost forever. Fay writes,

> The touch of the human hand in this world becomes an affront to what is truly divine. Cutting a single giant tree becomes a crime beyond any that a human court could invent, far worse than a Christian or a Muslim damning and spitting on the name of a prophet. The sight of a road bulldozed into this place, after living beyond the hand of man for so long, provoked in me a violent reaction, beyond reason. This was a hatred that was deep and absolute. I had been to the other side, living in a world that humans do not see, don't know, and thus can't care about. To see all of this perfection unraveled for the vanity of people was impossible for me to understand.
>
> The Congo Basin is a last great reservoir of healthy populations of chimpanzees, bonobos, gorillas, and so many other animals. Nothing could be more vital than saving it, for so much hangs in the balance.

✢ ✢ ✢ ✤ ✤ ✤

If John Muir has been reincarnated, he likely is cavorting unrecognized in the habitus of J. Michael Fay—yet another larger-than-life preservationist. Fay is the famous adventurer who walked 1,200 miles of otherwise-impassable Congo Basin jungle to make his case to the world that it is, as he calls it, "the last place on Earth" untouched by human presence—and that it deserves to remain forever so. The man seems to have Africa irrevocably embedded in his DNA because, like a moth drawn to a flame, he keeps returning, picking impossible fights—and winning more than his share.

Fay is an introvert, one with ideas and resolve like no one else's. Beginning with studies of gorillas in the 1980s, he went on to survey blocks of forest in the Republic of the Congo and the Central African Republic. Later, in 1996, his work involved aerial surveillance and surveys of the forest, and over the course of that work, he came to recognize that there is one last huge swath of forest, extending from the Oubangui River in the Republic of the Congo to the Atlantic Ocean in Gabon. What better way to catalogue and understand it, he thought, than to walk every inch of the way. The journey, begun in September 1999, would take him 454 days to complete.

Fay and his party of forest people stumbled through swamps, cut through walls of vegetation, and endured muck and foot worms, even applying duct tape to bad sores on their feet so they could continue the journey. Throughout, they encountered gorillas, chimps, elephants, and other animals, some of them unafraid because they had never seen humans before. The second part of the trip, through what he called "the green abyss," held nearly impassable plants of the genus *Marantaceae* with fifteen-foot-tall stalks that merged into a solid sea of vegetation. The final segment was dotted with *bai*s, clearings where animals congregate, seemingly as much for the socializing as for water and food. Fay recorded data on animal sightings, dung, and plants, tagging his observations to GPS information that updated every twenty seconds, in a meticulous effort to let the world know about this pristine African forest and why it was important to save.

Twenty months after completing his walk, his efforts were rewarded with a phone call from the president of Gabon: a historic initiative was agreed on to create a system of thirteen national parks in Gabon covering a total of some 11,000 square miles (about 28,500 square kilometers). Fay, who became technical director of the project, stayed for as many years as he could stand of Gabon's bureaucracy and false promises. After pursuing other projects for several years, he returned in 2010 for another difficult stint that was short lived, but he could see that his earlier years of effort had been all-important. Timber concessions now surrounded all the parks, and it seemed certain that the park forests would have been lost were it not for his great megatransect.

Fay, with the help of the National Geographic Society, brought Jane Goodall to the forest in 2002 to help accomplish yet another of his goals, this time to protect forests in the Republic of the Congo.[2] Jane spent a week with Fay in tropical rain forest that few sixty-eight-year-olds would have dreamed of venturing into. But Jane has never been one to miss out on a good fight—and this time, the stakes were the preservation of uninhabited forest critical to chimps of the Goualougo Triangle, whose territory was in jeopardy of being lost forever to timber concessions. Fay, who had surveyed the entire expanse in 1990, had successfully fought for creation of the extraordinary Nouabale-Ndoki National Park, even serving as project director. Now he was dead-set on seeing this additional thirty-seven-square-mile area added, and who better to bring along than Jane Goodall?

The pair succeeded, getting a nod from the Republic of the Congo's government in 2003. Along with the efforts of others, including Dave Morgan and Crickette Sanz, of the Goualougo Triangle Ape Project, the area was formally added to the national park in early 2012. Once again, Fay had recognized a "last place" that needed saving and given the world the one last chance to spare it. But this time, it was very clear that time is running out for the last forests of the Congo Basin and the wondrous animals and people whose lives depend on them.

✦ ✦ ✦

The Congo Basin is dotted with settlements and cities. It isn't pristine by any means, but portions still exist where humans are not a part. The central portions of the Congo Basin—remote and nearly impossible to traverse because of swamps and vines—are places where only a small number of people have glimpsed gorillas wading up to their chests in water and families of forest elephants having a morning bath.

The Congo River, for which the basin is named, is the source of a wonderful mystery as to why it so completely separates chimpanzees and bonobos and how the two could be so different. The irascible chimpanzees, found on the northern banks of the river, are far more aggressive than their cousins and have a male-dominated society in which displays and fights determine the social hierarchy. Bonobos, found only on the southern banks, have a matriarchal society and seem to substitute sex for fighting to maintain their social communities. Bonobos walk upright more often than other great apes, have a more slender body than chimps, and often have pink lips and a shock of hair surrounding their dark faces.

Despite these differences, both bonobos and chimps have keen intellects, complex relationships with one another, an acumen for language, and the ability to use tools. Scientists have disagreed for years as to which of them is truly humanity's closest relative. But recently, the genome of an eighteen-year-old captive bonobo named Ulindi has provided preliminary evidence that humans are probably as closely related to bonobos as they are to chimps, all three having descended from a common ancestor some six to eight million years ago in Africa.[3]

So, what explains these differences between chimpanzees and bonobos, and how is it possible that bonobos are as closely related to chimpanzees living just across the Congo River as they are to chimpanzees living more than two thousand miles away in Côte d'Ivoire? Genome studies offer some fascinating educated guesses, one leading theory being that the mysterious separation occurred rapidly, resulting in the bonobos becoming isolated in a region devoid of other great apes with which they would have to compete. The chimpanzees, on the other hand, were in habitat shared with gorillas and other animals that posed more competition for survival—and rewarded a more aggressive nature.

Bonobos, like chimpanzees, are now designated by the International Union for Conservation of Nature as an endangered species.[4] Even though they inhabit some of the most inaccessible forests on the planet, their populations are small—on the order of thirty thousand to fifty thousand—and they are being decimated by bushmeat hunters and losing critical forests to timber operations and human settlements. Several thousand members of the known bonobo population are protected within the confines of Salonga National Park, in the DRC, but thousands are in less well-protected areas. The Bonobo Conservation Initiative, led by its president and cofounder, Sally Jewell Coxe, is making great strides in working with locals to create community-managed protected areas—even, in some cases, repurposing forests that were designated for timber harvesting to conservation and the livelihoods of local forest people. The eleven sites, collectively referred to as the Bonobo Peace Forest, protect more than fifty thousand square miles of habitat that will be critical to their future survival.

Almost all of the world's remaining gorilla populations also call the Congo Basin home, and at the rate at which they are losing habitat or dying from exposure to human disease and poaching, projections are that most of them will have disappeared by as early as 2020 to 2025. Three of the four gorilla subspecies (eastern lowland gorillas, mountain gorillas, and Cross River gorillas) have become so threatened that they are listed as critically endangered, and even the survival of the more populous western lowland gorillas depends heavily on protecting the Congo Basin forests.

Conflict is a constant concern in this region, particularly complicating protection of mountain gorillas, eastern lowland gorillas, and eastern chimpanzees. This is where the militias are in force, posing danger to local people and particularly to law-enforcement officers and park rangers. Periodic incursions into the park can last months, and skirmishes sometimes take place squarely in the mountain gorilla regions; rangers were recently forced from well-known Virunga National Park, leaving the gorillas in real peril. Thankfully, when the rangers were finally allowed to reenter the park months later, they found that most of the gorillas had survived. The rangers believed that the gorillas appeared relieved to see them—members of one gorilla family circled them and wanted to touch and smell them. The courage and persistence of the rangers are impressive, given that more than 150 of them have been killed since 1995.

Chimpanzees survive in relatively greater numbers than other great apes, but their circumstances are similar.[5] Bushmeat, disease, and habitat loss and degradation—each of these is fragmenting their populations, even in the Congo Basin forests. The numbers of each of the four subspecies of chimpanzees have dropped drastically over the past hundred years, and they seem to be decreasing at a rate proportional to that at which the human population is growing. There are now an estimated 21,000 to 56,000 western chimpanzees, a mere 3,500 to 9,000 Cameroon chimpanzees, and somewhere between 70,000 and 115,000 central chimpanzees. Estimates for eastern chimpanzees dropped to somewhere between 76,000 and 120,000, but it was enormously good news to learn in 2010 that there may be 150,000 to 200,000 as-yet-uncounted eastern chimpanzees still surviving in the Congo Basin.[6]

And so, it seems, we have one last chance to get it right.

❦ ❦ ❦

Stemming the loss of the Congo Basin's forests won't be easy. Only about 11 percent of the forest lies in legally protected areas, just 10 percent has a management plan of any kind, and just 4 percent is considered to be under sustainable management. Its rapidly growing human population is expected to more than double to 170 million people by 2030, raising demand for food, fuel, and economic growth.[7] At the same time, international corporations, and countries like China, are increasingly looking to the region for timber, for land on which to grow palm oil, food, and other products, and for new sources of oil, minerals, and precious metals. Outsiders are even eyeing places sacrosanct to conservationists—like Virunga National Park. French and British companies have already begun exploring for oil in this World Heritage Site, despite the searing protests of the World Heritage Committee, the World Wildlife Fund, and even the British government. Small and medium-sized Chinese companies are funding destructive mining practices by buying products from small-operation miners, obtaining permits to log millions of hectares of forest-land, and increasingly buying large parcels of agricultural land for food and palm oil production.[8]

Important strides have been made in recent years, however. Satellite imaging, coupled with more sophisticated research methods, has finally allowed us to see what is happening to Africa's forests, and with that knowledge, we have become smarter in our approach to saving great apes and forests. We've grown the notion of conservation landscapes and moved away from thinking that protected areas alone hold sufficient answers. We've become savvier scientists, performing better evaluations of what does and does not work—and we've scaled up the programs with the most promise. We have become far better collaborators, realizing that big successes come when African leadership is supported by the international community and by NGOs.

＊　＊　＊

We know we are capable of fixing one of the major problems driving deforestation in the Congo Basin: the continued use of archaic slash-and-burn agricultural methods. The Asian Green Revolution in the 1960s transformed agriculture across the continent, resulting in higher crop yields and greater food security. But in Africa, these same years were part of the postcolonial transition, during which there was little infrastructure to support a science-based development campaign. Thus, the Green Revolution largely passed the continent by. Consequently, African farmers still use traditional methods that call for rotating crops like cassava, maize, groundnuts, and peanuts for two to three years, then letting the field lay fallow for ten to twenty years. With enormous pressure to produce enough food to feed expanding households, however, fallow periods have shortened, resulting in lower yields, damaged soils, and the need to clear yet more forest.[9]

It is time for developed countries and NGOs to bring Africa's agricultural practices into the twenty-first century by enabling family farmers to grow crops more sustainably and effectively.[10] Offering farming aid and crop-substitution programs to implement sounder agricultural practices is essential for averting climate-change scenarios of mass starvation and for slowing deforestation. By encouraging ecoagriculture, Africans could also become more resilient against international corporations that encourage the growing of destructive cash crops like tobacco. Problems of food insecurity and unsustainable agriculture are two problems we can fix, and it is time that we do so.

As the Congo Basin's population grows, it will have greater energy needs, especially for cooking. Fuelwood and charcoal already account for 90 percent of all wood harvesting in Africa and are a driving force for deforestation around towns and villages.[11] The Congo Basin's population is growing so rapidly that it would be impossible to immediately mobilize the quantities of alternative fuels like liquefied natural gas needed to replace fuelwood, even if the funds to do so were available. Community agroforestry plantations—local stands of fast-growing trees for fuel and other community needs—will be vital in the short term, coupled with restoration of native forests, serious efforts to introduce energy solutions, and family planning.

Efforts to fight corruption and trafficking rings have to become smarter. Interpol is working to develop new means of supporting law enforcement in its fight against wildlife crime, as is the International Consortium on Combating Wildlife Crime, consisting of the CITES Secretariat of the United Nations Environment Programme, Interpol, the United Nations Office on Drugs and Crime, the World Bank, and the World Customs Organization. Meanwhile, SYVBAC (Système des suivi de la Filiere Viande de Brousse en Afrique Centrale, or Central African Bushmeat Monitoring System) will amass valuable tracking information regarding areas where bushmeat is particularly problematic and intervention urgently needed. Organizations like Ofir Drori's Last Great Ape Organization are making change every day and confronting corruption by holding governments and courts accountable—but they need more activists willing to get involved. Aggressive efforts are also urgently needed to harness social media and to educate people throughout Southeast Asia about the toll of the illegal ivory trade on elephants and rhinos and those in Africa of the impact of the bushmeat trade.

Our ability to detect illegal harvesting of timber and bushmeat in real time, which is rapidly becoming more sophisticated, will significantly improve response to violations of existing wildlife laws. The World Resources Institute's Global Forest Watch 2.0 harnesses advances in satellite imagery, cloud computing, and social media to allow anyone with a computer and Internet access to receive alerts within two weeks of deforestation in high-conservation value forests and to support efforts to combat it. The information can go to government officials responsible for enforcing forest protections, as well as to advocates, the media, and locals, who can verify the episodes, take photos with their cell phones, investigate the circumstances further, and share the information with an international community of people linked by social media. The capability of this new platform, according to the organization's website, holds the potential to "put pressure on governments, companies, and others to curtail forest conversion and illegal logging in time."[12]

A host of other innovative technologies are also adding to the arsenal of conservationists. One example is use of conservation drones, hobby shop airplanes fitted with cameras and free software to create a highly affordable means of monitoring critical habitats and forests. Another is Cargo Tracck, developed in Brazil, a small tracking device that can be placed on a sampling of trees in protected forests. If the trees are illegally cut down and transported, the device will send a signal to monitors when they come within twenty miles of a cellular network, allowing the monitors to track the tree's movement to the mill and arrest the criminals. Creation of an array of affordable technologies like these will be vital in this conservation battle.

The single factor most associated with loss of great apes from protected areas is lack of eco-guards and law enforcement, and although the presence of tourists or researchers helps prevent such loss, it appears that nothing saves great apes like effective patrols and prolonged conservation efforts.[13] Wilderness areas are disappearing at a rate that most of us simply cannot imagine. Uganda, for example, lost a third of its five million hectares of forests in just fifteen years (1990–2005) and at this rate will lose all its forests by 2050.[14] There is urgency to truly safeguarding the so-called protected areas. Here, our support of on-the-ground conservation efforts can have a big impact. At the same time, many African countries must examine their oversight of forest areas so that the authorities concerned with forest management have aligned objectives. Currently, many countries' forestry ministries are working to maximize timber harvesting at cross-purposes with wildlife authorities fighting to preserve intact forests.

Highly trained eco-guards are critical to protecting apes and forests—but their work can be supplemented by recruiting locals to volunteer as forest monitors. One hundred such volunteers, equipped with smart phones that allow them to collect simple bits of useful information, report threats to the local environment, take photos, and input location coordinates, have been recruited near Gombe National Park. The information is automatically transmitted to a master program that integrates the observations, acts as a monitoring system, and generates alerts where there are threats to the park or the areas immediately surrounding it that have been slated to remain as woodlands.

We need to begin holding international companies more responsible for sourcing environmentally destructive products in the Congo Basin's most environmentally sensitive regions. The world needs to take notice when companies like British oil company SOCO International and the French firm Total engage in oil exploration in a World Heritage Site like Virunga National Park. In addition, the tobacco industry is having a huge impact on the forests of Uganda and elsewhere, raising serious ethical questions about not only the long-term toll of this crop on local soils and forests but also the health of the local populations. These are but two examples of a wide array of disturbing actions industry has taken.

Some environmentally minded businesspeople have been promoting greater corporate responsibility for decades. One nonprofit organization, Ceres, mobilizes investors and business leadership to promote sustainability. Its Investor Network on Climate Risk, for example, influences one hundred leading investors who collectively manage more than $10 trillion in assets. Meanwhile, groups like Global Witness are reporting to the world on the impact of corruption and conflict minerals and calling on businesses to ensure that their products do not use these minerals, and a global coalition known as Transparency International includes among its purposes holding companies accountable for their business practices, both abroad and at home.

Palm oil production has savaged the largest tropical forests in Asia, putting orangutans and other animals at extreme threat of extinction, and now is rapidly expanding in Africa. Agribusinesses from North America, Europe, and Asia are clearing African forest to establish megaplantations. The world market for palm oil greatly increased in recent years because the oil is free of trans fats and was thought to offer health benefits over a number of other oils. And although it proved to be a poor alternative because of its high saturated-fat content, it remains an ingredient in a stunningly broad array of foods and household products, appearing on labels as palm oil, palmitate, glyceryl stearate, sodium lauryl sulfate, and stearic acid, and sometimes as vegetable oil. Thankfully, world opinion is changing, and companies are being pressured to obtain it only from certified sources. A campaign in Norway led to an 87 percent reduction in use of palm oil among eight major food companies, and in the United States, a number of businesses, including Johnson & Johnson and Unilever, have committed to use of certified sustainable palm oil by 2015. Free iPhone applications, like one developed by the Cincinnati Zoo, are beginning to allow us to make smarter decisions at the market and helping us avoid items that use uncertified palm oil.

Programs developed by Reducing Emissions from Deforestation and Forest Degradation (REDD+), an initiative of the United Nations, will soon begin having major impacts in the Congo Basin, scaling up finances to conserve forests while improving the livelihoods of people in African forest communities. These programs will need the financial support that only a handful of countries, particularly Norway, are offering. The United States needs to match Norway's recent REDD+ spending levels, on the order of $400 million annually, while simultaneously expanding its climate mitigation efforts. Lest this sound unrealistic, it is a relatively small dollar amount compared to the $6 billion-plus the United States has been spending annually on its President's Emergency Plan for AIDS Relief and the Global Fund to Fight AIDS, Tuberculosis, and Malaria. The Congo Basin countries are completing the initial groundwork and infrastructure essential to beginning REDD+ programs in earnest. Already, REDD+ has had a big impact in improving land-use planning and, with sufficient funding, could play a crucial role in climate mitigation and protection of existing carbon stocks through preservation of rain forests.

Efforts are under way to develop a vaccine to prevent the Ebola virus in chimps and gorillas, since it is feared that a new outbreak could be disastrous. One such vaccine tested on captive chimps appears to be protective, but as yet it is not practical to administer to wild chimps and gorillas. Instead, an oral form of the vaccine will be essential, since it would likely need to be provided in the field in food items. Although the current vaccine can be administered by darting, that is only practical when giving it to chimpanzees accustomed to human presence. Getting it to the truly wild populations means having a vaccine that can be injected, for example, into a banana or another food item and that will remain stable over time and in relatively warm temperatures.[15]

Finally, saving the last great populations of chimpanzees will require an integrated approach that brings the weight of an international community of web-connected advocates to bear in ensuring that governments and international corporations adhere to wildlife-protection and environmental-protection laws. Thanks to huge advances like Global Forest Watch 2.0, coupled with a web-connected planet, the opportunity will be ours.[16] As forest monitors and satellites alert us to developments in those last great forests, we will have our opportunity to speak out and to take action. Advocates like Imazon, in Brazil, have already shown how powerful this approach can be in fighting against deforestation. Now it is time to save the Congo Basin—not just for chimps but also for the locals whose lives depend on its resources.

Scientists tell us that twelve to fifteen million hectares of forest are being lost each year, the equivalent of thirty-six football fields per minute. Still, there are solutions for the Congo Basin, the Amazon, and the last Asian forests. It is not too late to save the great apes, biodiversity, and the last places on Earth—but we are at a critical juncture. It will require advocacy, awareness, funding pivotal organizations, and using the power of our pocketbooks. It is doable, but only if we can wake our communities to the problem of looming extinctions and the loss of our last great forests.

CHAPTER 23

HAIL MARY:
WHAT ONE PERSON CAN DO

*The clock is standing at one minute to midnight for
the great apes, animals that share more than 98 percent
of their DNA with humans. If we lose any great ape species,
we will be destroying a bridge to our own origins,
and with it, part of our own humanity.*

KLAUS TOEPFER, DIRECTOR OF THE

UNITED NATIONS PROGRAMME[1]

*If you think you are too small to make a difference,
try sleeping in a closed room with a mosquito.*

AFRICAN PROVERB

It is now undeniably clear that unless we take action, our children will witness the loss of the great apes from all but the most protected of national parks in their lifetime. It will progress over the next five to ten years, during which we risk losing the Cross River gorilla subspecies and Sumatran orangutans, which could be followed within several years by the loss of the eastern lowland gorillas. Bornean orangutans and Nigerian-Cameroon chimpanzees could be gone within the next ten to twenty years. And so it will go over the next thirty to sixty years with, eventually, the picking off of western lowland and mountain gorillas, bonobos, and chimps, virtually all the last remaining great apes. They will be lost to habitat destruction, exponential human population growth, poaching, disease, the live-animal trade, and civil wars. Perhaps what is most disturbing is that most people on the planet—even those living near the chimp forests—have little idea how endangered the great apes are.

But what if the planet knew that humanity's closest relatives are in dire straits? Could it lead to a sea change in attitude? Is there any hope for preserving the Earth's animal diversity and for saving the chimps and other great apes? Dr. Goodall thinks there is. She writes,

My four reasons for hope . . . are simple—naïve perhaps, but they work for me: our quite extraordinary intellect, the resilience of nature, the energy and commitment of informed young people who are empowered to act, and the indomitable human spirit. When human know-how and the resilience of nature are combined with the resourcefulness of dedicated individuals, desecrated landscapes can be given another chance—just as animal and plant species can be saved from extinction.[2]

Like Jane, I believe there is much reason for hope, particularly because scientists and conservationists have stepped up their game in the last twenty years by using technology and collaboration to develop far better means of protecting the great apes. The concept of conservation landscapes, REDD+, huge advances in technology for monitoring forests, and better management of protected areas—all these are important advances. But these efforts will need to be sustained—and intensified—and that will require advocacy on our part, as well as a groundswell of new support. It will demand that you and I get ardently involved by writing letters, sending contributions, insisting that our congressional representatives do their part to make it happen, and advocate, Advocate, ADVOCATE. There is so much each of us can do—using social media, signing petitions, donating dollars, and getting the word out. It has got to be a grassroots effort—one not just about chimps but also about a fight for the planet's last great forests and iconic animals, a fight to ensure that the human species doesn't lose its sacred connection to nature. Here is my own list of places to start.

1. CONNECT

As you finish reading this chapter, go to Facebook and become a friend of GRASP, the Great Apes Survival Partnership. This five-minute task will instantly connect you to the latest developments in protecting great apes. Their updates are interesting and on the cutting edge.

Next, visit ChimpSaver.org and join the site's mailing list to stay abreast of important campaigns, alerts, and ways to help. Explore its pages to experience firsthand just how remarkable chimps and other great apes are, and check ChimpSaver.org's links to organizations that are making a difference. Most important, use the site to view Google Earth time-lapse maps of the Congo Basin forests and become part of a social media community of advocates committed to saving the basin. For the first time, every one of us with a computer and Internet access is able to view the forests of the Congo in near real time, to know when they are in jeopardy, and to collectively and meaningfully raise our voices on behalf of not just chimps but also the people that so need those forests to endure.

2. CONTRIBUTE

NGOs have been key players in great ape causes for years, and supporting them is a big step in helping in a significant way. The Jane Goodall Institute has been essential in creating conservation action plans and innovative social programs, improving satellite monitoring of chimp habitats, creating and supporting chimp sanctuaries, and fighting to create new protected areas. Two other important organizations are the Wildlife Conservation Society, which has also played a part in many of these efforts, and the World Wildlife Fund, which has helped forge the Congo Basin Forest Partnership, promoted landscape management, and called for international collaborations.

Direct contributions to sanctuaries via the Internet can also make a world of difference. These organizations usually have shoestring budgets and enormous unmet needs, yet they carry the potential to not only rescue orphaned chimps but also directly influence the attitudes of thousands and thousands of Africans.

These are but a few among an array of NGOs worth your contributions. A partial but larger list of those helping wild and captive chimps can be found at ChimpSaver.org.

3. ADVOCATE
Become a voice for chimpanzees.

Captive Chimpanzees
Groups such as the Humane Society of the United States, the International Primate Protection League, the New England Antivivisection Society, and Project R&R are actively involved in campaigns to protect and promote the well-being of chimps, but they need a groundswell of new advocates to pressure legislators to enact long-overdue protections and provide needed funding. Although the National Institutes of Health

has announced that it plans to retire all but fifty of its laboratory chimps to sanctuaries, funding to enact this change will be critical. A number of states prohibit having primates as pets, but every state critically needs to enact such laws. Several hundred chimps are still held in wayside and unaccredited zoos and in laboratories of pharmaceutical and other businesses. Invasive research on chimps can no longer be justified, given new breakthroughs and past experience, and these chimps, like those at the NIH, need our help.

Support advocacy organizations with donations and signatures and share their petitions. Actions frequently involve contacting lawmakers about important legislation or agencies implementing new regulations. It is time to retire chimps from laboratories and stem the illegal pet trade and to prohibit use of chimps and other primates as pets.

Wild Chimps and Other Great Apes

It is easy to get involved by signing up with efforts like the World Wildlife Fund's Conservation Action Network or subscribing to the Take Action section of the Jane Goodall Institute's website (www.janegoodall.org/action). Stay informed on the latest news about conservation of tropical rain forests by signing up to receive the free weekly newsletter from Mongabay.com and alerts from the Rainforest Action Network.

An uproar must be raised against companies that grow unsustainable products like tobacco on African soil and against corporations irresponsibly violating international agreements or degrading critical habitats in order to obtain oil and other resources. Support the efforts of groups like Ceres and Global Witness and conservation organizations that promote greater corporate responsibility or draw attention to violations. Be familiar with the corporate responsibility of businesses you support through mutual funds or stock purchases.

4. EXERT YOUR POWER AS A CONSUMER

Be sure that the companies you buy from are environmentally minded. If you are about to buy new furniture or lumber, go to the Forest Stewardship Council's Marketplace or the Rainforest Alliance to find businesses that sell products made from certified materials. Although most furniture in the United States does not use timber from the Congo Basin, you can still support the FSC's efforts by ensuring that your purchases use certified materials from forests in the United States, Canada, and other countries. Buying certified has caught fire in Europe and is increasing worldwide.

Insist on purchasing products made with certified palm oil. Few Americans know what a devastating impact palm oil is having on the forests of Southeast Asia and on orangutans, and international companies are now moving on to the forests of Africa. We need to get behind efforts that pressure suppliers to grow it responsibly. Currently, only about 10 percent of palm oil is certified sustainable, but consumers can help increase this amount by buying from conscientious businesses. Avon, Johnson & Johnson, Nestlé, and Unilever are among some of the best-known companies pledged to source certified palm oil, but that is only a start. We need grocery and drugstore chains to consider the source of the products they sell, and we all need to print and carry the Philadelphia Zoo's wallet card (unless.philadelphiazoo.org/resources) or install shopping-guide apps from the Cincinnati Zoo and Botanical Gardens (www.cincinnatizoo.org/sustainable-shopper) or the Cheyenne Mountain Zoo (www.cmzoo.org/conservation/PalmOilCrisis), both of which list products made from sustainable palm oil.[3]

Let companies that use chimp actors in their advertisements know that you will not be using their products, and why. We know the miserable track record of Hollywood chimp trainers and the tragic impact they have on chimps. Commercials confuse the public into believing that chimps are thriving in the wild and perpetuate the belief of traffickers that there is still an international market for them.[4] By educating companies and insisting that they stop using entertainment chimps, we can bring an end to such exploitation.

5. SEE FOR YOURSELF

Visit your local accredited zoo or go to a sanctuary for chimps if there is one in your area. Better yet, spend a day or a week at Ngamba Island Chimpanzee Sanctuary, in Uganda (www.ngambaisland.org), travel with the Jane Goodall Institute to the Tchimpounga Chimpanzee Rehabilitation Center, in the Republic of the Congo, or visit one of the other chimp sanctuaries in Equatorial Africa (see www.pasaprimates.org). You can also visit some of the conservation programs described in this book or travel to Africa with groups like the African Wildlife Foundation, the Great Primate Handshake, and the World Wildlife Fund.

Thanks to the Internet, you can become more connected to Africa without traveling there yourself. You can support an African by loaning twenty-five dollars to microfinance his or her business project through Kiva (www.kiva.org). You'll connect not only with Africans but also with others throughout the world who are supporting that same project, and you'll even be paid back if the venture you've funded is successful. You can also sponsor the education of an African student through groups like the Kasiisi Project or fight hunger by contributing to UNICEF and others.

Follow the work of sanctuaries in the United States and Africa. They offer videos and updates, connecting you with the individual chimps they are caring for. Some of my favorites are Save the Chimps, in Florida; the Tchimpounga Chimpanzee Rehabilitation Center, in the Republic of the Congo; the Pandrillus Foundation with wildlife centers in Cameroon and Nigeria; and the JACK Sanctuary, in the DRC.

6. VOLUNTEER

Quite a number of sanctuaries welcome volunteers, both here in the United States and in Africa. To learn more, go to ChimpSaver.org or the website of the Pan African Sanctuary Alliance (www.pasaprimates.org). Some conservation NGOs also welcome help with office duties, fund-raising, and other volunteering.

7. SHARE WITH FRIENDS AND COMMUNITY

Creating a grassroots movement is as close as your computer, your cell phone, and your favorite social media. Share news stories about great apes, Africa, and forests with your community and post links to important campaigns.

Hold fund-raisers and educate the people in your community. Sponsor a Gorilla Run to raise funds for Africa's sanctuaries and conservation groups or hold a Walk for Hunger whose proceeds benefit UNICEF and others. Start a Roots & Shoots group of children—or even adults. If you're already working with a youth group, whether in scouting, church, or school, consider enrolling it as a Roots & Shoots group.

Talk to your friends, and be sure they know that forests are vanishing. They need to know that humanity's closest relatives and a host of other species are disappearing fast but that there are things they can do about it. Then create a community, and start growing the number of people where you live who are networking for change.

8. LIVE MORE SUSTAINABLY

If everyone on the planet lived an American lifestyle, it would take the natural resources of four Earths to sustain them. It is time to start looking critically at the amount of waste and stuff in our lives and to make changes.[5] Check an online carbon-footprint calculator such as the one found on the website of the Nature Conservancy (www.nature.org/green living/carboncalculator/index.htm) for help on where to start. Be sure to recycle your phone and electronic devices with a program such as Eco-Cell (www.eco-cell.com), remembering the impact that coltan and tantalum capacitors are having on forests and wildlife. Eat locally, waste less, and be energy-wise.

When you travel, be carbon-neutral by buying carbon offsets. Check out TerraPass (www.terrapass.com) and CarbonFund.org to learn more and to better understand the amount of CO_2 emissions we generate regularly. My trip from Los Angeles to Uganda, for example, caused twice the CO_2 that driving my Prius generates in an entire year—four tons of CO_2. By purchasing forty-eight dollars' worth of carbon offsets at TerraPass, I provided money to invest in projects that reduce carbon dioxide emissions, such as wind farms. Be sure to include offsets for land travel and hotel stays as well.

9. HELP FIND SOLUTIONS TO THE UNSOLVED PROBLEMS

Some conservation issues still lack champions and dollars, ones where immediate out-of-the-box thinking is desperately needed. Among the most urgent concerns are the chimpanzees living in unprotected forests adjacent to growing human communities. These chimps are at risk every day from snares and traps and from the local people with whom they compete for the last remnant forests. They don't have much time left, and they are in drastic need of help.

These chimps do not have many advocates. Given limited conservation dollars, NGOs generally target their funds toward efforts in intact forests, and most experts count other chimps as a lost cause. Past efforts to help them have involved removing snares, funding patrols, and establishing programs to reduce human-wildlife conflict, but they have generally been run on tiny budgets and have had limited success. Clearly, these disenfranchised chimps are going to survive only if locals perceive them as worth saving. At the same time, these are areas where wildlife ecotourism is no longer a possibility.[6]

These chimps need organizations to take up their cause with the same intensity as those that benefit tigers and other iconic species. Multifaceted programs are needed to educate local communities, maintain critical chimp food and water resources within the remaining forests, manage and reduce dangerous human-chimp encounters, and promote alternative human livelihoods and sources of income. Groups like the Chimpanzee Sanctuary & Wildlife Conservation Trust are a prototype for this work, but they are operating on minimal funding. We have not yet seen what a better-funded program could achieve. At the same time, we need technology to better monitor the remaining forest and to detect dangerous mantraps and snares and provide educational programs to influence locals. Agricultural programs to help farmers transition to more sustainable crops with higher yields could also be transformative. All this is achievable, but the groundwork needs to be laid quickly, or thousands of chimpanzees will continue to be lost from these areas—and people will lose their forests and watersheds.

10. CONNECT WITH NATURE

Make certain that the next generations of your family know the joy of camping, growing a vegetable garden, or visiting a park. We all need to stay connected to the sanity and spirituality of the natural world and to say no to paving paradise.

❧ ❧ ❧

Iroquois legends hold that peace is the will of the Creator and the natural order of humanity, something acquired through reason and spirituality. In the beginning, the legends say, the Creator provided the people with all that they needed, asking only that they never forget to appreciate the gifts of the Earth. But when they stopped obeying and the world slipped into injustice and war, the Creator sent an emissary with a message urging them to be righteous and to make a good future for our children for seven generations to come.

Many of us live in a time and place of plenty, and often, our actions are driven primarily by personal comfort rather than consideration for other creatures. Now it is time to begin to consider the impact of our every decision on the planet. Each of us needs to live sustainably and for the benefit of our children's children. If we remain on our current trajectory, our grandchildren will inherit an Earth devoid not only of the species we most cherish but also of many of its foundation species, which are so fundamental to the health of the planet's ecosystems. It is a critical time and a solemn responsibility. Let us work to ensure that our seventh generation inherits a planet with trees, clean oceans and streams, and chimps and gorillas.

CHAPTER 24

ROOTS & SHOOTS, AND
FINAL REFLECTIONS

Running away from any problem only increases the distance from
the solution; the easiest way to escape from the problem is to solve it.
ANONYMOUS

✤ ✤ ✤ ✦ ✦ ✦

Jane has gone through many seasons, as have I. She has been a world-famous scientist, a wife, a mother. She has dealt with divorce from her first husband and the death of her second. She began by teaching the world about the complex lives of intelligent animals, then became a champion for captive chimps and later a defender of wild chimps against the bushmeat trade and habitat loss. And now, in her next chapter, Jane has added Earth and its children to her list of causes. Firmly resolved that the best hope for the future is to win the hearts and minds of youth, the eighty-year-old Jane travels three hundred days a year to win support for an international youth program she created in 1991, Roots & Shoots.

✤ ✤ ✤ ✦ ✦ ✦

It is no small thing to make a promise to someone like Jane Goodall and then try to make good on it. I had promised her when I first arrived at Gombe that I would strive throughout my life to help chimps. Some of Jane's other former students have gone on to great accomplishments as professors and conservationists, but that was not the path that I chose. So, over the years, I have worked to be an advocate for Dr. Goodall and the chimps however I can. This has meant being a supporter of the Jane Goodall Institute and other conservation organizations, reading each of her latest books, trying to stay as informed as possible about primate conservation, and supporting campaigns to improve conditions for captive chimps. Until my family's trip to East Africa in 2008, I honestly thought

I had been doing a reasonably good job, but in retrospect, that clearly was not really so.

One thing that I did very right, however, was to become a leader in Dr. Goodall's youth organization, Roots & Shoots, in 1994, soon after its creation, once again looking for ways to support her newest initiative. The organization now consists of thousands of groups in more than 120 countries around the world, including more than six hundred groups in mainland China, each working to serve its local community, animals, and environment—and developing a sense of empowerment in the process.[1] Jane's purpose was to instill in the world's young people a deep respect for people of other cultures, religions, and nations, as well as an irrevocable connection to the natural world. As the idealistic mother of a six-year-old daughter, I could see Jane was on to an inspiring and passionate new cause, and I wanted to be part of it.

When I started with a group of third, fourth, and fifth graders from my daughter's school, the concepts of R&S caught fire with them. We talked about chimpanzees and what makes them such fascinating animals. At one of the meetings, we discovered how easily chimps become bored in captivity and why they need stimulating activities. The children enthusiastically undertook their first project, drawing what they thought would be the perfect environment for chimps living in a zoo, a place full of things to keep them occupied and to provide as normal a situation as possible.

Soon after, I phoned the Los Angeles Zoo, hoping to arrange a visit for the group. When I spoke to the zoo's director of education, she mentioned that a new, multimillion-dollar chimp environment was soon to be unveiled and that Jane, along with Los Angeles mayor Richard Riordan, would be dedicating it. She invited the children to bring their drawings to share and to attend the opening. Weeks later, two busloads of our kids arrived at the zoo for the dedication. The children sat at the foot of the podium as Jane spoke, intent on every word. She talked directly to each of them, and her warmth instantly christened ninety new ambassadors for her youth program. It was the first of many Roots & Shoots events my family and I would be a part of, watching the inspirational Jane pour her heart into inspiring youth, encouraging them as they described their dreams and accomplishments.

By 1998, the Jane Goodall Institute had established an annual Roots & Shoots national youth summit for teens, and our Ventura contingent traveled to Mount Hood, in Oregon, to be a part of it. Teens from all over the country attended—a group of Native Americans representing four tribes, children from an inner-city school in Harlem, middle school students from an affluent private school in Cape Cod—all of them imbued with youthful passion to make the world a better place. As I caught my first glimpse of Jane at the event, I could sense the renewal of spirit she was getting from being among them. This was her sustenance, her time to be with young people, engaged in what matters most.

I stood with her at the back of the room as each group told about its work. We heard about conservation efforts to protect the endangered Channel Island foxes, protests against experimentation on monkeys, a campaign to create a greener tourist industry on Cape Cod, and a project to restore an Oregon wetland. Jane listened attentively, praising each group and suggesting how to grow their efforts. It was exciting to see their work and how the youth themselves had selected and developed their projects. But of all the impressive groups that spoke that day, it was the elementary school kids from Harlem that brought her to tears. Eleven- and twelve-year-old disadvantaged African American children presented a flawless PowerPoint talk about how they had persuaded the school to eliminate polystyrene foam from the cafeteria. Their talk was the perfect embodiment of what Jane most hoped for from Roots & Shoots. These inner-city children had been empowered to make change for the better and to say no to the status quo.

The conference stands out in my mind for another reason as well, for this was the only time, in all the years I have known her, I have ever seen Jane appear overwrought. I have undoubtedly heard her lecture more than fifty times, attended more events featuring her than I can count, and seen her in quite an array of situations. But here, on this next-to-last night of the summit, Jane delivered a lecture of despair.

When she began her talk that night, I don't believe she intended to be pessimistic. After all, she founded Roots & Shoots in order to provide children with hope and to empower them to fight back against hopelessness. But as she got to the slide showing the well-demarcated park periphery at Gombe National Park, something broke within her. She described the moment in 1992 when she flew over Gombe and felt the awful recognition of how cut off it had become. The local people were so desperately in need of fuelwood that they had used every branch, every tree, right up to the very edge of the park.

As she spoke, she seemed utterly exasperated, appalled that humankind was looking the other way and failing to find solutions for Africa's people and wildlife. It surprised me because it seemed so out of character for her. Perhaps she had finally encountered deaf ears one too many times or had just received bad news. Or perhaps even world-class warriors are entitled to wear down once in a while.

She went on for a few more minutes, almost pleading with us, with herself, for a solution or a better bit of news. The looks on the faces of the roomful of people were dour. All these hopeful youth, here for inspiration, were witnessing what I had never seen—the momentary fatigue and surrender of the unconquerable Dr. Jane Goodall. It was hard not to jump up as a shield and declare that even a heroine like Jane gets to have a moment of doubt. Soon, on recognizing that she had unintentionally gone to a dark place, she brought the lecture to a premature close, reminded us of the Native American blessing ceremony in the morning, and quietly left the podium. The lights came up and we mumbled a few words to others at our tables and went off to our cabins. It was a low moment at the summit, and each of us went to bed that evening not knowing how to feel.

The next morning, we woke at daybreak for the blessing ceremony, led by a Native American man who had dedicated his career to preserving nearly lost tribal languages and traditions. Chitcus, who Jane refers to as her Native American spirit brother, was a steady presence, someone you could not help but like. His long silver hair spilled down his back, and he wore jeans and a western shirt. As he wafted the burning sage toward us with eagle feathers, we held hands, looked toward snow-covered Mount Hood, and hoped for some kind of inspiration. We went around the circle, sharing thoughts and whatever bits of hope we could dredge up. Little by little, bits of resilience emerged, enough to sustain us for now.

That evening, the Jane I knew returned full force. She took her place at the podium, briefly cleared her throat, and launched into a message of hope that evoked relief in all of us. She reminded us of the many obstacles that humankind has successfully overcome, even in the bleakest of situations, and of the power of the human spirit.

She told us the story of a chimp named Old Man, a lab chimp for twelve years who was later retired to an island at a Florida zoo. One day, when a keeper accidentally scared a new baby chimp on Old Man's island, the mother and two other female chimps began to attack the man, throwing him to the ground and threatening his life. But Old Man, despite years of abuse at the hands of humans, intervened. He charged at the females, dispersing them until the keeper could get to his boat and safety. Days later, when leaving the hospital, the keeper told Jane, "You know, there's no doubt in my mind that Old Man saved my life." Jane noted that if a chimp who has suffered all his life at the hands of humans can show this kind of compassion, surely we humans can do the same for chimps and other animals.

Reminded why the fight is so important, the group of one hundred of us embraced one another, formed a circle, and sang. But even as we did so, a part of me knew we had entered a new stage. If Jane had been that worried, the Gombe chimpanzees must be in dire circumstances.

❖ ❖ ❖

Over the years, I would attend numerous other conferences and summits, each time bringing a new group of initiates to receive Jane's blessing and inspiration. My own children's lives would be profoundly influenced by hers, and they would grow up believing that their purpose is to work for the greater good and to protect the natural world. As they joined Roots & Shoots leadership councils, they had amazing opportunities to represent the organization all over the world. My daughter went to St. Petersburg, Russia, and to the Amazon, and my son was a representative at the first international youth summit, which was attended even by youth from African refugee camps. Both were part of the group that traveled to Tanzania to work with local Roots & Shoots members in their tree nursery and, after returning home, launched a campaign to benefit the nursery and to plant trees here in the United States.

Our Roots & Shoots group in Ventura evolved and grew. We walked dogs for the local animal shelter, threw parties for the needy, restored local nature areas, created ponds for rescued native turtles, raised money for needy Peruvians and Hurricane Katrina victims, and supported the education of a young African. One of our best projects started with a visit to the local wintering site of monarch butterflies. The kids were mesmerized, and when the opportunity came to help a scientist tag butterflies as part of a migration study, they jumped at the opportunity. The kids were becoming monarch butterfly experts, and soon they established a monarch festival and convinced Ventura's mayor to create a day officially honoring the butterflies—a small step, but a big win for a group of children wanting to make a difference. Other local groups raised money for medical supplies to support the successful rescue of endangered local foxes from extinction and held an annual festival at the zoo to create greater awareness. High school students began assisting the needy with tax preparation and relief efforts, while others raised money for microfilters to send to African villages that have unsafe water sources. The list goes on.

❖ ❖ ❖

The late Paul Epstein, former associate director of Harvard Medical School's Center for Health and the Global Environment, once remarked on the potential mental toll of issues like global warming, adding, "Getting involved can be an antidote to the depression that can come from the overwhelming realizations that we have to face. It can be empowering to realize that what you do is effective."[2]

And that is one purpose of Jane Goodall's Roots & Shoots, a means of immunizing children against hopelessness in the face of enormous obstacles like climate change and population growth. By giving children experiences in overcoming problems, they learn about their own effectiveness against powerful outside forces and become the leaders who will guide the future.

In 2001, Jane described the program to Kofi Annan, then secretary-general of the United Nations, and it was not long after that he appointed her the UN's tenth Messenger of Peace, praising her "dedication to what is best in mankind." It was an immense honor, one entrusted to only a small number of distinguished individuals, and she passionately undertook its duties, helping support the mission of the UN in improving lives. The honor is bestowed initially for two years, but Jane has put in more than a decade of crusading for peace and tolerance as a Messenger of Peace.

Jane's years of inspiring others would deeply and forever ingrain two principles: the importance of educating others in order to accomplish change and the value of sitting down and talking with the people we disagree with. She writes,

> When I first talked with timber, petroleum, and lab scientists, I was reviled by some conservation groups. How could I have a cup of tea with a chimp experimenter? But if you don't talk, how can you ever expect to change things. The only way is to reach the heart by telling stories. Change often works best when it comes from within.[3]

Time and again, she tells us, these conversations lead to respectful relationships and, often, to solutions.

Jane's Roots & Shoots is even playing an important role in the Jane Goodall Institute's efforts to save the Congo Basin. As programs resembling the Lake Tanganyika Catchment Reforestation and Education Project are created in regions critical to gorilla and chimp populations, the Roots & Shoots program is rapidly growing, inspiring youth to not only appreciate their natural world but also be active and concerned citizens in protecting it. Dario Merlo, executive director of the institute's programs in the DRC, tells how a group of nine- and ten-year-olds came to him one day, asking to reforest a hill that had long been held as sacred and that lay in an area ravaged by a local militia. Merlo got involved, convincing the militia leader to allow it. However, the leader insisted that soldiers monitor the children as they planted. It was a hot day and a difficult job, and one child in particular struggled with digging a hole. Noticing her difficulty, one soldier put down his gun and went to help. Soon, all four soldiers were working side by side with the children. Jane reports that the sacred hill is now green with trees and some vestige of hope.

❧ ❧ ❧

Jane travels extensively, even now at age eighty, and much of her travel is devoted to spreading the good word of Roots & Shoots. The program is her passion, and it is clear that she believes that empowering youth is the best hope for the future. She spends days with youth at leadership conferences, trains new leaders, and listens to umpteen young people tell about the work and service that they are doing as part of Roots & Shoots. Her travel schedule is jam-packed, one that very few people could withstand, but such is the level of her commitment that she labors on for the cause.

Many of Jane's former students are starting to retire from their careers as college professors and as leaders in primate studies, while other, younger students are assuming their places as some of the world's most influential figures in the battle to save Africa's chimpanzees. She has fostered generations of them while continuing her own integral part as the planet's most famous chimpanzee scientist. Yet, it is probably safe to say that no one has had a greater impact on the chimpanzees of this world than Jane herself. She still stands alone because of her unparalleled ability to inspire something great within each of us. Mention her name almost anywhere on the planet, and people will instantly remark on what an inspirational figure she is and testify to the importance of her work.

It would probably take a hundred other people to equal Jane's impact, and—take it from me—she is a tough yardstick by which to measure oneself. I know I would have long ago sunk under the weight of all those interviews and appearances, the constant travel, her unyielding advocacy. I would have bawled and whimpered, not entertained guests, after falling down a cliff and dislocating my shoulder. Undoubtedly, I would have packed it all up years ago, feeling that early retirement was entirely justified.

But here I am—like so many others—ever the soldier in Jane's army. And like the rest of the troops, I intend to do all that I can, preaching the gospel of chimps, and Jane, and peace, and respect for the world's people . . . of the importance of simplicity in all things . . . of how essential nature is to humanity's happiness and well-being. And I intend to look the problems more squarely in the eye from now on, instead of simply hoping for the best. It is hard to live a purpose-driven life when one is constantly looking the other way.

Chimps suffer much at the hand of humans, be it in the wild, in laboratories, at Hollywood performing-animal farms, or as pets. Discovering the full extent of this cruelty has been disturbing at times, sometimes agonizing. I suppose it is the fact that chimps are so like us that leads humans to abuse them. Precisely because they are our closest relatives, we do to chimps exactly what we can't bring ourselves to do to humans, ignoring the fact that they suffer equally. We need to be their voice. They are so like children, and we need to protect them as such.

I don't expect to ever equal the heroes I have met and known, but I suspect that I am far from alone in this. The limitless zeal of great people drives them to be bold and persevere when others of us retreat. Few of us would take on the cause of world peace and find a way to engage world leaders in their vision—but that's what David Hamburg did. No conventional person would conceive of accepting 250 chimpanzee orphans, then find $4 million to care for them, but that is the dimension of Carole Noon's grit. And there is the unyielding Jane, still on a mission. Yet in knowing them, I have learned a valuable lesson: It is people like you and me that sustain these heroes. We are the threads in their rich fabrics, and when we create movements for grassroots change, we can play a vital role in accomplishing the near impossible.

I am a Forrest Gump of sorts, someone who has had the uncommon opportunity to work with my heroes and the most extraordinary animals on Earth. Perhaps this book, in some small way, can be an encouragement to others to actively seek out our heroes, drawing from their inspiration and genius, and trying to build on it in whatever way we can. Thankfully, my life journey with chimpanzees isn't over. I was granted an epiphany in 2008, and now I am back, ready to advocate in every way possible. There will be blogs, books, lectures, visits to my congressional representatives, and work in Africa. Whatever it takes.

And although not all of us have the stamina or an unswerving drive for greatness, I can't help but believe that each of us has our own unique spark to drive change and make a meaningful difference for the better. Mine is a work in progress, newly fortified. Now, let us all begin the work of saving African forests, people, and, yes, chimpanzees.

Fall 2013. We are back in Uganda to gauge how the country's chimpanzees are faring, and today is the most crucial day of the trip. PhD candidate Maureen McCarthy has been studying the movements of the 280 chimpanzees living precarious existences in an unprotected forest corridor, and she is sharing her final day in the field with us. Research assistant Tom Sabiiti is also along to introduce us to one community of those chimps, "the Bulindi Survivors." Numbering thirty to thirty-five chimps just five years ago, the group has now dwindled to nineteen. As luck would have it, the chimps are clustered just ahead.

We tromp through farmers' fields of beans, rice, and cassava, past cooped chickens and even cattle. Women working in their modest fields warn us of the gathered chimpanzees ahead. Maureen and her boyfriend, Jack Lester, wait behind to talk with them as we move toward a fragile stand of trees along the river.

There we spot Murry and Keeta, two of the group's four adult males, grooming one another below the last grand *Pseudospondias* tree in this tiny grove. Above them, latched on tree branches, play juveniles Jemima and Jenny. It is an idyllic scene reminiscent of Gombe, if minus the forest. Just over our shoulders comes the patter of the farmers.

Tom tells us that even this last remaining *Pseudospondias* tree is now marked for clearing at the end of the rainy season. We stand, absorbed in watching the chimps, cognizant that there are 260 others like them having to steal from farmers' crops just to survive as their last bits of forest are cut.

Maureen joins us, reminding us that these chimps are incredibly resourceful at surviving, as long as their human neighbors do not kill them. But perhaps she has hit on the rub. Just last week, Maureen experienced the agonizing pain of finding a three-year-old chimp struggling in a snare. She urgently summoned a veterinary team, but it unavoidably took them hours to arrive, and proved too late.

❧ ❧ ❧

We leave the chimps in their bucolic grove to wander the river, finding mostly small patches of scrub vegetation or complete clearing right up to the river's edge. This watershed, so vital to local people as well as chimps, cannot long withstand such losses. What, we wonder, will become of these farmers once they have destroyed the vegetation? How can they survive?

We stop to talk with the village chairman, seating ourselves in his parlor made from wood poles and mud. We want to hear the human side of this conflict, and he obliges, describing how the chimps have eaten his mangos, papayas, and crops, even threatened his children and made it unsafe for them to walk alone. There are now more chimpanzees than ever, he mistakenly tells us, based on his now frequent encounters with them.

He turns solemnly to Maureen and asks, "Then what would be the advice for us? To keep both the human beings and the chimps, to live together?"

Maureen answers, emphasizing the importance of keeping what little forest is left. The chairman glances aside, then responds, "That is the advice you are giving me, and we are trying, but some are not hearing you." His small portion of land is not enough to provide the fruits the chimps need.

We ask about Uganda's laws that prohibit killing of the endangered chimps and if people obey them. The chairman responds that they do. If not, he says, people would be killing them. "There are so many ways to kill them."

"And what are the ways?" we ask.

"There are very many ways. We trap them. We kill them by any means. We kill them one by one. Eh? One by one, using spears or arrows or even poison. There are so many ways." And though he tells us that locals are not attempting these things, in our hearts, we know better.

We leave Bulindi with our heads hung, as though we have just been a witness to a modern-day Trail of Tears. Will these young chimps, Jemima and Jenny, survive? Will thousands and thousands of chimps across Africa die, one by one? And what about the farmers? These chimpanzees are their bellwether. If chimps are lost, so are the forests and watersheds that people's lives depend on. It doesn't make sense.

Arriving home a week later, I write Drs. Goodall and Wrangham about our chilling experience, and the next evening, much to my amazement, I tune in to a live-streamed conversation between the two during which they describe the Bulindi survivors to an international audience of great ape experts. Agriculture, Jane says, is the primary driver of loss of critical great ape habitats, and Richard describes the example of the Bulindi survivors, sharing photos and our reports of the beleaguered chimpanzees, so representative of thousands of others.

It is a work in progress, this campaign to save forests and people and apes—but it will take much more. Some solutions will be as small as providing Uganda the resources it needs to enforce its protections on riverine forest. Others will be as big as programs across sub-Saharan Africa to give farmers the tools they need to survive and reason enough to believe that preserving forests and biodiversity is essential. Countries such as China, India, and Rwanda suggest it is possible to pull highly endangered animals like tigers and gorillas back from the brink. Now it is time for the chimps—and others.

In the end, one thing is clear—it is a frightening new day for the world's remaining chimpanzees, particularly those living outside protected areas. Any hope of saving them will require a wealth of funding, urgent and novel approaches, and a host of new advocates.

✦ ✦ ✦

The stories of the Bulindi Survivors will be updated regularly on the ChimpSaver website by field researcher Dr. Matthew McLennan.

ACKNOWLEDGMENTS

There are many to thank. First, the teachers and students at Stanford University's Writer's Studio, particularly Stephanie Reents and Malena Watrous; my writing circle, Karin Carrington, Kim Aikens, Jo Lynn Bailey, Joanne Godley, Nancy Hachisu, and Melanie Moore; and friends from the Bread Loaf Writers' Conference 2010. Special gratitude goes to the remarkable Rebecca Solnit for reviewing an early version.

Second, the forever-bonded Gombe community. Many helped me recount memories, particularly Faye Benedict, Julie Johnson, Patrick McGinnis, Palmer Midgett, and Jim Moore. Jane and Dr. David Hamburg were, of course, pivotal.

Thanks to agent Penny Nelson and editor Alexis Rizzuto for making this book possible. Thanks, too, to Craig Stanford, Candace Sclimenti, Ofir Drori, Elizabeth Ross, Richard Wrangham, Kate Wrangham-Briggs, Gladys Kalema-Zikusoka, Matthew McLennan, Lilly Ajarova, Maureen McCarthy, and Jess Hartel. Thanks, Ronan Donovan, for your phenomenal photography, and Caroline Riss, for hosting us.

The story is inspired by my Roots & Shoots family, including Sheri Mandel, Gloria van Santen, Karen Oxrider, Megan Nelson, Hans Cole, Marion Soloway, Dar and John Zalvaney, Jordan Robbins, Susan Morris, Melissa Kirkegaard, Jayne Kulzer, and Erin Viera. And special appreciation goes to the young people of our Ventura group, who've amazed me with their kindness and energy.

Thanks to supportive friends: Diane Bean, Jill George, Pat McCart-Malloy, Robin Weber, Joan Whitley, Kathy Dunlop, Wendy Francke, Kay Giles, Gail Myers, Leslie Lynn Pawson, Cathy Puccetti, Lynn Rockney, Andrea Schenk, and Sandy Spota. Particular appreciation goes to Carrie Hunter for providing articles, good advice, and friendship.

Finally, profound thanks to my astonishingly wonderful family. My sister, Beth Merrick, contributed the map and so much more in helping create ChimpSaver.org. My mother, Evea Merrick, has read every version, and my son, Bryan, has been a constant advocate. Kate and Gary, thank you for living this book with me every day. Credit is truly shared with you, too.

PREFACE

1. Takayoshi Kano et al., *Ecological Study of Wild Chimpanzees in the Savanna Woodland: Distribution and Population Density of Chimpanzees in Tanzania in 1994–2003*, report to TAWIRI (2005); David Moyer et al., *Surveys of Chimpanzees and Other Biodiversity in Western Tanzania*, unpublished report to the US Fish and Wildlife Service (2006): 1–65.

CHAPTER 1

1. Chimpanzee Sanctuary and Wildlife Conservation Trust (now Chimpanzee Trust Uganda), "Guidelines and Regulations for All Visitors to Ngamba Island Chimpanzee Sanctuary," July 2008.

CHAPTER 2

1. Lilly Ajarova, author interview, June 2008.
2. Andrew Plumptree et al., "The Status of Chimpanzees in Uganda," *Albertine Rift Technical Report Series* (New York: Wildlife Conservation Society, 2003).
3. Geza Teleki, *Hunting and Trapping Wildlife in Sierra Leone: Aspects of Exploitation and Exportation*, report submitted to the Office of the President, Sierra Leone (World Wildlife Fund-International, 1980).
4. Hope Ferdowsian et al., "Signs of Generalized Anxiety and Compulsive Disorder in Chimpanzees," *Journal of Veterinary Behavior: Clinical Applications and Research* 7, no. 6 (2012): 353–61.

CHAPTER 3

1. Jane Goodall with Phillip Berman, *Reason for Hope: A Spiritual Journey* (New York: Grand Central Publishing, 1999).

CHAPTER 4

1. Jane Goodall, personal and e-mail communications, June 2008.
2. Jane Goodall, *My Life with the Chimpanzees* (New York: First Minstrel Books, 1988).

CHAPTER 5

1. Eveline Wolfcarius, "UNHCR Helps Congolese Refugees Return Home Across Lake Tanganyika," United Nations High Commissioner for Refugees (UNHCR) News Stories, September 5, 2008, http://www.unhcr.org.
2. Eveline Wolfcarius and Bernard Ntwari, "Repatriation of 1972 Burundian Refugees from Tanzania Enters Final Phase," UNHCR News Stories, April 24, 2009, http://www.unhcr.org.

CHAPTER 8

1. Dale Peterson, *Jane Goodall: The Woman Who Redefined Man* (Boston: Houghton Mifflin, 2006).
2. See Jane Goodall, *The Chimpanzees of Gombe: Patterns of Behavior* (Cambridge, MA: Harvard University Press, 1986), and Jane Goodall, *Through a Window: My Thirty Years with the Chimpanzees of Gombe* (Boston: Houghton Mifflin, 1990).
3. Jane Van Lawick-Goodall, *In the Shadow of Man* (Boston: Houghton Mifflin, 1971).
4. Caroline E. G. Tutin, "Mating Patterns and Reproductive Strategies in a Community of Wild Chimpanzees," *Behavioral Ecology and Sociobiology* 6 (1979): 29–38.
5. Andrew Whiten et al., "Cultures in Chimpanzees," *Nature* 399 (1999): 682–85.

CHAPTER 9

1. Kim Bard and Kathryn Gardner, "Influences on Development in Infant Chimpanzees: Enculturation, Temperament and Cognition," in *Reaching into Thought: The Minds of the Great Apes*, ed. A. Russon et al. (Cambridge, UK: Cambridge University Press, 1999).
2. Robert Sapolsky, "The 2% Difference," *Discover*, April 2006.
3. Wolfgang Kohler, *The Mentality of Apes* (New York: Vintage, 1959).
4. Videos of the 1930s experiments with Gua may be viewed at http://archive.org/embed/comparative_tests_on_human_chimp_infants.
5. Roger Fouts with Stephen Tukel Mills, *Next of Kin: My Conversations with Chimpanzees* (New York: Avon, 1997).

CHAPTER 11

1. *Wild Film History: 100 Years of Wildlife Filmmaking*, http://www.wildfilmhistory.org.
2. "Information about Northern Tanzania: A Personal Scrapbook of 'Cuttings' from Published Sources," http://www.ntz.info.

CHAPTER 12

1. Anne Pusey et al., "The Contribution of Long-Term Research at Gombe National Park to Chimpanzee Conservation," *Conservation Biology* 21, no. 3 (2007): 623–34.
2. "Chimpanzees," GRASP Fact Sheet, accessed September 2009, http://ww.un-grasp.org (previously, http://www.unep.org/grasp).
3. Ian Redmond, "Year of the Gorilla," lecture to the Greater Los Angeles Zoo Association, October 23, 2009.

4. David Wilkie and Nadine Laporte, "Forest Area and Deforestation in Central Africa: Current Knowledge and Future Directions," in *African Rainforest Ecology and Conservation*, ed. W. Weber et al. (New Haven, CT: Yale University Press, 2001), 119–39.

5. Danae Maniatis, *Ecosystem Services of the Congo Basin Forests* (Oxford, UK: Global Canopy Programme, May 2008).

6. Jane Goodall, keynote address, Wildlife Conservation Expo of the Wildlife Conservation Network, San Francisco, October 2009.

CHAPTER 13

1. Dian Fossey, *Gorillas in the Mist: A Remarkable Woman's Thirteen-Year Adventure in Remote African Rain Forests with the Greatest of the Great Apes* (Boston: Houghton Mifflin, 1983).

2. Camilla Bedoyere, *No One Loved Gorillas More: Dian Fossey: Letters from the Mist* (Washington, DC: National Geographic, 2005).

3. Bill Weber, "The Evolving Practice of Conservation in Rwanda," in *State of the Wild: A Global Portrait, 2010–2011* (Washington, DC: Island Press/Wildlife Conservation Society, 2010).

4. Jody Bourton, "Scale of Gorilla Poaching Exposed," BBC Earth News Portal, September 18, 2009, http://news.bbc.co.uk/.

5. Gene Eckhart and Annette Lanjoux, *Mountain Gorillas: Biology, Conservation, and Coexistence* (Baltimore: Johns Hopkins University Press, 2008).

6. Julian Caldecott and Lera Miles, eds., *World Atlas of Great Apes and Their Conservation* (Berkeley: University of California Press, 2005).

CHAPTER 14

1. Richard Wrangham and Elizabeth Ross, eds., *Science and Conservation in African Forests: The Benefits of Long-Term Research* (Cambridge, UK: Cambridge University Press, 2008).

2. Richard Wrangham, "Moral Decisions about Wild Chimpanzees," in *Great Apes & Humans: The Ethics of Coexistence*, ed. Benjamin Beck et al. (Washington, DC: Smithsonian Institution Press, 2001).

3. The Kasiisi Project, http://www.KasiisiProject.org.

4. The Kasiisi Porridge Project, http://www.KasiisiPorridge.org.

5. Kate Wrangham-Briggs, e-mail communications, 2011–2013.

6. Dax Biondi et al., "Risk Factors and Trends in Childhood Stunting in a District in Western Uganda," *Journal of Tropical Pediatrics* 57, no. 1 (February 2011): 24–33.

7. F. M. Turyashemererwa et al., "Prevalence of Early Childhood Malnutrition and Influencing Factors in Peri Urban Areas of Kabarole District, Western Uganda," *African Journal of Food, Agriculture, Nutrition, and Development* (June 1, 2009).

8. Conservation Through Public Health, http://www.ctph.org.

9. Gladys Kalema-Zikusoka and Stephen Rubanga, author interview, July 2011.

CHAPTER 15

1. Edward Ssekika, "Government Suspends Timber Harvesting," *Observer* (Uganda), March 9, 2012.

2. Matthew McLennan et al., "Chimpanzees in Mantraps: Lethal Crop Protection and Conservation in Uganda," *Oryx* 46, no. 4 (2012): 598–603.

3. Bob Winterbottom and Gerald Eilu, *Uganda Biodiversity and Tropical Forest Assessment*, report by International Resources Group for USAID/Uganda, July 2006.

4. Uganda National Environment Management Authority, *Status of Forests, Wetlands, Riverbanks, Lakeshores, and Land Resources* (2007).

5. Tommie Herbert and Paul Hatanga, "Massive Ugandan Experiment Asks: Does PES Really Promote Sustainable Land Use?" http://www.ecosystemmarketplace.com, May 25, 2012.

6. Uganda Bureau of Statistics, 2006.

7. Matthew McLennan, "Beleaguered Chimpanzees in the Agricultural District of Hoima, Western Uganda," *Primate Conservation* 23 (2008): 45–54.

8. Matthew McLennan, "Diet and Feeding Ecology of Chimpanzees (*Pan troglodytes*) in Bulindi, Uganda: Foraging Strategies at the Forest-Farm Interface," *International Journal of Primatology* 34 (May 2013): 585–614.

9. Samuel Sejjaaka, "From Seed to Leaf: British American Tobacco and Supplier Relations in Uganda," in *International Business and the Challenge of Poverty in Developing Areas*, ed. F. Bird and S. Herman (New York: Palgrave-Macmillan, April 2004).

10. Center for Tobacco Control in Africa, *Report of "Alternative Livelihoods to Tobacco Growing and Environmental Conservation Meeting" in Kampala, Uganda*, February 6, 2012.

11. Conference of the Parties to the WHO Framework Convention on Tobacco Control, "Economically Sustainable Alternatives to Tobacco Growing," July 17, 2012.

12. Gideon Munaabi, "Why Do Tobacco Firms Thrive in Developing Countries Despite the Industry's Health Concerns?" UGPulse.com, November 2007.

13. Dale Lewis et al., "Community Markets for Conservation (COMAC) Links Biodiversity Conservation with Sustainable Improvements in Livelihoods and Food Production," *Proceedings of the National Academy of Sciences*, http://www.pnas.org, 2011.

14. Cristina Lasch et al., "Report of the Tanzania Chimpanzee Conservation Action Planning Workshop Report," posted to the Internet by the Nature Conservancy, February 2011 at http://conpro.tnc.org/.

15. Monique Grouter et al., eds., *Living Planet Report 2012: Biodiversity, Biocapacity, and Better Choices* (Washington, DC: World Wildlife Fund, 2012).

16. John F. Oates, "Is the Chimpanzee, Pan troglodytes, an Endangered Species? It Depends on What 'Endangered' Means," *Primates* 46 (2006): 102–12.

17. Caroline E. G. Tutin, "Saving the Gorillas and Chimpanzees of the Congo Basin," *Reproduction, Fertility and Development* 13 (2001): 469–76.

18. Christian Nellemann et al., eds., *The Last Stand of the Gorilla: Environmental Crime and Conflict in the Congo Basin*, United Nations Environment Programme (Arendal, Norway: GRID-Arendal, 2010), http://www.grida.no.

CHAPTER 16

1. Robert Nasi et al., *Conservation and Use of Wildlife-Based Resources: The Bushmeat Crisis*, Technical Series no. 33 (Montreal: Secretariat of the Convention of Biological Diversity and Center for International Forestry Research, 2008).

2. Danay Downing, "The Effect of the Bushmeat Trade on African Ape Populations: Critical Evaluation of the Evidence and Potential Solutions," *Collegiate Journal of Anthropology* (January 16, 2012), http://anthrojournal.com/.

3. Nasi et al., *Conservation and Use of Wildlife-Based Resources*.

4. Julie Stein, *Species Affected by the Bushmeat Crisis* (Washington, DC: Bushmeat Crisis Task Force, 2001).

5. Peter Walsh et al., "Catastrophic Ape Decline in Western Equatorial Africa," *Nature* (April 6, 2003): 1–3.

6. Elizabeth Bennett et al., "Hunting the World's Wildlife to Extinction," *Oryx* 36, no. 4 (2002): 328–29; Ian Redmond et al., *Recipes for Survival: Controlling the Bushmeat Trade* (Ape Alliance, 2006).

7. Graham Boynton, "Is This the End of the Wild Rhino?" *Condé Nast Traveler*, January 2013.

8. WildAid, "About: The WildAid Difference," http://www.wildaid.org.

9. Great Apes Film Initiative, "Pedal Powered Cinema," http://www.gafi4apes.org.

10. Tom Clynes, "Confronting Corruption," *Conservation* 11, no. 4 (December 2010).

11. Last Great Ape Organization, http://www.laga-enforcement.org.

12. Susan Hack, "Force of Nature," *Condé Nast Traveler*, November 2012.

13. J. Terborgh and C. van Schaik, "Why the World Needs Parks," in *Making Parks Work: Strategies for Preserving Tropical Nature*, ed. J. Terborgh et al. (Washington, DC: Island Press, 2002), 3–14.

14. Jeffrey Gittleman, "Elephants Dying in Epic Frenzy as Ivory Fuels Wars and Profits," *New York Times*, September 3, 2012.

15. Natalie Laporte et al., "Expansion of Industrial Logging in Central Africa," *Science* 316 (2007): 1451.

16. Francis Putz et al., "Sustaining Conservation Values in Selectively Logged Tropical Forests: the Attained and the Attainable," *Conservation Letters* (May 16, 2012).

17. Central Africa Regional Program for the Environment, *Regional Development Cooperation Strategy: 2012–2020* (May 1, 2012).

18. E.J. Stokes et al., "Monitoring Great Ape and Elephant Abundance at Large Spatial Scales: Measuring Effectiveness of a Conservation Landscape," *PLoS Hubs: Biodiversity* (April 23, 2010).

CHAPTER 17

1. Jeffrey McNeely, "Conservation Amid War," in *State of the Wild: A Global Portrait, 2010–2011*, ed. Wildlife Conservation Society (Washington: Island Press, 2010).

2. David A. Hamburg, *No More Killing Fields: Preventing Deadly Conflict* (Lanham, MD: Rowman and Littlefield, 2002).

3. Mary Marshall Clark interview with David A. Hamburg, December 10, 1998, Carnegie Oral History Project, http://www.columbia.edu/.

4. David Hamburg, *Preventing Genocide: Practical Steps Toward Early Detection and Effective Action* (Boulder, CO: Paradigm, 2008).

5. Robert Strauss, "A Different Kind of Peace Process," *Stanford Magazine Online* (May/June 2009), http://alumni.stanford.edu/.

6. David Hamburg and Eric Hamburg, prods., *Preventing Genocide*, Stanford University Digital Collections (2008), http://lib.stanford.edu/pg.

7. Carnegie Commission on Preventing Deadly Conflict, *Preventing Deadly Conflict* (New York: Carnegie Corporation, December 1997).

8. Jeffrey Sachs interview, *Preventing Genocide*, Stanford University Digital Collections, March 17, 2008, http://lib.stanford.edu/.

9. Eran Bendavid and Jayanta Bhattacharya, "The President's Emergency Plan for AIDS Relief in Africa: An Evaluation of Outcomes," *Annals of Internal Medicine* 150, no. 10 (May 19, 2009): 688–95.

10. McNeely, "Conservation Amid War."

11. Christian Nellemann et al., eds., *The Last Stand of the Gorilla: Environmental Crime and Conflict in the Congo Basin*, United Nations Environment Programme (Arendal, Norway: GRID-Arendal, 2010), http://www.grida.no.

CHAPTER 18

1. Save the Chimps, "Baby Chimp Discovers Ultimate Form of Transportation," You Tube.com.

2. Jane Goodall, "A Plea for the Chimpanzees," *American Scientist* 75 (1987): 574–77.

3. Roumiana Boneva et al., "Infectious Disease Issues in Xenotransplantation," *Microbiology Review* 14, no. 1 (January 2001): 1–14.

4. Christiaan Barnard, "Good Life, Good Death," quoted in Jon Wynne-Tyson, *The Extended Circle: A Commonplace Book of Animal Rights* (New York: Paragon House, 1989), 9.

5. D. M. Asher et al., "Experimental Kuru in the Chimpanzee: Physical Findings and Clinical Laboratory Studies," Symposia of the IVth International Congress of Primatology, *Nonhuman Primates and Human Diseases* (Basel: Karger, 1973), 43–90.

6. Joseph Patterson et al., "Cross-Circulation Between Humans in Hepatic Coma and Chimpanzees," in *Non-Human Primates and Medical Research*, ed. Geoffrey Bourne (New York: Academic, 1973), 256–68.

7. National Association for Biomedical Research, "Fact Sheet: The Chimpanzee's Critical Contribution to Biomedical Research," October 2010, http://www.nabr.org.

8. Jerrod Bailey, "An Examination of Chimpanzee Use in Human Cancer," *Alternatives to Laboratory Animals* 37 (2009): 399–416.

9. National Research Council, *Chimpanzees in Biomedical and Behavioral Research: Assessing the Necessity* (Washington, DC: National Academies Press, 2011).

10. "US National Health Agency to Retire Most Research Chimps," Environment News Service, July 3, 2013, http://ens-newswire.com/.

11. National Research Council, *Chimpanzees in Biomedical and Behavioral Research*.

CHAPTER 19

1. Candace Sclimenti, author interview, April 2012.

2. James Anderson et al., "Pan Thanatology," *Current Biology* 20, no. 8 (April 27, 2010): R349–51.

CHAPTER 20

1. Patti Ragan, founding director of the Center for Great Apes, e-mail communication, August 11, 2013, http://www.centerforgreatapes.org.

2. Sarah Baeckler, "Campaign to End the Use of Chimpanzees in Entertainment: Tes-

timony at a Briefing of the Chimpanzee Collaboratory and the Environmental Media Association," briefing cohosted by the Chimpanzee Collaboratory and the Environmental Media Association, Los Angeles, October 14, 2003.

3. Stephen Ross et al., "Specific Image Characteristics Influence Attitudes About Chimpanzee Conservation and Use as Pets," *PLOS One* 6, no. 7 (2011): e22050, doi:10.1371/journal.pone.0022050.

4. Project ChimpCare, http://www.chimpcare.org, accessed April 2013.

5. Cleve Hicks, "A New Home for the Aketi Five Chimpanzee Orphans," *International Primate Protection League Newsletter*, May 2009.

6. Asami Kabasawa, "Current State of the Chimpanzee Pet Trade in Sierra Leone," *African Study Monograph* 30, no. 1 (March 2009): 37–54.

7. Daniel Stiles et al., *Stolen Apes—The Illicit Trade in Chimpanzees, Gorillas, Bonobos, and Orangutans*, United Nations Environmental Programme (Arendal, Norway: GRID-Arendal, 2013), http://www.grida.no.

CHAPTER 21

1. Jane Goodall Institute, *Conservation Action Plan for the Greater Gombe Ecosystem, Western Tanzania 2009–2039* (April 2009).

2. Cristina Lasch et al., "Tanzania Chimpanzee Conservation Action Planning Workshop Report, January 19–21, 2010," posted to the Internet by the Nature Conservancy February 2011 at http://conpro.tnc.org/.

3. Peter Walsh et al., "Catastrophic Ape Decline in Western Equatorial Africa," *Nature* (April 6, 2003): 1–3.

4. 2nd GRASP Council Meeting, Paris, November 6–8, 2012.

5. Andrew Plumptree et al., *Eastern Chimpanzee (Pan troglodytes schweinfurthii): Status Survey and Conservation Action Plan 2010–2020* (Gland: IUCN, 2010).

6. Rebecca Kormos et al., eds., *West African Chimpanzees: Status Survey and Conservation Action Plan* (Gland: IUCN, 2003).

7. Nick Oakes et al., eds., *The Little Forest Finance Book: 14 Catalysts to Scale Up Forest-Friendly Finance* (Oxford, UK: Global Canopy Programme, 2012).

8. Mary Humphrey and Lilian Pintea, "Health of the Habitat" webinar, Jane Goodall Institute, May 14, 2013.

9. B. Huijbregts et al., "Ebola and the Decline of Gorilla (Gorilla gorilla) and Chimpanzee (Pan troglodytes) Populations in Minkebe Forest, North-Eastern Gabon," *Oryx* 37 (2003): 437–43.

10. J. G. Collomb et al., *A First Look at Logging in Gabon* (Washington, DC: World Resources Institute, 2000).

11. Toshisada Nishida et al., "Do Chimpanzees Survive the 21st Century?" in *The Apes: Challenges for the 21st Century*, conference proceedings, ed. Chicago Zoological Society (Brookfield, IL: Chicago Zoological Society, May 10–13, 2000), 43–51.

CHAPTER 22

1. Mike Fay, *The Last Place on Earth* (Washington, DC: National Geographic, 2005).

2. David Quammen, "Jane in the Forest Again: New Hope in Goualougo, Congo," *National Geographic* 203, no. 4 (April 2003): 90.

3. Kay Prufer et al., "The Bonobo Genome Compared with the Chimpanzee and Human Genome," *Nature* (June 23, 2012); Kevin Langergraber et al., "Generation Times in Wild Chimpanzees and Gorillas Suggest Earlier Divergence Time," *Proceedings of the National Academy of Sciences* 109, no. 39 (July 13, 2012): 15716–21.

4. International Union for Conservation of Nature (IUCN), "Red List of Threatened Species," http://www.iucn.org.

5. Craig Stanford, *Planet Without Apes* (Cambridge, MA: Belknap/Harvard University Press, 2012).

6. Thomas Butynski, "The Chimpanzee Pan troglodytes: Taxonomy, Distribution, Abundance, and Conservation Status," in *West African Chimpanzees: Status Survey and Conservation Action Plan*, ed. R. Kormos et al. (Gland: IUCN, 2003), 5–12.

7. Food and Agriculture Organization, *The State of Forests in the Amazon Basin, Congo Basin, and Southeast Asia: Report Prepared for the Summit of the Three Rainforest Basins, Brazzaville, Republic of Congo* (Rome: FAO, May 2011).

8. Louis Putzel et al., *Chinese Trade and Investment and the Forests of the Congo Basin*, Center for International Forestry (Indonesia: CIFOR, 2011).

9. C. de Wasseige et al., eds., *The Forests of the Congo Basin—State of the Forest 2010* (Luxembourg: European Union Publications Office, 2012).

10. Gebisa Ejeta, "Revitalizing Agricultural Research for Global Food Security," *Food Security*, 1 (2009): 391–401.

11. Food and Agriculture Organization, *State of the World's Forests 2011* (Rome: FAO, 2011).

12. Global Forest Watch 2.0, http://www.wri/org/gfw2.

13. Sandra Tranquilli et al., "Lack of Conservation Effort Rapidly Increases African Great Ape Extinction Risk," *Conservation Letters* 5, no. 1 (2011): 48–55.

14. National Environmental Management Authority (Uganda), *State of the Environment for Uganda, 2008*, June 2009.

15. John VandeBerg, "Apes Need Vaccines, Too," *New York Times*, August 2, 2013.

16. Global Forest Watch 2.0.

CHAPTER 23

1. Klaus Toepfer, "Humankind's Closest Living Relatives on the Brink of Extinction," speech, Paris, 2003, http://www.unep.org/.

2. Jane Goodall with Thane Maynard and Gail Hudson, *Hope for Animals and Their World: How Endangered Species Are Being Rescued from the Brink* (New York: Grand Central, 2009).

3. http://unless.philadelphiazoo.org/resources, http://cincinnatizoo.org/sustainable-shopper, http://www.cmzoo.org/conservation/PalmOilCrisis.

4. Kara Schroepfer et al., "Use of 'Entertainment' Chimpanzees in Commercials Distorts Public Perception Regarding Their Conservation Status," *PLOS One* (October 12, 2011).

5. Andrew Balmford, *Wild Hope: On the Front Lines of Conservation Success* (Chicago: University of Chicago Press, 2012).

6. Matthew McLennan, blog at Chimpsaver.org.

CHAPTER 24

1. Jane Goodall, *Jane Goodall: 50 Years at Gombe—A Tribute to Five Decades of Wildlife Research, Education, and Conservation* (New York: Stewart, Tabori, and Chang, October 2010).

2. Emily Anthes, "Climate Change Takes a Mental Toll," *Boston Globe*, February 9, 2009.

3. Jane Goodall, personal communication, May 28, 2013.